FAMOUS FIGHTING SHIPS

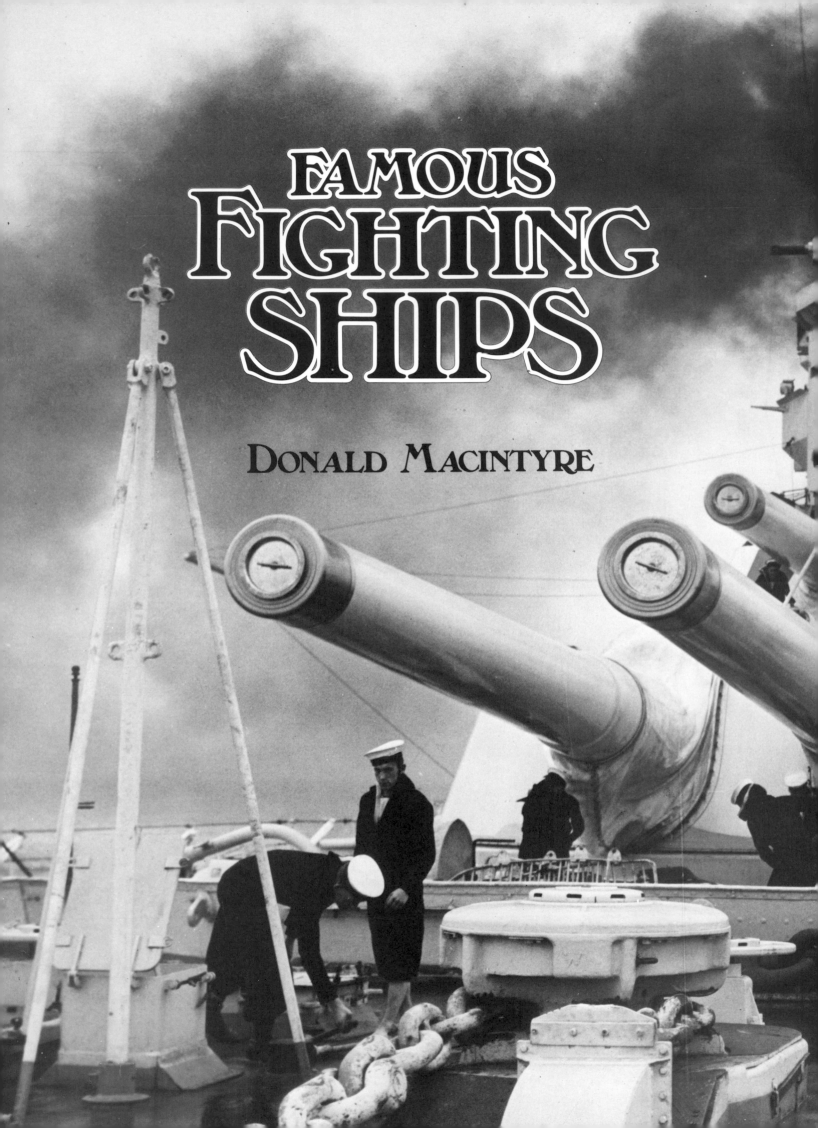

FAMOUS FIGHTING SHIPS

DONALD MACINTYRE

HAMLYN
LONDON   NEW YORK   SYDNEY   TORONTO

CONTENTS

REVENGE 6
REDOUTABLE 18
'OLD IRONSIDES'—USS CONSTITUTION 34
MIKASA 46
SEYDLITZ 56
HMS WARSPITE 72
USS WASHINGTON 90
SCHARNHORST 100
HMS ARK ROYAL 116
USS ENTERPRISE 138
Acknowledgments 158
Index 159

Published by
The Hamlyn Publishing Group Limited, 1975
London   New York   Sydney   Toronto
Astronaut House
Feltham, Middlesex
England
Copyright © The Hamlyn Publishing Group Limited 1975
All Rights Reserved

ISBN 0 600 35486 5

Printed in England by Jarrold and Sons Limited, Norwich

REVENGE

The royal shipyard at Deptford on the Thames was chiefly occupied in 1577 with the fitting out of one of the new fighting warships being built for the Queen. Responsible for the programme of eighteen such ships of between 300 and 500 tons, and its inspiration, was the Treasurer of the Navy, John Hawkins; and, no doubt, it was memories of the Spanish treachery which had brought catastrophe and ruin to his trading fleet at San Juan de Ulua on the Spanish Main in 1568 that made *Revenge* a suitable name for this, the first royal ship to bear it.

Of a design worked out by English shipwrights who at this time were well in advance of their rivals–a design perhaps by Matthew Baker, examples of whose work survive–the ship was a galleon, one of a class that was to make all existing warships obsolete. As compared to the latter, instead of a hull two and a half times as long as it was broad, the dimensions became roughly 4 to 1. This not only made for much better sailing capabilities, but provided a long lower deck on which could be mounted seven of the long-range 18-pounder guns, known as culverins, on wooden carriages with four small wheels or 'trucks'. The upper gun-deck, or main deck, open in the waist but covered elsewhere by the fore and after castles, carried a similar number of smaller guns, 9-pounder demi-culverins or 5-pounder sakers. The *Revenge*, which was of 441 tons burthen, actually mounted 46 guns in all, which included a number of smaller 'man-killing' (as opposed to ship-smashing) guns such as the little falcons and robinets.

Both fore and after castles were cut down from the towering structures of earlier ships to two decks above the main deck, and that portion of the forecastle which had previously projected beyond the stern disappeared, replaced by a flat beak-head. The after castle's two decks were the half-deck and poop. When the former was cut back to leave the area between mainmast and mizen open, the half-deck became the quarter-deck. In the covered part of the after castle were the officers' quarters and, right aft, the 'great cabin'.

No contemporary picture of the *Revenge* exists; but as one of the largest of the galleons she probably had four masts–fore, main, mizen and bonaventure mizen. Fore and main-masts each carried three square sails–course, topsail and topgallant, the mizens a lateen sail each. Below the bowsprit, for use in following winds, could be spread a square spritsail.

The ship was manœuvred by a tiller attached to the rudder head, the helmsman being assisted by others hauling on relieving tackles running between the tiller head and the ship's sides.

To steer a steady course in fair weather from the poop or the deck below it, there was the device known as the whip-staff. This was a long vertical pole, attached at its bottom end to the tiller head and pivoted where it passed through the deck in such a way that besides rotating on the pivot it could slide up and down. The whipstaff could thus be tilted to one side or the other, moving the tiller through its horizontal arc.

Such ships could sail closer to the wind than the bigger, more heavily armed men-of-war of Spain. They could thus fight at a range of their own choosing, both avoiding being boarded by the numerous soldiers carried by the latter and, with their culverins, engaging them outside the range of the heavier cannon and demi-cannon which made up the main armament of the lofty Spanish carracks. England and Spain were not yet officially at war and Queen Elizabeth was still using every artifice to avoid open hostilities; but the seamen, such as Hawkins, Drake, Frobisher, Grenville and others whom she supported in their expeditions to the Spanish Main, knew that war must come soon if England was to preserve her independence.

In the meantime hostilities took the form of privateering in which merchant or other privately owned ships, armed with letters of marque and reprisal could legally attack the ships of the countries mentioned in these licences, ostensibly to recover damages suffered. From Dunkirk in the Spanish Netherlands such corsairs swarmed into the Channel and the Irish Sea and a Channel Guard was

maintained by the English to protect their sea-borne commerce. In 1579 the *Revenge* was commissioned as flagship of that squadron and was to carry out such duties, going as far afield as the coast of Portugal, over the next eight years. Few details have survived of her activities except that, like another famous warship in this volume, the twentieth-century *Warspite*, she displayed a wayward nature in twice going aground–in Dublin Bay in 1582 and at Spithead in 1586–each time narrowly escaping total loss.

It was perhaps because she was still under repair that she did not take part in Sir Francis Drake's famous expedition to Cadiz in 1587– his pre-emptive attack on the Armada being prepared for the 'Enterprise of England' in which the great seamen, as he claimed 'singed the King of Spain's beard'. For in May 1585 open war between Spain and England had finally broken out when King Philip II of Spain had treacherously seized all English merchant ships in his ports. In reprisal Drake had set out that September in the royal galleon

Elizabeth Bonaventure with a squadron of twenty-five ships for his 'Descent on the Indies', to sack the fortress cities of San Domingo, capital of Hispaniola, and Cartagena on the Spanish Main, returning in triumph in time to set out for the expedition against Cadiz on 18 April 1587.

So England was made safe against invasion for that year. But by the spring of 1588 the Spaniards had made good their losses and were preparing to set out again. At a painful cost to the thrifty Queen, the English fleet was kept in commission, an Eastern Squadron in the Medway under the Lord High Admiral, Lord Howard of Effingham, and a Western Squadron at Plymouth. It was as commander of the latter that Drake hoisted his flag in the *Revenge*. Drake and Hawkins urged the Queen to let them repeat the exploit of the previous year. Whether her refusal was strategically wrong or wisely prudent is matter for argument; but certainly it permitted William Hawkins, Mayor of Plymouth, and his brother John at Chatham to refit and careen the ships

A model of a royal galleon, one of the specialized fighting ships of the Elizabethan navy. Such ships, of which the *Revenge* was one, with their improved hull design could outsail the heavily armed but clumsy war carracks and, with their long-range culverins, engage them at the range of their choice. Science Museum, London.

7

Typical 'high-charged' Spanish carracks—round-bellied with tall fore and after-castles as compared to the improved, fast-sailing English galleons with their cut-down castles and slimmer hull design. Escorial, Madrid.

Sir John Hawkins, Devon merchant and seaman who led the first trading ventures to break the Spanish monopoly in the New World. One of these ventures was treacherously overwhelmed in 1568. Hawkins later rose to be Treasurer of the Navy and inspired the design and construction of the new fighting galleons such as the *Revenge*. National Maritime Museum, London.

so that by April all were in full commission and seaworthy.

As news of the Invincible Armada's preparations came in, the fleet concentrated at Plymouth where on 2 June* Howard arrived with the Eastern Squadron flying the Commander-in-Chief's flag in the galleon *Ark Royal*, and Drake, as second-in-command, hoisted the Vice-Admiral's flag. There the fleet was at first cooped up by a westerly gale – a storm which, unknown to Howard, was at the same time scattering the Armada. When news at last arrived that the enemy fleet had reconcentrated at Corunna, much battered, Howard and Drake were permitted to set out, only to be headed by contrary winds and driven back to Plymouth where they anchored on 22 July.

The same winds, of course, favoured the Armada which had left Corunna the previous day. So on 29 July there was enacted the historic scene on Plymouth Hoe when Captain Thomas Fleming of the bark *Golden Hind*, who had been scouting in the Channel approaches, brought the news to Howard and Drake of a large group of Spanish ships off the Scilly Isles. The famous Invincible Armada had arrived and seemingly caught the English fleet wind and tide-bound in Plymouth Sound. Drake, in the middle of a game of bowls is said to have nevertheless calmly declared: 'We have time enough to finish the game and beat the Spaniards, too!'

It was the good seamanship of the English sailors that was to make his boast come true. On the ebb-tide that evening and the following one early on the 30th, fifty-one ships, including all the galleons and the most powerful merchant ships, were warped out of the Sound to an anchorage in the lee of Rame Head. And while the Spanish Admiral, now lying off the Lizard, held a council of war to debate whether to attack Plymouth where, as he thought, the English fleet was trapped, Howard was beating out to sea on the edge of a westerly wind. On the following morning the astonished Spaniards saw his ships gathered to windward. Holding thus the weather-gauge and able to sail closer to the wind than the Spanish ships, the English controlled the situation, being able to decide whether or not to attack and at what range.

This was crucial to the situation, for the Spanish fleet was not only more powerful, but it assumed an ingenious defensive battle formation. Round the fleet flagship and a centre squadron of powerful ships there gathered the large body of unwieldy transports and supply ships that formed an important but vulnerable element. Stretching back to windward from the ends of this central bulk were two wings of the best

* Dates are given in New Style, i.e. in accordance with the Gregorian Calendar in modern use.

fighting units to entrap between them any attacker venturing into the curve of the rough crescent in which the Spaniards confidently awaited the English attack.

Never before had the new type of English galleon taken part in a pitched battle at sea. The tactics were all to be newly devised. On the morning of the 31st the Spanish commander, the Duke of Medina Sidonia, hoisted to the masthead of his flagship, *San Martín*, the sacred battle banner. The Lord Admiral of England sent his personal pinnace, the *Disdain*, to deliver his knightly challenge. This done, he led his division in line ahead to attack the northern Spanish wing while Drake in the *Revenge* led the other division against the southern horn of the crescent.

Neither had any intention of engaging the lofty Spanish ships at close quarters, exposing themselves to their heavy cannon fire, or to boarding by the soldiers crowding their decks and castles. Using their superior sailing qualities they held off at culverin range, suffering no damage themselves, but, as they were to discover, doing only minor damage to the stout timbers of the enemy. When Medina Sidonia with the bulk of his fighting men-of-war turned and beat defiantly to windward, the English drew back to wait for the remainder of their fleet to join from Plymouth. The Armada re-formed and, followed at a distance by the English, continued its stately way up-Channel.

Its feathers had been ruffled, nevertheless; and it can perhaps be attributed to the manœuvring forced on it by the English attack, that during the afternoon *Nuestra Señora del Rosario*, flagship of Don Pedro de Valdès, commanding the Andalusian squadron, collided with another ship and lost her bowsprit. And while the rest of the Armada was heaving-to to wait for repairs to be made, a second and worse catastrophe took place when gunpowder stored aft in the *San Salvador* blew up, setting her ablaze. The *San Salvador* was temporarily saved, her fires being extinguished and she herself taken in tow by two galleasses – half galleys, half sailing ships. But as evening approached, squally and rough, the *Rosario*, which had still not managed to rig a jury bowsprit, was suddenly taken aback. Lacking a forestay, her foremast collapsed. The *San Martín* tried vainly to take her also in tow; but as darkness fell the need to re-form the huge confused array became essential and the *Rosario* was left with a small galleon and four pinnaces to assist her.

Meanwhile, as night closed over the English fleet, Lord Howard entrusted the task of guide to Drake who lighted the *Revenge*'s great poop lantern as a beacon. The wind had dropped to a fresh westerly breeze before which, through a clear night, the *Ark Royal* led the remainder, keeping the light in view until, of a sudden, it disappeared. Doubts have been cast on what had occurred. According to Drake, he sighted through the darkness vague shapes passing on the starboard (seaward) side. Dowsing his poop lantern so as not to mislead the fleet, he turned aside, followed by the privateer, *Roebuck*, to investigate, and discovered a group of neutral German merchantmen. By the time he identified them and turned back to rejoin, dawn was approaching

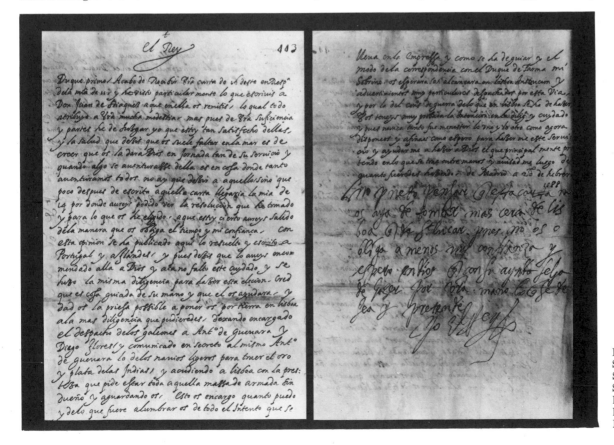

Letter from King Philip II of Spain to the Duke of Medina Sidonia, Commander of the Spanish Armada (1588). The last lines were added by the king in his own hand. National Maritime Museum, London.

Lord Howard of Effingham, Lord High Admiral of England who, flying his flag in the galleon *Ark Royal*, commanded the English fleet which defeated the Spanish Armada in 1588. National Maritime Museum, London.

and, in the early light, right ahead of him there appeared the crippled *Rosario*. Though Don Pedro's flagship had as many men as in both the English ships combined and a powerful main armament, he thought it no shame to surrender to the famous Drake without a fight. He was taken on board the *Revenge*, a prisoner, while the *Roebuck* escorted the *Rosario* into Tor Bay. Drake's proverbial luck with rich prizes had served him well once again. In the *Rosario*'s strong room were 55,000 gold ducats.

While Drake was thus taking possession of the richest prize to be taken from the Armada, his Commander-in-Chief, who had unwittingly followed the enemy flagship's lantern through the night, had found himself at dawn, accompanied only by the galleons *Bear* and *Mary Rose* within culverin shot of the enemy's rear, the remainder of his fleet being hull-down to the west. Fortunately the good sailing qualities of his ships enabled him to extricate himself from a perilous plight and by the evening the English fleet was again concentrated.

That afternoon the Spaniards suffered their second loss when the *San Salvador* had to be abandoned. Instead of being scuttled she was left to drift and fell into the hands of the

English, being towed to Weymouth by Captain Fleming's *Golden Hind*. Meanwhile the Spaniards reorganized their fighting ships into a powerful rearguard under Don Alonso de Leiva in the *Rata Coronada* and a smaller vanguard led by the Duke's *San Martín*. Early on 2 August, off Portland Bill, the wind backed round to the east and Howard led his galleons close-hauled to try to regain the windward gauge, firstly on a northerly tack when he was headed off by the enemy's vanguard. He reversed course and tried for the rest of the morning to work his way round to seaward, only to be similarly frustrated by de Leiva. A violent cannonade erupted but again without any decisive result on either side.

In the afternoon the wind shifted into the south and further separate actions developed with, at one time the *San Juan de Portugal* flagship of the Spanish Vice-Admiral, Juan Martinez de Recalde, cut off and being cannonaded by a dozen of the English ships led by the *Revenge*; at another it was the *San Martín* that was surrounded, exchanging broadsides with the *Ark Royal* and other English galleons as they sailed back and forth past her. In each case the English made use of their superior sailing qualities to draw off to windward when other Spanish galleons bore down to the rescue. By the end of the day it was clear to the Spanish that even with the weather-gauge they could not force their opponents into the close action which they desired; at the same time the English were realizing that the tactics adopted with the new galleons were not working. With powder and shot already running low, they had been able to inflict little serious damage with their culverins or to disrupt the Spaniards' excellent tight defensive formation which was again taken up as dusk approached. When the wind veered round to the west again, Medina Sidonia resumed his ponderous passage up Channel to the hoped-for rendezvous with the transports of the Duke of Parma which were to come out of Dunkirk.

Dawn on Wednesday, 3 August revealed a tall Spanish carrack straggling on the Armada's southern quarter. It was the *Gran Grifon*, flagship of the great round-bellied merchant-ship transports herded in the Armada's centre. As the *Revenge* led off to attack her, she crowded on sail to gain the shelter of the galleons of the right wing. From the centre, galleasses under oars put out to take her in tow. But before she reached safety, the *Revenge* and her consorts had time to sail past her several times and, though their culverins could not greatly damage her hull, they inflicted heavy casualties amongst the carrack's crew and soldiers and damage to her masts and rigging. By noon the skirmish was over and as the wind dropped away to light airs the two huge fleets drifted slowly onwards.

During the night two more Spanish ships fell behind, a royal galleon, the *San Luis de Portugal*, and a merchant carrack. At daybreak, off the Isle of Wight, it was flat calm and Hawkins hoisted out his boats to tow the *Victory* into action; the Spaniards responded with their galleasses towing de Leiva's *Rata Coronada*, whereupon the *Ark Royal* and Lord Thomas Howard's *Golden Lion* manœuvred to join in the fray. Then, as the breeze freshened, the battle spread, with the Spanish van under Medina Sidonia himself engaging Martin Frobisher's squadron on the left wing, while to the south the main body of the English joined the *Revenge* in attacking that horn of the crescent.

As before, much expenditure of powder and shot achieved a disappointing amount of damage as the English galleons tacked to and fro and by the end of the day both sides (though unknown to each other) were almost out of ammunition. Nevertheless the engagements put an end to any hopes Medina Sidonia still retained of entering Spithead and seizing the Isle of Wight. They also came near to causing a catastrophe to the Spanish who, all the while, were being edged northwards towards the long rocky hazard, the Owers. In the nick of time

the Duke's pilot warned him of the danger; the galleons were recalled and the Armada bore away south-eastwards on a long slant that was to take them to anchorage on Saturday the 5th in Calais Roads.

During Friday the English contented themselves with following close behind the Armada and when the Spanish anchored on the following morning they followed suit, little more than a culverin shot away. Medina Sidonia was now in touch with Parma. As he was no doubt planning their rendezvous, the English seamen knew they must give him no respite. Although they had now been joined by a fresh squadron under Lord Henry Seymour, including five of the Queen's best galleons, and by a swarm of little ships bringing urgently needed ammunition, they had no intention as yet of fighting at close quarters as the Spaniards would have liked. At a council on board the *Ark Royal* it was decided to use fireships to drive them from their anchorage.

That the situation was ideal for such a tactic with a gale from the west working up and the Spanish throng to leeward of the English, Medina Sidonia well knew, and he organized a screen of pinnaces to grapple any drifting fireships and tow them clear. Thus,

Contemporary view (from a tapestry design) of the encounter between the Spanish Armada and the English fleet. In the centre foreground is seen a galleass – a fighting ship propelled by oars as well as sails. Astern of her is an English galleon; ahead a typical, high-charged Spanish carrack. National Maritime Museum, London.

when at about midnight on Sunday, 7 August eight fires in a line were seen to blaze up as the flames caught hold of the tarred rigging and timbers of a line of ships drifting down on them, the Spaniards were prepared. Two of the fireships were smartly caught and diverted. But when the fireships' guns, which had been left loaded, heated up and began to explode, hurling all kinds of shot in every direction, the pinnace crews sheered off in panic leaving the other six to sweep on towards the anchored fleet.

The Spanish Admiral was ready for this also; having fired a signal gun, the *San Martín* slipped her cable and having beat to sea a short distance, went about and returned to drop her sheet anchor a mile or so to the northward of her original anchorage. Four other royal men-of-war, including Recalde's *San Juan* conformed with this movement; but the rest of the great array which had maintained such admirable order during the week of running fight now broke up and scattered in confusion as captains cut their cables and fled down wind from that terror of all sailors – fire at sea. By dawn all were out of sight except the five galleons and, crippled and struggling along the shore, the *San Lorenzo*, flagship of the galleasses.

Now at last it seemed, the time had come to annihilate the scattered enemy. The whole English fleet spread their sails in pursuit. Though by now it was some 150 strong, the main fighting would be between the galleons and larger armed merchantmen on either side. And while Howard led his own squadron to deal with the *San Lorenzo*, which they drove ashore and plundered, Drake steered the *Revenge*, leading the remainder after the Duke's squadron of five. At first it was a slow stern chase, but when the *Revenge* drew near, the *San Martín* luffed up and lay-to in defiance.

The English commanders had by now come to realize that to achieve a decision they must close to a much shorter range – no more 'playing at long bowls'. Not until the *Revenge* had sailed within 'half musket shot' did she open fire and in turn accept the fire of the Spanish flagship before sailing on to seek out others of the enemy galleons, followed by the *Nonpareil* and the remainder of his own squadron, each of whom exchanged broadsides with the *San Martín* as they passed.

The next squadron to come up was that of Martin Frobisher in the *Triumph* who stayed to hammer the *San Martín* in hopes, no doubt, of achieving the destruction of the enemy flagship. The irascible Yorkshireman, no friend of Drake's, criticized the latter's conduct as cowardly or treacherous. But Drake's keen tactical sense had shown him that it was more important to drive on to bring to action the other Spanish galleons to leeward before they could re-form and support one another.

Had Frobisher followed him, the battle might have reached a decisive point that day. As it was, Frobisher's squadron, joined by that of Hawkins and later by Seymour's and,

eventually the Lord Admiral's, concentrated on the *San Martín*. Medina Sidonia was supported at first only by the *San Marco de Portugal* but gradually by others of his galleons until a fighting shield had formed itself behind which the unwieldy mass of weaker ships could reorganize. The Spanish galleons and carracks nevertheless suffered fearful damage and casualties from the superior English guns and gunnery to which they could reply only indifferently owing to their greater shortage of ammunition. As the afternoon wore on the Armada was driven ever closer to the sandbanks of the Flanders coast. It seemed to the English as though the Battle of Gravelines, as it was to be known, must end in its total destruction.

Suddenly, however, there came a violent squall, forcing both sides to concentrate on dealing with the fury of the elements; a blinding screen of rain hid the Armada for some fifteen minutes; when it cleared the English saw, with grudging admiration, that it was standing away to the northward, once again forming up in the crescent formation which had defied all attacks during the previous week. Furthermore, the *San Martín* was seen to shorten sail and offer to renew the battle.

The fate of the Armada had been sealed nevertheless. Many of its fighting ships were no longer battleworthy. A great carrack, the *Maria Juan* had foundered during the squall. The same evening the men-of-war *San*

Mateo and *San Felipe* were driven ashore on the Flemish shoals to be captured by the Dutch. Another merchantman sank the next morning. The Armada, in fact, was in the hands of the elements. The wind had veered round to the north-west, sailing as close-hauled as they could, they were still being inexorably driven to leeward towards the Zeeland sands. Only a miracle could save them: a miracle indeed it was when at the last moment, with less than five fathoms under the keel of the *San Martín*, the wind suddenly backed again to south-west.

The Armada was able to haul off the shoals and steer out into the North Sea. Doggedly in their wake followed the English galleons with powder rooms almost empty, their stock of round shot exhausted. It was not feasible to force close action on the Spaniards under those conditions. But so long as the prevailing westerly winds held, the Armada, many of its principal units in so shattered a state that they could barely be kept afloat, could do nothing but drive on northwards. All hopes of achieving its object of covering Parma's invasion of England had vanished. And, in fact, there was to be no more fighting; nor was there need for it.

The tragic story of the long journey north-about round the British Isles of the 66 ships (44 of them fighting units) which staggered back to Spain out of the 130 which set out, and the loss by shipwreck or foundering of the remainder, is no part of the story of the

The Spanish carrack *San Salvador*, of the Spanish Armada, on fire from an explosion of gunpowder. She was later abandoned and captured by the English.

Revenge. With the remainder of Howard's fighting fleet she trailed the Spanish ships as far as the latitude of the Firth of Forth before, satisfied that no danger remained from them, she turned back to the Thames to report victory and, no doubt, to pay off by the thrifty Queen's command. Certainly the plight of the wounded and sick from among the *Revenge*'s crew, unpaid and neglected once the danger was over, must have inspired Drake to found that year, in collaboration with Hawkins, the 'Chatham Chest', the first charitable fund for the relief of poor sailors.

At the same time Drake and Hawkins pressed the Queen and her Council to follow up the victory over the Armada with a renewed attack on Spanish sea-power. With an Exchequer almost emptied by the expenses of 1588, a government-financed operation was out of the question; but a joint-stock expedition on similar lines to Drake's earlier forays

was organized. The Queen supplied £20,000 in cash and six of her galleons, including the *Revenge*, to serve again as Drake's flagship. The remainder was privately financed.

In April 1589 the expedition set out, some 150 ships strong, including transports carrying 10,000 soldiers under Sir John Norreys. The objective was the capture of Lisbon, and subsequently the Azores and the installation on the throne of Portugal of the pretender, Don Antonio. In addition, on the way, an attack was to be mounted on the Biscayan port of Santander to destroy remnants of the Armada refitting there. This was the largest undertaking of its kind ever launched by England at the time and it was to prove beyond her organizational capabilities. Instead of Santander a futile assault on Corunna was made. Moving on south, though the troops were successfully landed some 50 miles from Lisbon, drunkenness, typhus and a lack of siege artillery combined to make their advance a catastrophe and they were finally re-embarked from Cascais at the mouth of the Tagus.

On the way home Vigo was sacked and burned; but when Drake set out to attempt the capture of the Azores his fleet was scattered in confusion in a gale and even the *Revenge* came near to foundering. Drake returned to be made the Queen's scapegoat for her financial loss and was to remain in eclipse, if not in disgrace, for the next six years. When he set out in 1595 for his last, sadly unsuccessful and personally fatal expedition to the West Indies and the Spanish Main, the *Revenge*, his favourite ship, was no longer available to him.

During 1590 and 1591 the Queen's galleons were employed in attacking Spanish sea-borne commerce off the Azores and the coasts of Spain and Portugal instead of in over-ambitious amphibious operations. This *guerre-de-course* was the classic form of sea warfare open to a weaker naval power – as England still was compared to Spain. Like the U-boats of 350 years later, the Queen's ships were organized in small squadrons or 'wolf packs' to prey upon enemy shipping. Sir John Hawkins led one of these in 1590 to operate off the coast of Spain, while Sir Martin Frobisher hoisted his flag in the *Revenge* to lead the group stationed off the Azores.

The threat was enough to stop the sailing home that year of the treasure fleet upon which the economy of Spain depended. It was decided to repeat the operation in 1591; but, in the hope of intercepting the huge treasure convoy by then awaiting passage home, the main force of six galleons under Lord Thomas Howard in the *Defiance* was sent to the Azores. Under him, as Vice-Admiral in the *Revenge*, was Sir Richard Grenville. A smaller force under the Earl of Cumberland, sent to cruise off the Spanish coast would, it was hoped, prevent any reinforcements for the convoy escort being despatched.

In the three years since the Armada, however, the Spaniards had not only rebuilt their naval strength numerically; they had also taken a leaf out of English ship-designers books and built themselves new galleons on the English model—twelve of them each named after one of the Apostles. And it was with the whole of the fleet of Spain that the Captain-General Alonzo de Bazan set out in August 1591 to meet the treasure *flota* at the Azores.

There, on the 30th of that month, Howard's squadron was lying anchored under the lee of Delgada Point on the north coast of Flores when a pinnace from the Earl of Cumberland came winging round the cape to round up alongside the *Defiance*. Her Captain had shadowed Bazan's fleet until he was certain of its destination and then sped on to warn the English Admiral. The situation that now arose presented an acute problem. After many weeks of cruising in search of the Spanish convoy, typhus and scurvy had made their inevitable appearance and spread until almost half the ships' companies were down with it. The sick had been sent ashore to a temporary camp. Meanwhile, the opportunity was being taken to freshen the foul ballast and to embark fresh water when this news of the approaching enemy arrived.

Orders were at once given to prepare for sea and to start re-embarking the sick; but before the latter had been completed the enemy were reported in the offing. Faced with a greatly superior enemy force, Howard prudently decided that he must get under way and to sea without delay. Cables were cut, sails shaken out and the galleons followed the *Defiance* out of harbour—all but the *Revenge*. There, it is said and generally accepted, Grenville delayed to embark the last of the sick, refusing to let them fall into the hands of Spain where, as Protestant heretics they were likely to suffer the horrors of the Inquisition.

It may be that Grenville believed that the *Revenge* could outsail the enemy ships as during the Armada campaign. But when he finally got under way to follow Howard, he found himself trapped between one Spanish squadron which had encircled the island of Corvo to the north and was now beating southwards and the main fleet coming up to meet it. He could perhaps have fled down wind; but Grenville was a Devon sea-dog with a fierce, fighting spirit ('of unquiet mind, and greatly affected to wars', as Linschoten, who was with the Spanish fleet, was to describe him), as well as a contempt and hatred for the traditional enemies of his country and religion. He had been frustrated from leading expeditions against them in the past—those which Drake eventually led in circumnavigation of the world and again at the time of the Armada

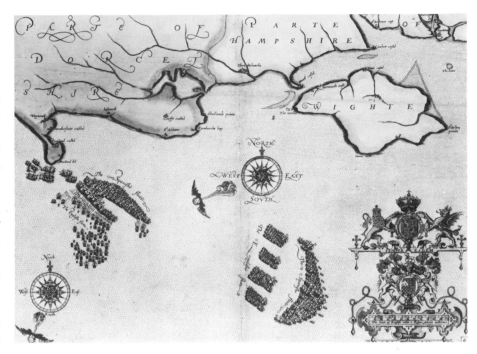

The Armada. The action off Portland Bill.

when he had been held ashore to command the local levies. Now he determined to sail between or fight his way through the converging enemy squadrons.

The latter it proved to be and the ensuing action is perhaps the most famous fight against odds in sea warfare—between the 'one and the fifty-three' in Tennyson's famous Ballad of the *Revenge*—which lasted for fifteen hours during which two of the Spanish men-of-war were sunk and two more so disabled that they had to be abandoned. The *Revenge* was reduced to

Alessandro Farnese, Duke of Parma, Philip II's Governor and Commander-in-Chief in the Netherlands, whose army was to have been escorted over to England by the Spanish Armada. Musées Royaux des Beaux-Arts de Belgique, Brussels.

15

a wreck; her powder was spent; forty had been killed of the hundred fit men she had at the outset and nearly all the remainder had been wounded when, ignoring the order of the dying Grenville to his master gunner to split and sink the ship, she was at last surrendered. Sir Richard was transferred to Bazan's flagship, the *San Pablo*, where, shortly before he died, the indomitable man said in Spanish to his awe-struck captors:

Here die I, Richard Grenville, with a joyful and a quiet mind, for that I have ended my life as a true soldier ought to do that hath fought for his country, queen, religion and honour.

The *Revenge* did not survive to grace a Spanish triumph. She was still with Bazan's fleet at the end of September amongst the Azores. The Captain-General had been joined by the *flota* (which had still not brought the expected treasure) when a hurricane struck during which more than half of the Spanish fleet as well as the *Revenge* were sunk, the latter with a Spanish prize crew of 200 men on board. The Queen's best galleon had indeed been aptly named.

Over the centuries eight more ships of the Royal Navy have borne the honoured name. Today H.M.S. *Revenge* is a nuclear-powered submarine armed with the ballistic-missiles with which the Royal Navy plays its part in helping to deter aggression.

HMS *Revenge*, super-dreadnought battleship mounting eight 15-inch guns, which served in both World Wars.

HMS *Revenge*, nuclear-powered submarine armed with Polaris ballistic missiles with nuclear warheads, being launched from Cammell Laird's shipyard, Birkenhead, on 15 March 1968.

REDOUTABLE

The French 74-gun ship-of-the-line *Redoutable*, when her hull first took the water from a building slip at Lorient in 1792, was given the name of that most brilliant of French admirals, the Bailli de Suffren. But times were out of joint; if not for France herself, as her people indulged in violent revolution to replace her absolute monarchy by a Republic, for her navy, where discipline for a time collapsed when the majority of senior officers were removed, many to die under the guillotine as aristocrats. At the request of the sailors, it was said, the name was changed to *Redoutable*. Suffren's name had smacked too much of the *ancien régime*.

The republican government inherited the imperial ambitions of its royal predecessors, though ostensibly for ideological purposes. When its armies overran the Austrian Netherlands (Belgium) and Antwerp became the 'pistol pointed at the heart of England' in 1793, war with Britain became inevitable. With her navy's efficiency brought low by the loss of virtually the whole of its officer corps, France had challenged the foremost naval power in the world. The consequences were first made apparent when the Brest fleet under Vice-Admiral Villaret-Joyeuse (promoted at a bound from Lieutenant) met the Channel Fleet under Lord Howe in 1794 in the battle known to the British as the 'Glorious First of June'. The French fleet succeeded in its strategic aim of covering the return of the Atlantic convoy laden with a vital supply of American grain; but tactically and professionally it was outclassed. In spite of all efforts to avoid a decisive clash, it lost seven ships of the line. The *Redoutable* did not take part in this battle.

Thereafter the stranglehold of blockade was to grip the French Atlantic fleet, holding it penned in harbour with only occasional breaks in continuity. One of these occurred at the end of December 1794 when the Brest squadron was ordered to sea. The upshot was catastrophic: at first only two ships, the *Républicain* and *Redoutable* were able to obey the order; finding they were not followed, they dropped anchor in Le Goulet, the outer harbour, only to have their cables part when a north-east gale blew up. The *Républicain* was driven ashore and wrecked; the *Redoutable* made sail and reached the open sea where she was joined by the remainder of the squadron four days later. Hardly had this junction taken place when a violent gale from the south-west swept down upon the unpractised ships, four of which were wrecked. At the beginning of February 1795 the remainder, including *Redoutable*, re-entered the port of Brest.

In June of that year Villaret-Joyeuse led his squadron of nine ships-of-the-line and thirteen minor vessels out again to go to the assistance of the squadron of three ships-of-the-line and five frigates mewed up at Belle Isle. The lax blockade maintained by the Channel Fleet under Lord Bridport permitted the two squadrons to unite. In the indecisive clash which followed, the French lost three of their battleships and Villaret-Joyeuse castigated the conduct of some of his captains, three of whom were court-martialled and cashiered. But others, including Captain Moncousu of the *Redoutable*, were praised for their gallantry.

After that the *Redoutable* returned to Lorient where she lay in reserve during 1796 until the fleet was re-activated in midwinter to take part in an expedition in support of the Irish rebel Wolfe Tone. Once again Bridport failed to prevent the fleet's sortie and the expedition reached Ireland, but only to be driven back to Brest by a savage winter storm with nothing accomplished. The *Redoutable*, like a number of others, had to be paid off while extensive repairs were made.

Once again the French Atlantic fleet submitted to being held harbour-bound throughout 1797 at a time when the British Channel and North Sea fleets were for several months incapacitated by the great mutinies at Spithead and the Nore. Neither the French nor their puppet allies of the (Dutch) Batavian Republic were able to take advantage of this situation. By 16 May the Channel Fleet had returned to duty and put to sea to renew the blockade; but at the Nore all but two of Admiral Duncan's North Sea Fleet were in revolt and for a time the blockade of the Dutch in the Texel was nothing but an impudent bluff by frigates in the offing signalling to an imaginary battle fleet over the horizon. Before the Dutch decided to go to sea the mutiny had been settled and the sailors so recently defying discipline proceeded to inflict a crushing defeat upon them at the Battle of Camperdown.

Not until April 1799 did the *Redoutable* spread her sails again; this time, under command of Captain Maillard La Morandais, she was one of a squadron of twenty-four ships-of-the-line under Vice-Admiral Bruix which broke out of Brest, evaded the blockade, passed through the Straits of Gibraltar unchallenged and reached Toulon. But though this gave the French a naval superiority in the Mediterranean, Bruix failed to take advantage of it and by September he was back again in Brest. It was the last occasion on which a French fleet broke through the blockade before the conclusion of the brief Peace of Amiens in the spring of 1802.

Napoleon Bonaparte used the respite from war to prepare for its renewal by assembling an invasion fleet and army on the Channel coast, But French affairs across the Atlantic called also, with the populations of some of the French West Indian islands in revolt, inspired by the revolutionary promises of Liberty, Equality and Fraternity. The *Redoutable* was partly disarmed by the removal of one tier of great guns, to serve as a troopship (armed *en flute*). Having hoisted the flag of Rear-Admiral Bouvet and embarked a battalion of 500 soldiers and General Richepanse who was in command of the expedition, she sailed in April for Guadeloupe in company with the *Zélé*, another 74-gun ship-of-the-line, and four frigates all similarly laden. The troops were

duly landed under cover of the ships' guns and the squadron was back in Brest by 20 August 1802.

The *Redoutable* flying the flag of Rear-Admiral Bedout, was similarly employed that winter in connection with operations in Saint Domingue where the negroes had revolted and set up an independent republic under Toussaint L'Ouverture. The squadron was still there when war with Britain broke out again in May 1803; by the time he could get back, Bedout found Brest once again under close blockade; so he took his squadron to Ferrol in Spain to which port the blockade was at once extended.

There now began the two years which make up the period of the Trafalgar campaign during which Napoleon launched his unrealistic Grand Design aimed at concentrating his Franco-Spanish squadrons, scattered between the ports of Toulon, Cartagena, Cadiz, Ferrol, Rochefort and Brest in one huge Atlantic fleet which would dominate the Channel long enough to cover the passage of his invasion flotillas carrying the *Grande Armée* across from its camp at Boulogne. During the greater part of that time the *Redoutable* was to lie moored in Ferrol, where Rear-Admiral Gourdon had replaced Bedout, and was blockaded throughout 1804 and the following eight months.

For most of the French and Spanish ships thus held in port by the British blockade it was a demoralizing experience. Seamanship and gunnery inevitably deteriorated; the realization that both had become inferior to those of their opponents, who kept at sea summer and winter in calm or storm, ate away insidiously at self-confidence and enthusiasm. Indeed there had never been any opportunity to teach seamanship or gunnery to many of the conscripted crews, products of the *inscription maritime*—a method of manning the fleet which sent to sea at least as high a proportion of unwilling landsmen as British impressment.

But to the *Redoutable* there came in command in November 1803 a remarkable man, Captain Lucas. Almost a dwarf—he was less than five feet in height—he made up for any lack of inches with a more than ample supply of courage, efficiency and enthusiasm.

He had first come to the fore in the Battle of Algeciras in 1801 where, as First Lieutenant of the *Formidable* he had succeeded to the command when his captain was killed. His gallant conduct had subsequently earned him captain's rank and command of the captured *Hannibal*. Like many men of his stature, Lucas was blessed with a compensating self-conceit. He set about imposing efficiency upon his men, made up partly of soldiers brought back from the expedition to Saint Domingue and who now formed the crews for the replaced tier of guns, and he infused in them something of his own fiery spirit.

Faced with the difficulty of giving them realistic gunnery practice in the confines of Ferrol harbour, Lucas concentrated instead on the tactics of close action and boarding—musketry practice till every man was a marksman even when perched in the rigging, the casting of grappling irons, the hurling of hand grenades, cutlass drill and pistol firing. He discarded any idea of achieving a skill and efficiency with the great guns comparable with that of his seasoned foes. Once close alongside an enemy ship, the guns were to be run in, the gunports slammed shut to prevent the

The port of Brest during the Napoleonic Wars. Here a large part of the French Fleet was for long periods bottled up by the British blockade. Palais de Luxembourg, Paris.

enemy boarding through them, and the crews ordered to their assigned stations on deck, in the rigging or in the tops. Then, having swept his opponent's upper deck clear of men, the bugle would sound for the boarding.

These were the tactics of privateering, a form of irregular sea warfare in which the capture of the merchant ship as little damaged as possible and so the more value in the subsequent prize court proceedings was of paramount importance. It was the warfare in which the chief heroes of the French navy of the past such as Jean Bart and Duguay-Trouin had excelled and which Robert Surcouf was successfully waging in distant waters at that very time. It was not perhaps, a practical way of fighting in action with regular men-of-war; but Lucas either believed it could be, or he adopted it in default of any other method open to him in the circumstances. And he convinced his sailors of its efficacy. He had the best part of two years in which to perfect their training.

Had Napoleon's admirals been able to carry out the complex moves which made up his first plan, the *Redoutable*'s testing time could have come early in 1805. The Emperor's plan called for his Toulon squadron to break out past Nelson's blockade through the Straits of Gibraltar and cross the Atlantic, where it would meet the Rochefort squadron which would have similarly evaded the blockading force off that port. The Combined Fleet was then to have returned in company to drive off the blockading squadrons from Ferrol and Brest. The rest of the French fleet would have emerged to form an overwhelming force capable of brushing aside all opposition and proceeding up-Channel to convoy the invasion flotillas.

The Rochefort squadron duly broke out and sailed to Martinique; but the Toulon squadron under Admiral Villeneuve was driven back to harbour damaged by heavy weather with which his inexperienced crews were unable to cope. An even more intricate plan–the Grand Design as it was called–was now devised. Villeneuve was again to put to sea, evade Nelson, get through the Straits, call at Cadiz to add to his force any Spanish ships under Admiral Gravina which might be ready for sea and cross to the West Indies. Meanwhile, from Brest, the French Atlantic fleet under Admiral Ganteaume would also have broken out, steered for Ferrol to drive off the blockade and pick up the French and Spanish squadrons there and also head across the Atlantic to a rendezvous at Martinique where the Rochefort squadron was expected to be still waiting. The Combined Fleet, which would now total some forty sail-of-the-line, was then to steer for the Channel and overwhelm any British force that barred its way. On 30 March 1805 the first move was made when Villeneuve put to sea from Toulon.

The plan was doomed from the start by Napoleon's order that both Ganteaume and Villeneuve were to avoid action prior to their junction. Villeneuve, with eleven of the line, was able to give Nelson the slip in the Mediterranean and having picked up five Spanish ships from Cadiz under Admiral Gravina, he duly steered for Martinique. But Ganteaume's preparations for sea were immediately known to the British frigates keeping the inshore watch on Brest; and when the Western Squadron appeared to seaward, ready to give battle, the French Admiral had no choice but to re-enter harbour.

Pierre Villeneuve, French Commander-in-Chief of the Franco-Spanish Fleet defeated at the Battle of Trafalgar. He was captured in his flagship and brought to England. Soon after his release he committed suicide or was murdered at Rennes in Brittany. Bibliothèque Nationale, Paris.

Apart from this fatal flaw in the Grand Design, the standing orders for the British blockading squadrons – that if the section of the enemy fleet for which they were responsible got away to sea, they should at once fall back on the Western Squadron and reinforce it – meant that the French fleet would have to give battle to an approximately equal British force before they could hope to dominate the Channel.

Not knowing where Villeneuve had gone, Nelson waited for some time in the central Mediterranean in case the Toulon squadron had designs on Sicily or Egypt. When news finally reached him, westerly winds so delayed him that he was a full month behind Villeneuve when he at last worked clear of the Straits and set off across the Atlantic in pursuit. In spite of his ships' barnacle-infested hulls after their months of blockade service, Nelson gained ten days during his passage. Villeneuve found that the Rochefort squadron, having given up hope of his coming, had returned to France. Under orders to spend a month harrying and capturing the British West Indian islands, Villeneuve took three weeks to overcome the resistance of the tiny naval garrison of the islet of Diamond Rock off the coast of Martinique. Thus, when Nelson arrived at Barbados on 4 June 1805 he was within two days sailing of him. False intelligence now sent Nelson off in the wrong direction, however; and before he could retrace his steps, Villeneuve and Gravina had started back across the Atlantic. Lest their destination should be the Mediterranean for which Nelson was responsible, the latter made for Gibraltar. But Villeneuve's orders were to pick up the French and Spanish ships in Ferrol and then go north to rendezvous with Ganteaume off Brest.

There was never any prospect of such a move succeeding, but the French Admiral was bound to make the attempt. Off Finisterre his collection of battered ships manned by sickly crews was intercepted by Sir Robert Calder's blockading squadron on 22 July and was lucky to escape into Vigo after two Spanish ships had been captured. A few days later, when Calder was driven off station by a gale, Villeneuve took advantage of this to run north and join the Ferrol squadrons at Corunna.

The fleet of which the *Redoutable* now became a unit contained twenty-nine ships-of-the-line of which eighteen were French – impressive numerically but hardly so in quality, remembering that many of them had not put to sea since the beginning of the war. With such a force the French and Spanish admirals knew that the Emperor's plan was out of the question. When they put to sea on 13 August, therefore, Villeneuve, having driven off the watching British frigates, turned south and, as more recent orders from the disillusioned Napoleon by this time permitted, entered the harbour of Cadiz where four more Spanish ships were added to his command.

There Villeneuve hoped to refit and dock his foul and battered ships, to replace sails and cordage and to restore his 1,700 sick to health in the temporary camp established on shore. His proud Spanish allies, resentful of French command, refused at first to supply him with stores or victuals out of their own meagre stocks. It took an appeal to the Spanish government through the French ambassador in Madrid to secure a grudging, partial cooperation.

Indecisive engagement off Cape Finisterre on 22 July 1805 between the British blockading squadron under Sir Robert Calder and that of Villeneuve who was returning from the West Indies. The latter escaped with the loss of two Spanish ships. National Maritime Museum, London.

But more ominous for the future was the lack of confidence of many of the French and Spanish captains and senior officers in their Commander in Chief, in each other, or in the fighting efficiency of their ships and crews. Neither of Villeneuve's subordinate French admirals, Dumanoir and Magon, respected him; the latter, indeed, a man of hot, tempestuous and daring character, was said to have yelled contemptuous abuse at Villeneuve's passing flagship, and even hurled his telescope and wig at her, when the battle off Finisterre was broken off.

Of the eighteen French captains the majority were realistic enough to appreciate the impossibility of the Emperor's plan and the hopelessness of challenging the fleet of tautly trained British ships with their own landlubberly crews. Such a demoralizing situation bred disloyalty and intrigue. There were a few, however, who remained loyal and fatalistically prepared to fight and die under Villeneuve's leadership. Lucas, almost alone, not only remained loyal but was convinced that if other captains would only follow his example victory could be gained over the English.

Apart from the low morale among the French, there was a fatal lack of trust or respect between the allies. The Spaniards accused the French of having deserted the two ships lost off Finisterre; the French in reply attributed the loss to Spanish incompetence. With a fleet in such a state, it was with inexpressible relief that on 28 September Villeneuve received new orders from Paris which signalled the final abandonment of the Grand Design. Napoleon, indeed, had on the previous day ordered his invasion army at Boulogne to break camp and to begin the movements which were to lead them to the victory over the Austrians at Austerlitz.

Villeneuve's new orders to break out 'at a favourable moment' and take the Combined Fleet to the Mediterranean to land his French troops at Naples before retiring to Toulon, seemed to him at least feasible. Granted suitable conditions – primarily a brisk, fair wind to get his fleet to sea and along the coast to Gibraltar in a single night – he could avoid the pitched battle with Nelson which all feared. He gave orders for the troops to be embarked and for the fleet to be made ready to sail immediately afterwards.

At the same time he felt it necessary to issue a stirring message welcoming the prospect of a battle on the day of sailing. This alarmed the Spaniards, who had no illusions as to the efficiency of their ships, manned largely as they were by soldiers, gaol-birds or the pressgangs' indiscriminate sweepings. Their objections led Villeneuve to call a council-of-war during which feelings rose high with the French hinting at cowardice amongst their allies, the Spanish insisting that to challenge

above
Captain Jean Lucas of the *Redoutable*. His crew was probably the best of any of the Franco-Spanish fleet at Trafalgar. During the battle *Redoutable* engaged Nelson's flagship *Victory* alone for a long time before the arrival of the *Téméraire* finally forced the *Redoutable*'s surrender.

Vice-Admiral Horatio, Viscount Nelson, Commander-in-Chief of the British Fleet at Trafalgar, who died in the hour of victory, shot by a musketeer from the *Redoutable*. Royal Collection.

opposite
Sir Richard Grenville at the age of twenty-nine. Twenty years later, in the *Revenge*, Vice-Admiral of Sir Thomas Howard's 'wolf-pack' of fighting galleons, he was cut off and surrounded by a powerful Spanish squadron. The *Revenge* fought them off for fifteen hours, sinking two of them and disabling others before being surrendered, a shattered wreck, against the orders of the dying admiral to blow her up. National Portrait Gallery, London.

pages 26–27
The attack by English fireships on the Spanish Armada anchored in the Calais Roads. The Spaniards were forced to cut cables and run, harried by the English fleet and driven by the westerly gale out into the North Sea, and then north-about round the British Isles to get home. National Maritime Museum, London.

The Battle of Trafalgar. The *Redoutable* is attacked by the *Téméraire* after her long fight with the *Victory* (on her port side).

the British fleet was madness. It was the Spanish who had their way, and it was agreed that sailing should await the 'favourable moment' mentioned in Villeneuve's orders and which might arise 'if the enemy fleet is driven off by bad weather or obliged to divide its forces'.

Bound by such conditions the Combined Fleet's sortie might have been indefinitely postponed. But Villeneuve's hand was now to be forced. Behind his back the French General Lauriston, commanding the troops with the fleet, had been accusing him, in a series of letters to the Emperor, of cowardice and vacillation and, finally, of never having intended to try to go to Brest when he left Corunna. At this, Napoleon had ordered the Admiral's recall and his replacement by Admiral Rosily. No specific news of this was sent to Villeneuve, but rumours of his coming disgrace reached him; on 18 October it was known that Rosily had reached Madrid where a broken carriage spring had delayed him. The same evening a light north-easterly wind sprang up, suitable for working ships out of harbour and for a subsequent run for the Straits. From the French flagship, *Bucentaure*, the signal to sail was hoisted at dawn on the 19th.

Almost at once the breeze dropped to a whisper in which only seven ships of Admiral Magon's division and some frigates had been laboriously worked to the open sea before dark brought all movements to a halt. During the next forenoon the remainder, profiting by a fair wind from the south-south-west also got

to sea. Squalls, with heavy rain, assailed them. The Admiral signalled for reefs to be taken in; the untrained Spanish crews struggled inexpertly to obey but several ships suffered torn sails and fell away to leeward before they could do so. From the *Bucentaure* a man fell overboard: the *Redoutable*, next astern, displayed comparatively good seamanship as she was hove-to, a boat launched and the man picked up.

The fleet was in a sorry state of confusion, however, when at 1 p.m. the signal was made for a cruising order in three columns on a westerly course.

Lucas, whose station was at the head of the centre column, watched and recorded with contempt and fury the ineffectual efforts of his brother captains, French and Spanish, to comply. And when, at 4 p.m. the wind suddenly veered to west, dictating a southerly course, the confusion was made worse as some ships were taken aback; those which had tacked in time had to shorten sail to give the others a chance to take up station on the new course. The Combined Fleet was still an unformed mass of ships when darkness fell.

All this had been watched and reported by the scouting British frigates manoeuvring to windward, and, after dark the coloured lights and guns of their signals seen and heard in that direction kept up the alarm. Meanwhile, just before dusk, the French *Achille*, out ahead of the remainder had sighted the British fleet away to the south-south-west; when this

AN° · DÑI · 1571 ·
ÆTATIS · SVÆ
· 29 ·

25

28

news reached Villeneuve at 8.30 p.m. the admiral made the signal – one of the few simple night signals available to the Combined Fleet, using coloured flares – to form single line of battle.

Such order as had been painfully achieved now dissolved as, in the slackening wind and long uneasy swell from the west, ships steered independently to take up station. Even Lucas, who had been leading the centre column with the *Bucentaure* three ships astern of him, became lost as various ships repeated the flagship's signals. In accordance with the instructions for the manœuvre he bore away to form up on the most leeward ships which should have hoisted distinguishing lights at their mastheads. But he could see none of these and he eventually found himself alongside the *Principe de Asturias*, flagship of Rear-Admiral Gravina with whom he arranged that the *Redoutable* should go ahead and take the lead of those ships the Spanish Admiral had managed to assemble. Thus it was that at dawn Lucas found himself still leading the fleet. The windward horizon was studded with the white pyramids of Nelson's sails. A battle could not be avoided now, though in the faint westerly breeze it would be midday before it could be joined. Villeneuve – surely unwisely in the poor sailing conditions prevailing – signalled for 'single line ahead in normal sequence'. It called for a complete rearrangement of the rough array (it could not be described as a line) in which the fleet had

formed during the night.

The *Redoutable*, for instance, had to drop back past some fifteen ships to reach her station three ahead of the *Bucentaure*. Lucas wore ship immediately in compliance but it took two hours to cover the necessary two miles. Other ships were less promptly or less well handled and there was still much confusion when, at 8 a.m. Villeneuve signalled for the fleet to reverse course by wearing together and form line of battle in reverse order. For by that time he could see that the British fleet was steering in two groups in such a way as to concentrate on his rear – just as he had suggested would be their tactics in an order to his fleet; and, indeed, just as Nelson had propounded in his own Memorandum. By reversing order, making his rear into his van he hoped to be able to bring his new rear up to support the threatened part of his line when the clash came.

Alas for such hopes, at the speeds at which the two fleets were moving – the British, running before the breeze with every stitch of canvas spread, yet making barely three knots, the Combined Fleet, close-hauled, hardly moving – there was ample time, for the former, in the slow advance to battle, to adjust to the new situation. All that Villeneuve's signal accomplished was further confusion of his own formation; at the onset of the battle his fleet was in a rough crescent with the centre to leeward of his van and rear and with French and Spanish ships in random order, with

The scene round the *Redoutable* at the height of the Battle of Trafalgar.

some of them farther still to leeward. As the French *Fougueux* opened the battle at 11.50 a.m. with a broadside at the *Royal Sovereign*, leading the British squadron steering to engage the enemy's rear, the battle ensign was broken out from every ship in the Combined Fleet. In the *Redoutable* this was greeted, as Lucas was to report, in an imposing style: as the drums beat and the musketeers presented arms, it was saluted by the officers and crew with seven cries of 'Vive l'Empereur!'

The *Redoutable*'s station was now three ships astern of the *Bucentaure* and so, sixteenth in line, in the centre of the Allied formation. The two ships which should have been between the *Redoutable* and the French flagship had failed to take up their station. One of them, Lucas was to record, had fallen too far to leeward to be able to do so; the other 'turned aside to fire at the *Royal Sovereign* which was out of range'. Seeing the other British squadron headed by the *Victory* steering to pass under the *Bucentaure*'s stern, Lucas closed the gap and with his bowsprit overlapping the *Bucentaure*'s poop placed himself athwart Nelson's bows.

'Determined to sacrifice my ship for the defence of the flagship,' recorded Lucas, 'I explained this to my officer and crew who received my explanations with repeated shouts of "Vive l'Empereur! Vive l'Amiral! Vive le Commandant!" Preceded by fifes and drums I made a tour of the gun-decks: everywhere I found brave men, burning with impatience for the battle to begin; many of them called to me, "Captain, don't forget our boarding."

'At 11.30 (French times were an hour earlier than the British) the enemy squadron which was steering for our centre came within range and the *Bucentaure* and the ship ahead of her (the *Santissima Trinidad*, four-decker, 130-gun flagship of the Spanish Rear-Admiral, Cisneros) began to fire on the *Victory*. I called most of my gun-captains up on deck to show them how badly our ships were shooting: all their shots were falling short; I told them they must shoot to dismast and above all to aim straight.

'At 11.45 the *Redoutable* opened fire with a cannon shot from No. 1 Battery which shot away the fore topsail yard of the *Victory*, which was still steering for the *Redoutable*'s foremast. Cheers from the gun-decks; our fire was brisk; in less than ten minutes that ship had lost her mizzen mast, her fore topmast and her main top-gallant mast.

'The *Victory*'s damage in no way affected Admiral Nelson's bold tactics. He continued to steer to cut the line ahead of the *Redoutable* and threatened to ram us if we opposed that. The approach of this three-decker, followed closely by the *Téméraire*, far from overawing our intrepid crew, only increased their courage and, to show the English admiral that we had no fear of his boarding us, I had grapnels hoisted on all the yardarms.

'Finally the *Victory* having been unable to pass astern of the French admiral, crashed into our port side, overlapping us aft so that our poop was alongside and level with her quarter deck.

'In this position the grapnels were thrown over; the after ones were cut but those forward held; our broadsides were being fired with the gun muzzles touching the enemy's side and they caused a horrible carnage . . .'

It has to be said that at this stage in his report, the gallant Lucas permitted his imagination to run somewhat wild. The *Redoutable* was in fact thrust aside by her bigger opponent, which passed slowly across the *Bucentaure*'s wake to fire a terrible, raking broadside into the French flagship, killing or disabling 200 of her crew and dismounting twenty of her guns. And while the *Victory* lay with the *Redoutable* alongside her to starboard, she continued to fire her port broadsides at the *Bucentaure* and the *Santissima Trinidad*. Furthermore, the cannonade between the *Victory* and *Redoutable* was to a great extent a one-sided affair.

The *Victory*'s men had seen the *Redoutable*'s gunports slammed shut. Thus Lucas was romancing when he went on to say: 'For some time we continued to cannonade . . .; and, using our small arms at the gun positions we so successfully prevented the enemy from loading their guns that they ceased to fire at us. What a glorious day for the *Redoutable* if she had had the *Victory* alone to fight! Finally the *Victory*'s batteries were no longer able to reply to us.

'I saw that the crew of that ship were preparing to board us – her deck was crowded with men. I ordered the trumpet to sound, the signal arranged during our exercises for boarding stations. They paraded in such good order, officers and midshipmen at the head of their divisions, that one would have thought it a rehearsal. In less than a minute our decks were covered with armed men running up to the poop . . .

'There developed a brisk musketry duel which the Admiral Nelson fought at the head of his crew. Our fire was so superior to that of the enemy that in less than fifteen minutes the *Victory* was silent; more than 200 grenades were hurled on board her with the greatest success; her decks were a shambles of dead and dying.

'Admiral Nelson was killed by the musketry fire; at almost the same moment his ship completely ceased fighting us; but it was difficult to get on board her owing to the relative movement of the two ships and the greater height of her upper deck. I ordered the sling

of the main yard to be cut so that as it fell it made a bridge across. Midshipman Yon and four sailors scrambled over the *Victory*'s anchor to her deck and informed us that there was no-one at her guns; but just as our brave lads were about to leap after them the three-decker *Téméraire*, which had no doubt seen that the *Victory* fought no more and must inevitably be captured, sailed alongside us to starboard and riddled us with point-blank broadsides.

'It would be difficult to picture the carnage produced by these broadsides; more than 200 of our fellows were killed or wounded; I was myself wounded at this time, but not so severely as to put me out of action. Prevented thus from attempting anything further against the *Victory*, I ordered the survivors of my crew to man those starboard guns which had not been dismounted and to fire them at the *Téméraire*. This was done, but we were so weakened and so few guns remained in action that the *Téméraire*'s reply was far more effective . . . In less than a half-hour our ship was so riddled that she was just a heap of debris.

'In this condition the *Téméraire* hailed us to surrender and not prolong a useless resistance. I ordered some soldiers near me to reply with musket shots and this was smartly

carried out. At almost the same instant our mainmast fell across the *Téméraire* while her two topmasts fell on board the *Redoutable*.'

Lucas now goes on to give details of the fearful damage suffered by his ship and of the ghastly casualties amounting to 522 of the total crew of 643, of which 300 had been killed. Yet from the wounded came cries of '*Vive l'Empereur*! We're not taken yet! Is the Captain still alive?' The *Victory*, Lucas repeats, was no longer fighting and it was the fire of the *Téméraire* and another ship firing into her poop that was knocking the *Redoutable* to pieces. Only when he had made sure that his ship was so shattered and leaking that she could not stay afloat much longer, did Lucas at last order the flag to be struck.

Captain Lucas' account of the *Redoutable*'s part in the Battle of Trafalgar strays from the path of actuality in a number of points; but this is understandable from one trying to recall the details of so gallant and gory a fight against great odds amidst the deafening bellow of broadsides, the crash and confusion of falling masts and yards, the crackle of musketry and explosion of grenades, all seen through drifting, choking clouds of powder smoke.

Thus it was true enough that his tactics of concentrating his men aloft armed with

A painting of the action at Trafalgar made from the descriptions of officers who had served in the battle. The *Victory* is right, centre, with next to her the battered *Redoutable* and the *Téméraire*. By George Chambers after Clarkson Stanfield. National Maritime Museum, London.

After the Battle of Trafalgar. A storm was gathering, in which many of the captured French and Spanish ships were to be lost, including the *Redoutable*, which sank the following evening. National Maritime Museum, London.

muskets and grenades caused a great many casualties on the *Victory*'s upper decks, including Nelson's mortal wound from a musket ball. But far from there taking place any 'musketry duel during which Admiral Nelson fought at the head of his crew', the British grimly ignored the fusillade as far as they could and concentrated on the more decisive business of serving the great guns; while Nelson was struck down as he and Captain Hardy paced the quarter-deck with the *sang-froid* senior officers were expected to display on such occasions.

All the while the *Victory*'s two lower tiers of guns continued to fire into the *Redoutable*'s hull which their muzzles actually touched when they were run out. The lack of response by the *Redoutable*'s guns gave Hardy the impression that she had struck; and when he ordered a cease fire, Lucas thought he had silenced his opponent and attempted to take her by boarding; at which the *Victory*'s guns resumed the process of destroying the *Redoutable* under the mistakenly exultant feet of her exhilarated captain.

But it must indeed have seemed as though a magnificent capture was snatched from his hands when the *Téméraire* loomed out of the smoke clouds to run alongside to starboard.

So, as the *Redoutable*'s resistance came to an end and the firing died away, the three line-of-battle ships lay dismasted, locked together, only to drift down on to another French 74-gun, the *Fougeux* lying crippled and dismasted after a duel with the British *Belleisle*. The *Téméraire*'s guns roared out again briefly and when the tricolour was hauled down, a few men were sent across to take the *Fougeux* in prize.

Not yet, however, had the *Redoutable* been thus taken. The *Victory*'s prize crew were unable to get across to her and it was not until the British flagship managed to disentangle herself from the quartet of crippled ships and get under way that it was possible to send across two midshipmen in a boat. They found the *Redoutable* in a sinking condition with four of her six pumps destroyed; and Lucas now turned to the *Téméraire* to demand help in manning the remaining pumps—otherwise he would set his ship on fire, engulfing the *Téméraire* in the process.

Help was sent and when the *Téméraire* succeeded in disengaging about 7 o'clock that evening, the British sailors remained to strive alongside their recent enemies to keep the *Redoutable* afloat while the *Swiftsure* took her in tow. Conditions were far from easy owing to the increasing westerly swell in which the disabled ships rolled wildly; and during the following morning, as the storm which the swell presaged struck, it was soon evident that the *Redoutable* could not be saved. The *Swiftsure* hove-to and sent her boats to bring off the prize crew, Lucas and his officers and all other Frenchmen who could be moved. The end was recorded in the *Swiftsure*'s log: 'At a quarter past, the boats returned the last time with very few in them, the weather so bad and sea running high that rendered it impossible for the boat to pass. Got in the boats. At a quarter past ten the *Redoutable* sank by the stern.' She took with her five of the *Swiftsure*'s prize crew and thirteen of the *Téméraire*'s.

Lucas recorded this last scene: 'It was blowing hard and the sea was high, making embarkation of the wounded very difficult; these unfortunates, seeing that the ship was going to founder, crawled to the quarter deck whence it was possible to save some. At 7 o'clock in the evening . . . the *Redoutable* sank with the majority of these luckless men whose courage made them worthy of a better fate. The next day the captain of the *Swiftsure* seeing men clinging to wreckage, sent to rescue them; there were some fifty of them, almost all wounded.

'169 men, the survivors of the gallant crew of the *Redoutable* were thus gathered on board the English ship. Of these, 70 were severely wounded, 64 more lightly. All these wounded were sent back to Cadiz under a flag of truce, so that only 35 men were taken to England as prisoners.'

They had every reason to be proud of the part they had played in the battle. As Lucas reported, 'They had engaged throughout the action two English three-deckers where the great hero of the Royal Navy had been killed and more than 300 men, senior officers among them, had been put out of action. Both the *Victory* and *Téméraire* had been dismasted and had to be sent home for replacement of masts and extensive repairs.'

Lucas was one of those carried to England as a prisoner-of-war. He was released on parole in 1806 and on his return to France was presented to the Emperor who made him a Commander of the Legion of Honour. He was to serve again with distinction commanding the *Regulus* during the fireship attack by Lord Cochrane on the Rochefort squadron in the Aix Roads, twice refloating his stranded ship under enemy fire and reaching harbour safely.

Lucas' unfashionable loyalty to the defeated Villeneuve, whose conduct he defended, earned him the hostility of Decrés, Napoleon's Minister of Marine, however. Promotion was denied him: he retired in 1816 and, his health collapsing, died on 6 November 1819.

Bearing the *Redoutable*'s honoured name today is the French navy's first nuclear-powered, ballistic-missile submarine.

Le Redoutable, France's first nuclear-powered ballistic-missile submarine, built at Cherbourg and commissioned in 1969.

'OLD IRONSIDES' USS CONSTITUTION

Hartt's Naval Yard in Boston Harbour was crowded with excited citizens on the morning of 21 October 1797. The excitement was no doubt tempered with some mildly malicious anticipation; for the people had gathered to see the second attempt to launch one of the six frigates which were to comprise a reborn United States Navy.

On the first occasion a month earlier, in the presence of the President, the Governor and other notables, the slope of the slipway had proved inadequate: the new ship had failed to move when the shores were knocked out. On this occasion, however, having been fully baptised with a bottle of wine and named the *Constitution*, 'she commenced' in the words of an attendant journalist, 'a movement into the water with such steadiness, majesty and exactness as to fill almost every breast with sensations of joy and delight'.

The ship which had thus nobly entered the water for the first time was no ordinary frigate by the standards of the day. Her design and that of the other five ships authorized had been entrusted to Joshua Humphreys, a ship-builder of Philadelphia. He had had the perspicacity to appreciate that a navy so much smaller than those of the great powers could only make itself felt if it was composed of frigates powerful enough to outclass foreigners of a similar 'rate', sufficiently good seaboats to be a match for two-decker ships-of-the-line in heavy weather when the latter would have difficulty in operating their lower tiers, and fast and manoeuvrable enough to evade action with them in light winds.

As a first essential, therefore, the new frigates were to mount thirty long 24-pounder guns on the main or gun deck as compared to the 18-pounders carried by frigates of other navies. To withstand the consequent strains as well as to offer a stouter defence against an enemy's cannon fire, their scantlings were to be the equal of those of 74-gun battleships and built of tough red cedar and live oak. The side planking was to be from 17 to 20 inches thick as compared to 11 to 15 inches in contemporary frigates. For so heavy a ship to retain the fine lines necessary for good sailing

qualities, she would have to be larger than the normal frigate; and with an overall length of 204 feet, a waterline length of 175 feet and a beam of 43·6 feet, the *Constitution* was 20 feet longer and five feet broader than a contemporary British 38-gun frigate. Her displacement was 2200 tons.

In addition to her thirty 24-pounders she carried other guns on the quarter-deck and forecastle, originally ten long 12-pounders which were later replaced by carronades–the short-barrelled, light 'smashers' which fired a comparatively heavy ball to a shorter range. In her hey-day, the War of 1812, the *Constitution*, though rated a 44-gun ship was to mount thirty 24-pounders on the main deck, sixteen 32-pounder carronades on the quarter-deck and six on the forecastle as well as one long 18-pounder and two long 24-pounders as bow chasers, a total of 55. This rating anomaly was in fact a normal practice in all navies, a British 38-gun frigate, for instance, actually mounting 49 guns in all.

Like the launching of the *Constitution*, the renaissance of the United States Navy had suffered from delays and doubts. The laying-down of six frigates had been authorized by Congress in 1794. They were to form the backbone of a squadron whose first task was to have been to overawe the corsair states of the Barbary Coast–Algiers and Tunis–and force their rulers to cease molesting American merchant ships in the Mediterranean. They had been nearing completion at the end of 1795 when a treaty to that effect with the Dey of Algiers persuaded Congress that a navy was no longer necessary. Work on the frigates was halted.

In the meantime, however, the American merchant service had begun to suffer indignities and interference from the navies of both Britain and France, who had been at war with one another since 1792. British warships, perennially short of hands, were in the habit of stopping American merchantmen and impressing from amongst their crews men who could not prove their American citizenship. At the same time French privateers in the West Indies were seizing the same merchantmen on the grounds that the goods they carried between British possessions and the States were contraband.

With their sea-borne trade, so vital to American prosperity, thus threatened from two sides, Congress decided reluctantly to take action. In July 1797 work on three of the six frigates, the *Constitution*, the *United States* and the *Constellation* was resumed. By the summer of 1798 they were ready for sea. The quarrel with England was patched up temporarily. But an attempt to make a treaty with republican France foundered on the expectation by French ministers of bribes to obtain their signatures. Though war was never officially declared, Congress now authorized reprisals against French shipping; until March 1801, when a treaty at last brought hostilities to an end, small squadrons, each centred on one of the new men-of-war, operated amongst the West Indies in pursuit of French privateers. The big frigates were unsuitable for this service, which called rather for small, fast and handy armed schooners: the *Constitution* had thus seen very little action by the time she was paid off into reserve and dismantled at Boston Navy Yard. She had, nevertheless, had one success to confirm Josiah Humphreys' uncanny skill as a ship designer. Challenged by a British frigate to a day-long race beating to windward, she scored a clear victory to win the wager of a cask of Madeira for her Captain, Silas Talbot.

The *Constitution* did not remain long out of service on this occasion. On 14 August 1803 she sailed for the Mediterranean under Edward Preble. He was to assume command of the squadron which, since the summer of 1801 had been maintained there in defence of American shipping which had come under attack by the corsairs of Tripoli. The Dey, consumed by jealousy of the ruler of Algiers who had extracted a handsome annual tribute from the American government, as well as the gift of a frigate, in return for a promise not to molest their merchant ships, was determined to secure similar 'protection' payment.

Once again the big frigates proved too large and too deep draughted for the task of chasing the corsairs amongst the inshore shallows for which they invariably made. For that purpose the two brigs and three schooners which made up for the squadron were more effective and the *Constitution* herself gained no laurels. Her sister ship, the *Philadelphia*, ran aground off Tripoli in October 1803 while thus engaged; she was captured by the corsairs, and her crew were made prisoners. Preble achieved renown through his planning of an expedition to destroy the frigate which was being prepared for service by her captors in Tripoli harbour.

'Old Ironsides'–USS *Constitution*. Rated a 44-gun frigate, she mounted thirty long 24-pounders on the main deck, 32-pounder carronades on the quarter deck, six on the forecastle as well as two long 24-pounders and one 18-pounder bow chasers.

Commodore Edward Preble, who flew his pennant in the *Constitution* in operations against the Dey of Tripoli 1803–5. US Bureau of Ships.

A popular contemporary print showing Stephen Decatur's exploit in leading a boat party to burn the captured US frigate *Philadelphia* in Tripoli harbour.

But it was Stephen Decatur, leader of the actual exploit which succeeded in burning the *Philadelphia* without the loss of a man, whose name is best remembered in connection with it.

A peace treaty by which the payment of tribute to Tripoli was brought to an end and all American captives released, was signed on board the *Constitution* on 3 June 1805. The ship returned home in 1807 and was again placed in reserve for two years in the Navy Yard at New York. Recommissioned in 1809 she served on the home station until August 1811 when she again crossed the Atlantic to carry the new American Minister to France, returning in time to be refitted at Washington in readiness for the outbreak of war with England on 18 June 1812.

The causes of this most unnecessary of wars were twofold. Firstly, in the struggle between Britain and France, each side declared 'blockades' of their opponent's territory. The British, supreme at sea, were the more effective in enforcement, thus inflicting painful blows to American prosperity. The rigours of their blockade would have been relaxed to avoid war with the United States; and, indeed, the Orders in Council regulating it were in the process of being annulled at the very time that President Madison was declaring war.

But it was the second cause which made war inevitable – British insistence upon their right to stop and search American ships and to recover any British deserters found amongst their crews, a procedure which resulted in numerous cases of injustice and illegal arrest. American national pride was deeply wounded. Only war could adequately restore it.

In the long run the British naval predominance was to bring American sea-borne trade – and thereby American prosperity – to a halt; a mere fraction of the British fleet deployed off the American east coast was to be sufficient for the purpose; and although, of the six frigates first authorized by Congress, two were captured, three immobilized by the British blockade and only the *Constitution* remained in commission at the end of the war, the tiny United States Navy was to teach the arrogant and over-confident Royal Navy some sharp lessons and to gain evergreen laurels in the process.

The *Constitution* was still refitting when war was declared and it was not until 12 July 1812 that, under the command of Captain Isaac Hull, she cleared the Virginia Capes and shaped course for New York where she was to

join her sister ship the *President*, flagship of a small squadron under Commodore John Rodgers. The junction was never made, however: Rodgers had sailed out into the Atlantic in search of the British trade convoy from the West Indies: the *Constitution* on the evening of 17 July, sailed into the arms of a British squadron of four frigates and the 64-gun ship *Africa* which Hull at first mistook for his compatriots.

There were problems of identity also amongst the British but, after a night of uneasy manœuvring both sides realized the situation at dawn and in the light and fitful airs of a blue summer day a chase began which was to be remembered as something of an epic. The British were to windward; while the breeze lasted, it seemed that the *Constitution* must be caught and, indeed, cannon shots were for a while exchanged between the bow and stern chasers of either side. When the wind finally died away altogether Captain Broke of the leading British frigate, the *Shannon*, called for boats from all the squadrons to take him in tow. In this way the gap was being steadily reduced and, as the *Constitution*'s Lieutenant, Charles Morris, was to write in his account of the episode, 'this seemed to decide our fate'.

But it was not for nothing that Isaac Hull had been trained under Preble and had been sailing master of the *Constitution* when she won her famous race with the British frigate fourteen years earlier. Appreciating that there was only a depth of twenty-five fathoms under his keel where the ship was floating, he adopted a device used normally to get a ship out of harbour when the wind was unfavourable or lacking. All the available hawsers, totalling nearly a mile in length, were rove together and attached to a kedge anchor which was carried ahead in a boat. The anchor was dropped, the ship hauled up to it and the process repeated.

Slowly the American frigate drew away from her pursuers. But it was not long before the British copied and even improved upon Hull's device. By using two anchors in such a way that, while the ship was being hove up to one, the other was being laid out ahead, they again closed the gap during the afternoon of the 18th and the succeeding night. At dawn a light but steady breeze from the south got up; the *Constitution*, heading to the north-westward, found the four enemy frigates spread on a circle between her lee bow and lee quarter. Hull decided that the time had come to use his ship's sailing capabilities to break away even at the risk of being crippled in an exchange of fire. The smallest of the enemy was the 32-gun *Aeolus* on his lee quarter. Wearing ship, he steered close-hauled on the starboard tack which took him within gunshot of her. As the *Constitution* sped past, to Hull's

above
Commodore Stephen Decatur, US Navy, who first gained renown by leadership of the naval exploit which burned the captured *Philadelphia* in Tripoli harbour. In the War of 1812 he commanded the frigate *United States* and captured the British frigate *Macedonian* in a single-ship action in October 1812

Captain Isaac Hull, who commanded the *Constitution* at the beginning of the War of 1812. In her he defeated and forced the surrender of the British frigate *Guerrière* which mounted a total of forty-nine guns.

On 17 July 1812, less than one
month after the opening of the
War of 1812, the *Constitution*
ran unwittingly into the arms
of a British squadron of one
line-of-battle ship and four
frigates, a trap from which her
Captain, Isaac Hull, extracted
her by his outstanding
seamanship.

surprise, not a shot was fired at her; nor did he open fire on the *Aeolus*. The wind increased, the *Constitution* began to show her paces and by the afternoon at a spanking $12\frac{1}{2}$ knots she was drawing away. By daylight on the 20th the leading British frigate, the *Belvedere*, was hull-down to leeward; soon afterwards the chase was finally abandoned and Hull was able to return to Boston. Captain Byron, of the *Belvedere*, wrote to Captain Broke of the *Shannon*: 'Nothing can exceed my mortification from the extraordinary escape of the American frigate . . .'

Isaac Hull took the *Constitution* to sea again on 2 August 1812. Fate nearly deprived the diminutive (five feet tall), plump, little fire-eater of his place in the roll of American naval heroes; for the very next day orders reached Boston to hold the ship in harbour until her newly appointed commanding officer, Captain William Bainbridge could take over. Before that, the *Constitution* had been sailed out into the Atlantic to look for trouble; and, there, some 360 miles south-east of Halifax, Nova Scotia, at 2 p.m. on 19 August, she found it, the frigate *Guerrière*, which backed her main topsail and lay, hove-to to leeward, awaiting the American frigate's onset.

The *Guerrière*, as her name suggests, had been captured from the French. By the custom mentioned earlier, she was classified a 38-gun frigate though, in fact, she mounted thirty long 18-pounders on the gun-deck, sixteen 32-pounder carronades, one 18-pounder and a long 12-pounder on quarter-deck and forecastle, a total of 49, firing a broadside of 556 pounds. In the same way, as noted earlier, the *Constitution*, rated a 44-gun

frigate, carried 55 guns, those on the gun-deck being 24-pounders.

The American, with this more powerful armament and a crew of 456 as opposed to 282 in their opponent, was greatly superior materially. Nevertheless, Captain Dacres of the *Guerrière* accepted battle with the absolute confidence born of fourteen years of warfare during which the British had achieved complete supremacy over the navy of their French enemy. He had earlier, indeed, sent a challenge to Commodore Rodgers saying he would be happy to meet 'the United States frigate *President* . . . or any other American frigate of equal force off Sandy Hook, for the purpose of having a few minutes' *tête-a-tête*'. Unfortunately for him, however, whereas the long run of easy victories had led to a neglect of gunnery practice in his and other British men-of-war, and an over-emphasis on 'spit and polish', in the *Constitution* the men had been continually exercised at the guns since commissioned seven weeks before. Furthermore the Americans had devised a form of adjustable sights for their guns, while the British still aimed theirs by eye alone.

Nevertheless the action opened in conditions far from favourable for the American as Hull, coming down with the north-westerly breeze on his port quarter had to approach head-on to the enemy; the *Guerrière* was thus able to fire raking broadsides at the *Constitution* which could reply only with her bow chasers. Fortunately for the latter the British shooting was poor and some of the few shots which struck the *Constitution*'s hull were seen to bounce off her stout timbers, at which one of her sailors shouted 'Hurrah! Her sides are made of iron' causing the name 'Old Ironsides' to be applied to her for ever after.

As the *Constitution* drew closer, the *Guerrière* bore up, placing the wind on her port quarter, whereupon Hull also wore ship on to the same tack and gradually drew abreast of the enemy. While this was happening the *Guerrière* fired broadside after broadside; but the Americans, at Hull's orders, made no reply, though suffering casualties, until at last as the *Constitution* drew up abreast and her every gun could bear, their little captain, leaping so excitedly in the air that his tight breeches split, yelled: 'Now boys; pour it into them.'

The result was horrifying as the hail of round-shot lashed the *Guerrière* again and again. Within ten minutes her mizen-mast had fallen over the starboard side, her hull had received so much waterline damage that the inrush of water could not be controlled. As the American frigate began to draw ahead, Hull ordered the helm over and took her athwart the *Guerrière*'s course. Before the two ships came together with the *Guerrière*'s bowsprit enmeshed in the *Constitution*'s rigging, the latter had had time to pour in two devastating raking broadsides. Within a few minutes the British frigate was silenced and at 6.30 p.m. Hull disengaged from her to make repairs to his rigging. When he approached again, Captain Dacres, his ship now totally dismasted and making water fast and her decks red with blood, surrendered. Fifteen of his men had been killed, another 63 were wounded. In the *Constitution* seven had been lost, and seven more wounded. So shattered was the *Guerrière* that an attempt to get her into harbour had to be abandoned and she was burnt.

A civic welcome by the city of Boston, with a banquet in honour of Hull and his officers who also received commemorative medals and swords; prize money of 50,000 dollars voted by Congress – such were the marks of satisfaction by the delirious citizens of the United States at this triumph at a time when all was gloom elsewhere in respect of the progress of the war. In England the news was received with incredulous shocked dismay.

Before the *Constitution* got to sea again on 27 October 1812, another British frigate, the *Macedonian* (38) had similarly been shattered and set ablaze by the *United States*. Isaac Hull, having commanded for two years, had been relieved by William Bainbridge, who now hoisted a Commodore's flag and sailed in company with the 18-gun sloop *Hornet*. They had had an uneventful cruise through the West Indies and southward along the Brazilian coast when, early in December, the British 18-gun sloop *Bonne Citoyenne* was discovered in the neutral harbour of Bahia. In the hope that the British sloop would respond to a

challenge sent in by the *Hornet* to come out and fight, Bainbridge announced that he would not interfere with such a duel. He then sailed off up the coast; but the *Bonne Citoyenne*, laden with specie, correctly ignored the challenge and it was the luck of Old Ironsides to be the one to find an opponent.

On 29 December 1812 at 9 in the morning, running down towards her before a brisk north-easterly breeze, there came into view the British frigate *Java*. Like the *Guerrière*, she had been taken from the French; like her, too, though rated a 38 she had 49 guns in all– nearly as many as the *Constitution* but with the difference that her main, long-range armament was made up of 18-pounders only. Captain Lambert of the *Java* had not heard of the fate of the *Guerrière* and *Macedonian*; though he had an abnormally large crew of some 400 including a draft for other ships of the East Indies squadron, they were as indifferently drilled at the guns as most British frigates of the period; but he had no qualms at steering after the 'chase', as the *Constitution* drawing him to seaward was described in his log.

At 1.30, however, Bainbridge reversed course and steered to close the *Java*, wearing ship in time to set a parallel course on the port tack before exposing himself to raking fire from the enemy. Both ships now shortened sail and cleared for action. At about a half a mile the *Constitution*'s 24-pounders roared out and were able to inflict damage on her opponent at a range at which the *Java* could do little. It was now two o'clock; for the next forty minutes Lambert was forced to endure this falling situation, his efforts to close being foiled by Bainbridge's adroit manœuvres until the latter decided that the time had come for a decision. Setting his fore-mainsail he luffed up; the *Java*, trying to sail across his bow, failed to do so and succeeded only in thrusting her jib-boom into the *Constitution*'s mizen rigging.

Lambert called for boarders, but with many of his men he was shot down by Bainbridge's sharpshooters in the tops; and before an assault could be mounted the two ships pulled apart, the *Java*'s bowsprit and jib-boom being torn away in the process. In the exchange of broadsides that followed during the next hour the American shooting was far more effective than that of the *Java*, where great confusion existed as her masts were brought down one by one in a wild tangle of rigging. By four o'clock she was completely dismasted and virtually silenced. Bainbridge sailed out of range to make repairs. Lieutenant Henry Chads who had succeeded to the command of the *Java* in place of the mortally wounded Lambert, strove manfully to restore some degree of fighting capability; but when the *Constitution* was again brought back and

Captain Philip Broke of the British frigate *Shannon*, one of the ships from which the *Constitution* escaped on 18 July 1812. Later in the war the *Shannon* overwhelmed and captured the American frigate *Chesapeake*. National Maritime Museum, London.

HM frigate *Guerrière*, dismasted and shattered, about to surrender to the *Constitution*. Metropolitan Museum of Art, New York. Gift of Edgar William and Bernice Chrysler Garbisch, 1962.

Commodore William Bainbridge, who commanded the *Constitution* when she fought and captured the British frigate *Java* on 29 December 1812. The chivalry with which he treated his beaten foes was a feature of the episode.

stationed in position to fire raking broadsides, the hopelessness of the situation was obvious and at half past five Chads hauled down the ensign which had been nailed to the stump of a mast.

In the *Java* 48 men had been killed or mortally wounded, more than 100 more had been otherwise wounded. The *Constitution* had lost 12 with 22 more wounded including Bainbridge himself and Lieutenant John C. Aylwin. The latter was to die of his wound a month later. The British frigate was so shattered that, like the *Guerrière* she could not be got to harbour to grace an American triumph but had to be burnt. The *Constitution*, comparatively little damaged, took her prisoners into Bahia where they were released on parole.

The chivalry with which the two navies conducted themselves–in sharp contrast to the savage verbal assaults of contemporary journalists and historians–was displayed in Lieutenant Chad's 'grateful acknowledgement for the generous treatment Captain Lambert and his officers have received from our gallant enemy, Commodore Bainbridge and his officers', in his report to the Admiralty. Bainbridge, indeed, himself painfully

wounded, limped on deck to return his sword to the dying Lambert as he was carried ashore. Lieutenant General Hislop, who had been taking passage in the *Java* to take up his appointment as Governor of Bombay, presented Bainbridge with a gold-mounted sword in gratitude for the kindness and consideration with which he had been treated.

Once again, at the end of February 1813, the *Constitution* sailed into Boston Harbour to the cheers of the populace. Once again banquets and medals were lavished on officers and prize money on the men. The *Java* was to be the last regular frigate of the Royal Navy to succumb to one of the American superfrigates; for the Admiralty had learned their lesson. Henceforth British frigates would cruise only in pairs; they were enjoined to avoid pitting their 18-pounders against 24-pounders in single-ship actions if possible. Meanwhile, 74-gun two-deckers were cut down to act as 50-gun frigates and sent out to join the blockade of American ports.

This blockade was very effective in neutralizing the major units of the United States Navy. Though it could not prevent a swarm of American privateers from destructively harrying British merchant ships even

in the latter's own home waters, it kept the *Constitution* penned in harbour until the end of 1813. Then a brief cruise in the Caribbean under the command of Captain Charles Stewart which brought only a single prize – a 14-gun schooner, HMS *Pique* – came to an end early in April 1814 when she narrowly escaped from two British 38s to get back in Boston Harbour.

Winter storms disrupting the blockade enabled Stewart to get out again in December 1814 and cross the Atlantic to prey upon British shipping. By this time negotiations for peace were under way between delegates meeting at Ghent and on 8 February it was learned that a treaty had been signed. Hostilities would not come to an end until ratification by the two governments, however; in the meantime Stewart cruised along the trade route between Madeira and the coast of Africa, picking up the odd merchant-ship prize. But his crew, volunteers who had been attracted to Old Ironsides by her fighting reputation, were disgruntled at the thought of ending the war without a go at the 'Limeys'. Knowing this, Stewart was curiously inspired to prophesy to them on the morning of 19 February that 'before two suns have set you

will be in action with the enemy and it will not be with a single ship'.

And sure enough at one o'clock on the following afternoon, as the *Constitution* was running before a north-easterly breeze, two sail were sighted to leeward steering north-westerly on the starboard tack. They were British men-of-war; the frigate-built *Cyane*, commanded by Captain Gordon Thomas Falcon, mounting twenty-two 32-pounder carronades on her gun-deck and eight 18-pounder carronades on the spar deck as well as two long 12-pounders; and some ten miles to leeward of her the *Levant*, a sloop armed with eighteen 32-pounder carronades, two long 9-pounders and one 12-pounder commanded by Captain The Hon. George Douglas, senior officer of the two.

Stewart at once spread every stitch of canvas including studding sails and bore down on the *Cyane* in the hope of catching her out of supporting distance of her consort. He over-reached himself, however, carrying away his main royal mast; the delay in making repairs defeated his purpose and by 5.30 the *Cyane* was within hail of the *Levant*. Individually each was totally outclassed and outgunned by the *Constitution*; neither of the

The USS *Constitution* (Commodore Bainbridge) forces the surrender of the British frigate *Java*, mounting forty-nine guns. So shattered was the latter that she could not be got into harbour and had to be burned.

British captains wished to get involved in a decisive engagement even with the close support of the other. On the other hand they knew that two British convoys were somewhere in the area and they could not simply run from their big opponent, leaving her free, perhaps, to get amongst the merchantmen.

Douglas told Falcon that he intended to try to manœuvre so as to disable her; for the moment the two British ships sailed close-hauled on the starboard tack in the hope of gaining the weather-gauge; when this failed as well as other efforts to delay action until nightfall, they formed into line with the wind on the starboard beam, the *Levant* being some 200 yards ahead; they then hoisted their battle ensigns and awaited the enemy's onset as the sun was setting over the leeward horizon. At five minutes past six the *Constitution* turned on to the same tack on their weather side at a distance of some 1,500 yards at which she was able to do considerable damage to the *Cyane* with her long 24-pounders while staying out of range of her opponent's carronades. This, of course, gave the American ship an advantage that, in combination with her windward position, must have given her victory eventually. The action which followed, however, is notable, none the less, for the smart seamanship and skilful manœuvring of Captain Stewart and

his men which brought about the surrender of the *Cyane* within forty-five minutes of the first broadside.

Having cannonaded the *Cyane* for fifteen minutes, cutting up her rigging, the *Constitution* ranged ahead to give her attention to the *Levant*. At this Captain Falcon luffed up to close the range, bringing the *Cyane* on to the American's port quarter. The *Constitution* might now have found herself in difficulties with her two opponents, whose combined broadside totalled more than her own, engaging her simultaneously. Stewart's answer to the situation was to back his yards and go astern until he was able to pour a whole broadside into the *Cyane* at point-blank range.

In an effort to come to the *Cyane*'s assistance, Douglas was meanwhile wearing ship; so that when Stewart filled his sails again and shot ahead, this brought him across the *Levant*'s stern from which position two raking broadsides wreaked fearful damage on the little sloop which staggered away down wind to make repairs. It was the *Cyane*'s turn now to draw the enemy's fire again as Falcon took her ahead to cover the *Levant*'s retirement; she then turned down wind in the hope of escaping in the gathering darkness; but Stewart also wore ship and, crossing the *Cyane*'s stern, poured in such a destructive raking fire that, at 6.50 p.m., with his rigging cut to

The British 38-gun frigate *Macedonian* strikes her colours to the 44-gun American frigate *United States* (Captain Stephen Decatur), sister to the *Constitution*. National Maritime Museum, London.

pieces, his masts tottering and numerous shot holes between wind and water, Falcon decided that further resistance was hopeless. A shot fired to leeward and a light hoisted in the rigging signalled his surrender.

For the next hour Stewart was occupied in taking possession of his prize and repairing damage sufficiently to go after the *Levant*, in sight to leeward in the moonlight. At about the same time Douglas completed the reeving of new braces and, having made some other repairs to his battle damage, might perhaps have made good his escape. Rashly, however, it must be judged (though apparently he did not realize that the *Cyane* had surrendered), he now beat back towards the *Constitution* and at 8.40 p.m. the two ships passed on opposite tacks barely fifty yards apart. Broadsides were exchanged after which the *Constitution* immediately wore under the *Levant*'s stern to rake her cruelly once again. When Douglas at last realized the hopelessness of his situation and turned to escape down wind, it was too late. He was intercepted by his big opponent and hammered into surrender at 10.30 p.m.

So ended the last fight of Old Ironsides. Six Americans had been killed and nine wounded. On the British side, the figures were 19 and 42. To a modern generation this seems shocking, considering that it was known that a peace treaty had been signed and, in fact, had been ratified three days before the action. But in that age, when life was held more cheaply amongst Western nations, war was a matter of personal confrontation in which individual honour and that of 'the flag' was as much at stake as the more material consequence of any battle. Stewart and his men were determined to emulate the exploits of previous crews of the *Constitution* in defeating British men-of-war; they persuaded themselves that the combined strength of the two minor war vessels was as great as that of a single regular frigate. On the other side Douglas and Falcon no doubt felt that in face of the *Constitution*'s aggressive approach, something must be attempted for the sake of their personal honour and that of the Royal Navy. But Stewart's clever manoeuvring turned what they must have hoped would be an indecisive skirmish into a disastrous defeat.

The Americans themselves were now to have a narrow escape from an encounter with a similarly overwhelming superior force. Stewart had taken the frigate and her two prizes to the Cape Verde Islands and, at fifteen minutes after noon on 11 March 1815 they were lying in the harbour of Porto Praya, Santiago, about to trans-ship their prisoners into a merchant-brig. A low-lying haze covered the water, but above it were

43

The *Constitution*, under the command of Captain Charles Stewart, defeats and captures the British frigate *Cyane* in forty-five minutes and goes on to take the sloop-of-war *Levant*. Stewart's brilliant handling of his ship was a notable feature of the incident. US Bureau of Ships.

seen the masts and sails of three large ships approaching. They could be none other than British men-of-war; Stewart at once cut his cable and, followed by his two prizes, put to sea.

The strangers were, indeed, a British squadron, composed of two cut-down line-of-battle ships, the 50-gun *Leander*, Captain Sir George Ralph Collier, senior officer of the squadron and *Newcastle*, Captain Lord George Stuart, and the 40-gun frigate *Acasta*, Captain Alexander Robert Kerr. They had for the last three months been searching for the *Constitution* which, from false intelligence fed to them, was supposed to be operating in company with the *President* and *Congress*. And now, as Collier ordered his ships to tack in chase, he seems to have believed that such, indeed, was the force some four miles to windward, in spite of the great difference in size between the *Constitution* and her prizes.

Of the British ships the *Acasta* was the best sailer and she was soon overtaking and working to windward of the enemy. In the hope of dividing his pursuers, Stewart signalled to the lagging *Cyane* to tack; but Collier ignored

this—according to his subsequent report, not because he realized how much less important she was, but because he judged she must reach the neutral waters of Porto Praya before she could be overtaken. The *Cyane*, once out of sight, circled astern of the British and set course for New York where she eventually arrived safely.

Meanwhile, the *Acasta* was continuing to gain on the *Constitution* where dismay at the apparently certain prospect of being taken seized the American officers while Douglas and Falcon could scarce disguise their elation. Once again Stewart tried the same ruse, ordering the little *Levant* also to tack. As she did so, to the Americans' incredulous joy, not just one of their pursuers but all three tacked in pursuit, fading into the haze; by 3 o'clock the *Constitution* was alone and free to shape course for America and safety.

Although the bungling of this great opportunity by Sir George Collier was naturally a matter of much comment and criticism in naval circles, no court-martial was ordered and various specious excuses based on the thickness of the weather and some unfortunate

44

A model of 'Old Ironsides' in the US Naval Academy, Annapolis.

signalling mishaps were accepted. Stewart was certainly lucky to bring Old Ironsides safely to New York where he arrived on 15 May 1815.

The war was by this time over. The *Constitution* required refitting and was out of service for the next six years. However, in 1821 she was commissioned again as flagship of the American squadron in the Mediterranean and, with a break in 1823 to recomission, she continued in that service until 1828. A survey of her at that time reported her as unseaworthy. But when she was condemned to be broken up, a furious outcry was raised, encouraged by the heroic poem 'Old Ironsides' by Oliver Wendell Holmes of which the last stanza read:

Oh better that her shattered hulk
Should sink beneath the wave;
Her thunders shook the mighty deep,
And there should be her grave;
Nail to the mast her holy flag,
Set every threadbare sail,
And give her to the god of storms,
The lightning and the gale.

Congress was persuaded to vote the money to rebuild the *Constitution* on the lines of her original design. And in 1835 she was once again commissioned for service on the Mediterranean Station. From that time until 1851 she was kept in service with intervals of laying-up for refit. In 1860 she was again brought out of retirement to serve as a training ship for the US Naval Academy until 1871, when, once again, she was rebuilt, work which took until 1877. A period as training ship for apprentice boys followed; but in 1881 she went out of commission–for the last time it might have been thought–and on the hundredth anniversary of her launching was the central figure of a great reception at her birthplace in her honour.

Again, however, in 1907 the old ship was rebuilt to serve as a naval museum. In 1927 yet again she was reconstructed and even commissioned in 1930 to make exhibition cruises to United States ports. Today, Old Ironsides, pride of the United States Navy, lies in dry-dock at Boston, open to the public to let them see how sailors lived and fought in sailing ships in the brave days of old.

MIKASA

The Japanese Empire had been induced by a show of American naval force in 1853 to emerge from its self-imposed isolation from all contact with the outside world which had existed since 1637. A series of treaties with the leading Western powers had followed, opening a number of ports to trade and foreign residence.

Unlike the Chinese, who had been similarly coerced, the Japanese had quickly realized that to avoid exploitation they had to catch up with Western technology and acquire modern Western armaments. Having done so they joined, and, indeed, far exceeded the Western powers in aggression against the enfeebled Manchu government of China. Annexing the Ryukyu Islands in 1879, they went on to clash with the Chinese over the suzerainty of the kingdom of Korea; and in 1894 war broke out in which the Chinese were quickly and decisively defeated on land and sea.

At the Treaty of Shimonoseki which concluded the war, China ceded Formosa, the Pescadores and the Liaotung Peninsula—on which the naval base of Port Arthur was situated—to Japan, and agreed to pay a large indemnity. When Germany, Russia and France combined to force Japan to relinquish possession of the Liaotung Peninsula, she felt bitterly humiliated: and when Russia then obtained a lease of it for herself and proceeded to establish her influence over the Korean government, eventual hostilities became certain. Japan, therefore, devoted much of the Chinese indemnity to building up her armed strength, notably her navy for which she ordered six battleships of the latest type from British yards.

These ships, the *Fuji*, *Yashima*, *Shikishima*, *Hatsuse*, *Asahi* and the *Mikasa*, subject of this history, were examples of the ultimate development of the battleship prior to the revolutionary design of the *Dreadnought*, whose launch in 1906 made all previous battleships obsolete. Completed in 1902, the *Mikasa*, built by Vickers at Barrow-in-Furness, displacing 15,200 tons, mounted four 12-inch guns in twin turrets, fore and aft, with a secondary armament of seven 6-inch on each side and twenty 3-inch. The big guns were protected by armour 14 inches thick, her sides by an armoured belt 9 inches thick amidships, tapering to 4 inches at each end. There was also an armoured deck, 4 inches thick where it sloped towards the sides. Two triple expansion reciprocating engines, fed with steam by 25 Belleville water-tube boilers, generated a maximum power of 15,000 horse-power to drive her through twin propellers at 18 knots. Flying the flag of Vice-Admiral Heihachiro Togo, Commander-in-Chief of the Japanese fleet, the *Mikasa*, with the five other battleships mentioned above, formed the 1st Division of the 1st Squadron and the hard core around which the fleet was organized. The remainder of the fleet consisted of cruiser squadrons and a number of destroyers, little ships of some 350 tons at that date, and mounting two or three 18-inch torpedo tubes.

Negotiations between Russia and Japan, aimed at a compromise solution of their dispute over Korea and Russia's occupation of Chinese territory, were begun towards the end of 1902; but they dragged on inconclusively and with little trust on either side; and when, at the end of January 1904 it became clear that the Russians were merely trying to gain time to improve their military situation in the Far East, while the Japanese had achieved their maximum naval strength by the acquisition of two new armoured cruisers from Italy, the latter decided to begin hostilities without formal declaration by a surprise destroyer torpedo attack on the Russian fleet at Port Arthur.

So on the morning of 6 February 1904 the *Mikasa* led the Japanese fleet to sea from Sasebo out into the Yellow Sea; and on the evening of the 8th Togo detached his destroyers which, to cheers from the big ships, slipped away into the dusk with all lights extinguished, to make history with the first mass torpedo attack, later to become a regular feature of naval tactics. Their target lying at anchor in the open Roads outside Port Arthur, with normal lights burning, with guns unloaded, the crews turned in on their mess-decks and no torpedo nets spread, consisted of a squadron of seven pre-dreadnought battleships, a division of five cruisers and a number of destroyers. Only the two duty cruisers had steam on their main engines: the only warlike precautions taken were searchlights from these two ships sweeping to and fro and a patrol of two destroyers in the offing. The latter, all unknown to themselves, actually encountered the approaching attackers, passing between the two columns in which the Japanese were steering. The Japanese force of twelve destroyers nevertheless became somewhat disorganized so that it was only their 1st Division of four ships that enjoyed the advantage of the complete surprise achieved as they closed to about 800 yards to launch their torpedoes, scoring one hit on each of the battleships *Retvizan* and *Tsarevitch* and the cruiser *Pallada*, damaging them but not fatally. The remainder attacked later: dazzled by the searchlights' beams and forced by the gunfire which met them to launch at greater ranges, they achieved nothing. Not for the last time in that war and later ones, torpedo attacks by surface ships proved less effective than theoretically calculated.

So began the Russo-Japanese War. Had Togo appreciated the state of disorder and unreadiness prevailing in the Port Arthur squadron and followed up the destroyer attack with one by his heavy ships at daybreak it is probable that the Russian Far East Fleet would have been decisively defeated there and then. As it was, however, it was not until his scouting cruisers brought him this intelligence at 11.00 that he led his battle squadron into action. By that time the heavy

guns of the shore batteries covering the Roads had belatedly cleared for action; so that as the Japanese ships filed past cannonading the Russians, though they succeeded in inflicting considerable damage, they themselves suffered hits from the 10-inch guns ashore. One of these hit the *Mikasa* under her mainmast, wounding seven men on her after bridge, but her armour saved her from serious damage. The *Fuji*, *Hatsuse* and *Shikishima* were also damaged as well as two of the Japanese cruisers.

Togo's fleet was the only and irreplaceable Japanese one, whereas the Russians had replacements available, albeit half the world away in the Baltic. He therefore felt that only if the Russians challenged him in the open sea he would be justified in risking an all-out fight. He withdrew, allowing the Russians to retreat with their damaged ships into the inner harbour.

Naval operations were now restricted to Japanese attempts to blockade Port Arthur–physically and unsuccessfully by sinking blockships in the channel and strategically by maintaining a cruiser watch ready to call forward the Japanese battle squadron from its base on the Korean coast should the Russians put to sea. This they did on several occasions to exercise under their new and more forceful Commander-in-Chief, Admiral Makaroff; but while the *Retvizan* and *Tsarevitch* were still under repair, they did not venture so far as to risk a fleet action. The Japanese therefore laid a trap minefield and, when, on 13 April,

Port Arthur in 1904. Here the Russian Far Eastern Squadron was blockaded by the Japanese Fleet, suffering defeat on each occasion it made a sortie.

As a result of collision in dense fog, the light cruiser *Yoshino* was lost on 15 May with a heavy death toll and the armoured cruiser *Kasuga* was so damaged that she had to be withdrawn for extensive repairs. On the same disastrous day the battleships *Hatsuse* and *Yashima* ran foul of a Russian minefield and both were sunk.

With Togo's battleship strength thus suddenly reduced to four, he found himself faced with a superiority of two when repairs to the Russian ships were completed during June. The Japanese still enjoyed a clear advantage in morale and training, however, and when the Port Arthur squadron, under its new and pathetically ineffective Commander-in-Chief, Admiral Vitgeft, sortied on 23 June, it turned tail at sight of Togo's four battleships and squadron of armoured cruisers waiting outside. As the Russians returned to harbour harried by Japanese destroyer attacks, the battleship *Sevastopol* was damaged by a mine.

While she was being repaired the deadlock was re-established. The timid Vitgeft was being urged throughout July to go out and fight; but it was not until a direct order from the Tsar was received, that with a heavy heart and a premonition of his own death, he at last signalled to prepare for sea. And at first light on 10 August, with his flag in the *Tsarevitch*, Vitgeft led his fleet out. It comprised the battle squadron–*Tsarevitch*, *Retvizan*, *Pobieda*, *Peresviet*, *Sevastopol* and *Poltava*–and four light cruisers. His intention was to fight his way through the Yellow Sea, the Straits of Tsushima and the Sea of Japan to join the detachment of Russian cruisers at Vladivostok.

Togo's ships, assembled to oppose him, hoisted their huge battle ensigns to their mastheads as he came in sight. They comprised the battle squadron led by the *Mikasa* and restored to six units by the addition of the armoured cruisers obtained from Italy, the *Nisshin* and *Kasuga*, a cruiser squadron of two armoured and three light cruisers and another of five old cruisers. It was numerically greatly superior; but in the battle which ensued the prime tactical principle of the battleship era was to be demonstrated–that the battleship with its stoutly armoured sides and powerful armament would decide the issue. The cruisers, when they were able to bring their guns to range on the enemy, tended to confuse the fire-control problem with the splashes of their shells mixing with those of the battleships. For the same reason the secondary armament of the battleships also proved to be of little significance.

The forenoon was taken up by tactical manœuvres on either side, with Vitgeft trying to get past the Japanese who, spread across his route, steered back and forth to prevent him. Not until 13.00 did the first guns thunder

Makaroff came out in support of his light forces skirmishing with the blockading Japanese cruisers, his flagship *Petropavlovsk* struck one of these, blew up in a tremendous explosion and sank, taking with her the Admiral, 32 other officers and over 600 men. The battleship *Pobieda* was also mined but succeeded with the remainder in regaining the harbour. Command of the fleet devolved upon Admiral Vitgeft.

For the time being the Japanese naval superiority was unchallengeable. They tried to make this permanent by another operation to block the entrance to Port Arthur with sunken merchant ships. But when this was unsuccessful they reverted to their sea blockade, their cruisers alternating with the battle squadron on guard in the offing. This active policy kept their crews at a high pitch of seamanlike efficiency; but it exacted a price.

out at their maximum range of some 14,000 yards. And in spite of their lack of practice, it was the Russians who first drew blood, the *Mikasa* shuddering under the explosion of a 12-inch shell below her mainmast which killed eight men and wounded five others. This, and the knowledge that time and numbers were on his side, deterred the Japanese Admiral, concerned for the preservation of his country's only fleet, from closing to decisive range. Manœuvres and mutual cannonading at long range continued, therefore, without serious results until, as the Russians were once again reversing course to try to circle round the Japanese rear, the *Tsarevitch* and *Retvizan* received hits which, though causing only minor structural damage, started fires amidst the smoke of which their line fell into some confusion.

Taking advantage of this, Togo closed in to circle their rear and, at a range of less than 8,000 yards, poured in a concentrated fire with every gun from 6-inch upwards. Yet, incredibly, from the forest of shell splashes, the Russians emerged in good order, little damaged and returning the fire in great style. Furthermore, Togo had sacrificed his position of advantage across his enemy's route. The Russians had slipped by and he found himself committed to a chase, with the *Mikasa*, leading the Japanese line, abreast of the enemy rear and so exposed to their concentrated fire.

With a battle speed advantage of two knots, this situation might be improved; but in the meantime Togo's leading ships began to suffer severely. Astern of the *Mikasa*, the *Asahi* was heavily hit at 14.50. Ten minutes later the flagship was hit on the waterline and again below the quarter-deck. In reply the Japanese gunners were achieving little: the rear

Russian ship, *Poltava*, was dropping back; this was owing to breakdown of her main engines as they pounded at maximum revolutions to keep up with her faster squadron mates.

Their stout armour had saved the *Asahi* and *Mikasa* from crippling damage; but as they steamed on through the leaping shell splashes, Togo realized that further punishment could slow him down to such an extent as to allow the Russians to escape. He decided to make use of his speed advantage to break off the action temporarily and, steering a curving course, re-engage later on level terms. He led away, and by 15.20, after the *Mikasa* had been twice more hit by heavy shells, was out of range, and able to turn to a parallel course.

Even then, however, at his maximum sustained speed of 15 knots he was overtaking only with agonizing slowness until, at 16.30, the Russians reduced speed for a time to wait for the lagging *Poltava*. But when Togo then turned inwards, Vitgeft left the *Poltava* to her fate and resumed his best speed, only a knot less than that of the Japanese ships. So that when the cannonade resumed at 17.35 the *Mikasa* again became the target for the concentrated fire of the Russian battleships and almost at once shuddered under the shock of a 12-inch shell under the fore-bridge.

For the next hour, indeed, misfortune piled itself upon the Japanese. Perhaps owing to errors in gun-drill as turret-crews strove to increase the rate of fire, one of the *Shiki-shima*'s forward turret guns and both the

Asahi's after guns burst. At 18.00 the *Mikasa* also had her after-turret put out of action as two heavy shells struck almost simultaneously. Thus five out of the sixteen guns of Togo's main armament were silenced. The *Mikasa* continued to be hit again and again, suffering

a total of 125 casualties, including her Captain wounded. A 12-inch shell plunged through the middle deck before bursting, and tore a huge hole on the starboard side only two feet above the waterline.

Meanwhile, the Russian line, although the *Peresviet* and the *Retvizan* had each had a turret out of action for a time, seemed to bear a charmed life. The battle was clearly going in their favour: but then came a sudden reversal of fortune. Two 12-inch shells struck the *Tsarevitch* in quick succession: one, bursting at the foot of the mainmast, swept the bridge, killed the Commander-in-Chief and 16 others and wounded and knocked senseless the Chief of Staff and Flag Captain. The other burst on the armoured roof of the conning-tower and killed or stunned every man in it: with her wheel jammed hard to port, the flagship careered in a circular course through the Russian line, throwing it into confusion before coming to a halt.

Although the Captain of the *Retvizan*, followed by the *Pobieda*, made a gallant charge towards the enemy to cover the flagship until she could get under control again, all order had vanished in the Russian battle squadron. As they fled the Japanese circled at a killing range. But darkness was now quickly falling and under cover of it the Russians escaped. The crippled *Tsarevitch*, unable to keep up, bore away to the port of Kiaochow where she allowed herself to be interned. The five other battleships managed to regain Port Arthur.

Although the Battle of 10 August or the Battle of the Yellow Sea as it was alternatively called, had been far from decisive from a material point of view, morale in the Russian fleet had suffered a mortal blow. It was decided that any further attempt to break out was out of the question; guns and men were landed to assist the garrison defending the besieged fortress.

This was not known to the Japanese, however, and they felt obliged to keep up the blockade of Port Arthur. This exposed their fleet to danger from Russian mines: at the end of October 1904, the *Mikasa*, newly refitted and rearmed, was again leading the line when one of these sinister objects was sighted close ahead: prompt action avoided it, but the *Asahi* following was not so lucky: the mine exploded under her forefoot, but fortunately did only minor damage.

In January Port Arthur fell to the besieging Japanese army. For the time being Japanese sea-power was undisputed. The *Mikasa* and the remainder of the fleet could exercise and train ready to meet the Russian Baltic Fleet which, since 15 October 1904, had been on passage from Europe. Comprising four modern battleships, *Kniaz Suvarov* (fleet flagship), *Borodino*, *Alexander III* and *Orel*, of comparable strength to the *Mikasa* and her sisters, three older battleships, five old armoured cruisers and a mixed force of light cruisers, some modern but some veritable museum pieces more than twenty years old, it left its last

Admiral Makaroff's flagship, *Petropavlovsk*, sinking after striking a mine outside Port Arthur.

帝國艦隊旅順攻撃手

The Japanese battle squadron bombarding Port Arthur. From a Japanese print.

海洋中附近帝國軍艦敵砲之圖

Japanese 6-inch gun in action on board a cruiser. From a Japanese print.

A Japanese print showing Russian sailors abandoning their sinking ship.

anchorage on the coast of Indo-China on 9 May 1905. Unpractised, suffering from a plague of defects and handicapped by the presence of so many slow ships, it was no match for Togo's freshly refitted fleet which met it on 27 May in the Straits of Tsushima, between Japan and Korea.

The Russians were to fight courageously enough; but there was too great a difference between respective efficiency for the issue ever to be in doubt. The Russian Admiral Rozhest-venski at the outset tried to take advantage of a patch of mist to surprise the Japanese. The manœuvre was too complicated for his captains, however, and when the two fleets came in sight of one another again, the Russians were caught in the process of forming their line of battle. Togo's line was organized in two divisions, the 1st composed, as on 10 August, of his four battleships–*Mikasa, Shikishima, Fuji* and *Asahi* in that order–and the two armoured cruisers *Kasuga* and *Nisshin.* The 2nd Division was composed of six armoured cruisers: *Idzumo*–flag of Rear-Admiral Kamimura–*Adzumo, Tokiwa, Yakumo, Asama* and *Iwate.*

Togo had no need on this occasion to be concerned to preserve Japan's only battle fleet; for the Russians, too, had deployed their last naval force. Earlier he had signalled to his fleet–'The future of the Empire depends upon this battle.' Leading his battle line across the path of the distant Russians, therefore, he boldly manœuvred to turn up parallel with

Admiral Zinovi Rozhestvenski, who commanded the Russian Baltic Fleet which steamed half round the world to be massacred in the one-sided Battle of Tsushima. The admiral was severely wounded and taken prisoner after his flagship had been sunk.

them at the decisive range of 5,000–6,000 yards and, breaking out his great battle ensigns at the mastheads at 14.08, opened fire on the five leading Russian ships. These were soon reeling under a fearful battering, the leading ships of the two divisions, the *Suvarov* and *Oslyabya* in particular being set ablaze.

The *Mikasa,* too, was hit ten times early in the action by heavy shells, suffering more than 100 casualties. The premature explosion of a shell put one of her fore turret guns out of action. Except for this, however, the Japanese kept all their guns in operation and the damage they suffered did not force any reduction of their superior battle speed of 15 knots which enabled Togo to dictate the course

The Japanese battle squadron steaming into battle at Tsushima.

of the action. At 14.50 the *Oslyabya* staggered out of the line to capsize and sink fifteen minutes later. At 14.55 the *Suvarov*, heavily damaged and with the Admiral lying wounded and barely conscious amongst his staff, most of whom had been killed or wounded, swerved away and came to a halt.

From this time the battle became a massacre. The *Suvarov*, fighting gallantly to the end and driving off a number of torpedo attacks by destroyers, finally sank at about 19.20. Before that the *Alexander III* and the *Borodino* had both gone to the bottom. During the night the battleships *Sissoi Veliki* and *Navarin* and the cruisers *Nakhimoff* and *Vladimir Monomakh* succumbed to massed destroyer torpedo attacks. The following day the *Orel* and the old battleships *Nikolai I*, *Apraxin* and *Semavin* surrounded by the whole of Togo's force, surrendered. Three cruisers under Rear-Admiral Enquist escaped the holocaust and found refuge in Manila where they were interned. Of the remainder of Rozhestvenski's motley collection of ships, only one light cruiser and one destroyer reached Vladivostok. The Admiral himself was taken prisoner when the destroyer in which he was lying unconscious surrendered.

The Battle of Tsushima thus finally obliterated the Russian navy of the day, leaving the Japanese absolute control of the disputed sea area. Sea-power on its own cannot impose total defeat in war, however. This must

The *Mikasa*. From a Japanese postcard on which is written Togo's signal: 'The fate of the Empire depends on the result of this battle. Let every man do his utmost.'

eventually occur through the advance of the victorious power into the enemy's territory. Such a development was far beyond Japan's military capacity. She had captured Port Arthur and defeated the Russian armies in Manchuria; but she could not advance into Russia. Nor, indeed, could Russia, tottering on the brink of revolution, despatch reinforcements across the long and tenuous communications available to the Far East. The deadlock was brought to an end by President Theodore Roosevelt who persuaded the two antagonists to meet at Portsmouth, New Hampshire, in August 1905.

By the peace treaty signed on 4 September 1905 Japan was recognized as suzerain of Korea and she took over the Russian leasehold of the Liaotung Peninsula, including Port Arthur, and the railway and economic rights in Manchuria which Russia had obtained from China. This placed Japan amongst the great powers of the world.

Six days after the Peace of Portsmouth was signed, the *Mikasa* was lying in the harbour at Sasebo when a fire blazed up in her stern. While efforts to extinguish this were being made, there came, first, a series of small explosions and then, during the next hour, three much more violent as the ship's magazines detonated and she sank to the bottom,

leaving only her upper works above water. No less than 256 officers and men were lost in the disaster and many others died from amongst the 343 injured.

Rumours spread of sabotage by members of the crew or workers in Sasebo dockyard, dissatisfied with the terms obtained by Japan in the Treaty. But an official enquiry and an examination of the *Mikasa*'s hull when she was raised in August 1906 made it clear that she had in fact been an early instance of a succession of warships which, between 1898 and 1918 suffered such disasters through spontaneous fire or explosion of ammunition which had deteriorated and become unstable. These included the USS *Maine* whose sinking in Havana harbour after an explosion, attributed at the time to a Spanish mine, was made the ostensible reason for the American declaration of war. Others involved in similar disasters were the Brazilian *Aquidaban*, the French battleships *Iéna* and *Liberté*–the British *Bulwark*, *Natal* and *Vanguard*, the Italian *Benedetto Brin* and the Japanese *Matsushima*, *Kawachi* and *Tsakuba*.

In spite of her tragic accident the *Mikasa*, re-floated and refitted, was re-commissioned and served during the First World War. She was declared a national monument in 1961, and as such is preserved today.

SEYDLITZ

On 10 February 1906 the British battleship *Dreadnought* slid down the ways into the waters of Portsmouth Harbour to bring about a startling revolution in the design of such ships of every maritime nation. Hitherto they had been standardized with an armament of four 12-inch guns in twin, centre line turrets fore and aft, backed up by a mixed secondary armament of smaller guns between 9·2-inch and 6-inch. Their stoutly armoured hulls were driven at a maximum of 18 knots by steam, reciprocating engines. Progressive naval theorists, notably the Italian Cuniberti, had, however, since the turn of the century, been advocating the installation of a single calibre of big gun in larger numbers at the expense of the secondary armament.

The wisdom of this had been clearly demonstrated in the fleet engagements during the Russo-Japanese War (1904–05) when the main armament of the battleships on either side had dominated the action, while the secondary guns had merely served to confuse the fire-control problem with their different trajectories, rates of fire and times of projectile flight. The British Admiralty under Admiral Sir John Fisher had been the first to implement this concept of the all-big-gun battleship. The *Dreadnought*, with her armament of ten 12-inch guns in five twin turrets, and driven by Parsons steam turbines at a maximum speed of 21 knots–a speed which, unlike ships powered by reciprocating engines, she could maintain over long periods–made every other existing battleship obsolete.

An equally revolutionary application of the concept was to the design of armoured cruisers, soon to be renamed battle-cruisers, the first of which, HMS *Invincible*, at the sacrifice of armour protection, had a top speed of nearly 27 knots and an armament of eight 12-inch guns.

Other naval powers, their battle fleets made obsolete at a stroke, followed the British lead in respect of battleships. Only the Imperial German Navy, being built up under the leadership of Admiral von Tirpitz ultimately to challenge the British, immediately decided to acquire a battle-cruiser force. The *Invincible* and her sisters, *Indefatigable* and *Indomitable*, were commissioned in 1908. Two years later the Germans commissioned the *Von der Tann* which, at 19,000 tons displacement, was 1,400 tons heavier; powered also by Parsons turbines, she had a top speed of 28 knots; but by contenting themselves with a main armament of eight 11-inch guns, the Germans were able to give her better armour protection than the *Invincible*'s.

The ships which followed the *Von der Tann* over the next four years–*Moltke*, *Goeben*, *Seydlitz* and *Derfflinger*–compared similarly with their British contemporaries. In the case of the *Seydlitz* these were the *Lion* class. The table below compares their characteristics.

A feature in which the *Seydlitz*, like other German capital ships, held an advantage over her British counterparts, was her internal anti-torpedo bulkhead of 1·8-inch armour plate running fore and aft and covering her vitals.

Named after General Friedrich Wilhelm Freiherr von Seydlitz, Frederick the Great's best-known cavalry leader, she was commissioned in the spring of 1913 under the command of Captain von Egidy. Trials and working-up exercises completed early in 1914, she hoisted the flag of Rear-Admiral Franz Hipper. His command, the Scouting Forces of the High Seas Fleet, consisted of the three battle-cruisers in home waters–*Seydlitz*, *Moltke* and *Von der Tann*–the armoured cruiser *Blücher*, a squadron of light cruisers and some twenty attendant torpedo-boats.

During the eight years since the launching of HMS *Dreadnought* a naval armaments race had been running between Great Britain and Germany. The former, dependent primarily upon her sea-power for the security of her world-wide empire, had reacted firmly to maintain her naval supremacy in the face of Tirpitz's building programme. Thus, when the First World War broke out on 4 August 1914,

	Displacement (tons)	Main armament	Secondary armament	Armour belt	Turret armour	Speed
Lion class	26,350	Eight 13·5 in.	Sixteen 4 in.	9 in.	9 in.	27
Seydlitz	25,000	Ten 11 in.	Twelve 5·9 in.	12 in.	10 in.	27

the British Grand Fleet with 22 dreadnoughts, 8 older battleships and five battle-cruisers held a marked superiority over the High Seas Fleet's 14 dreadnoughts, a number of pre-dreadnoughts, three battle-cruisers and the *Blücher* which, mounting only twelve 8·2-inch guns, was unwisely included with the latter. A direct challenge by the High Seas Fleet was therefore impracticable; it remained safely immured at Wilhelmshaven behind the defensive mine barriers closing the Heligoland Bight.

To harass the British, however, and induce them to divide their fleet instead of keeping it concentrated at Scapa Flow and Cromarty, it was decided to use the high-speed Scouting Force in 'hit-and-run' sorties to bombard the English East Coast towns. So on 2 November 1914 the scheme was set in motion when the *Seydlitz* led the way out of the estuary of the Jade. Four light cruisers, of which one, the *Stralsund*, was laden with mines, accompanied the battle-cruisers. The following morning the town of Great Yarmouth woke to the sound of bursting shells and the crack of the guns of a nearby coastal battery firing ineffectively at the shapes dimly seen through the haze to seaward. Within twenty minutes it was all over and the German force was speeding back across the North Sea.

The exploit earned Hipper the epithet of 'Baby Killer' in the British press; but it also caused voices in England to ask, 'What is the Navy doing?'–as had been intended. The British Commander-in-Chief, Admiral Sir John Jellicoe, was not persuaded to move any of his fleet farther south. But when, a few weeks later, through British ability to decipher German operational radio messages, it became known that a similar raid was to take place on 16 December, he reacted as the Germans

hoped. From Cromarty, Admiral Beatty's squadron of four battle-cruisers and from Scapa the 2nd Battle Squadron of six dreadnoughts and a squadron of light cruisers were ordered out. They were so deployed at dawn on the 16th as to form a trap for Hipper, while light cruisers and destroyers from Harwich were spread to intercept, report and shadow.

However, on this occasion, unknown to the British Admiralty, the whole High Seas Fleet under Admiral von Ingenohl was following Hipper at a distance. The trappers were about to be themselves entrapped. And so it might have happened but for the fact that Ingenohl's hands were tied by the Kaiser's strict injunction not to risk his precious and irreplaceable battleships in action against any superior force. When destroyers and light cruisers of his screen encountered those of Beatty just before dawn, he feared lest they were outriders of the whole Grand Fleet: Ingenohl swung away eastwards, retiring and leaving his Scouting Force to their fate.

Hipper was, indeed, in great peril as he carried out his part of the scheme, the *Seydlitz, Moltke* and *Blücher* making for Hartlepool and Whitby, the *Von der Tann* and the recently commissioned *Derfflinger* for Scarborough. At Hartlepool where the bombardment was made at ranges of between three and four miles, the shore batteries of 6-inch guns replied, scoring four hits on the *Blücher*, killing nine men and putting two small guns out of action, three on the *Seydlitz* causing a good deal of superficial damage, and one on the *Moltke*. Scarborough and Whitby had no defences.

All was soon over and the re-united battle-cruiser force had melted back into the mist, steering through heavy seas for its planned

The battle-cruiser *Seydlitz*, first commissioned in 1913, displaced 25,000 tons and mounted ten 11-inch guns in twin turrets. She had a top speed of 27 knots. Compared to contemporary British battle-cruisers she had better armour protection, with a 12-inch belt and 10-inch turret armour. The former, however, mounted eight 13·5-inch guns.

rendezvous with the German battle fleet. But this time its way was barred, unknown as yet to Hipper, by the British battleships and battle-cruisers. Fortunately, however, the worsening weather had caused him to order his light forces home earlier. In the low visibility they suddenly encountered Beatty's light cruisers: their report warned Hipper in good time and he was able to circle to the north and east round the enemy battle force which was left groping vainly for him in the mist and spray.

Both sides had had narrow escapes from confrontation with superior forces, though the British, at least, did not at the time realize it. Nevertheless Admiral Ingenohl decided to send his Scouting Force again across the North Sea, this time unsupported by his battle fleet, to raid the Dogger Bank fishing fleet. For this trivial object, the *Seydlitz* led Hipper's three battle-cruisers (the *Von der Tann* was under repair) and the *Blücher* to sea, accompanied by four light cruisers and twenty torpedo-boats on the evening of 23 January 1915.

The radio signal ordering the operation was intercepted and decoded by the British; so when at dawn on the following day the German force arrived off the Dogger Bank they found Beatty with the battle-cruisers *Lion* (flagship), *Tiger*, *Princess Royal*, *New Zealand* and *Indomitable* waiting for them, with a scouting screen of light cruisers spread ahead. It was with Commodore Tyrwhitt's light cruisers from Harwich that contact was first made by the German light cruiser *Kolberg* at first light. It was a clear, overcast morning and both the *Kolberg* and Tyrwhitt's flagship *Arethusa* made good shooting, each scoring several hits before the

German ship turned away to fall back in answer to Hipper's recall. For the Scouting Force Admiral realized at once that his sortie must have been somehow revealed to the enemy: he had not forgotten his previous narrow escape and he now reversed course for home. And so, when Beatty's battle-cruisers sighted him against the clear-cut eastern horizon, fourteen miles away at 07.50, it was a stern chase that developed.

Each side was at first limited by the speed of its slowest ship to twenty-five knots; but when Beatty decided to go ahead with his three fastest ships in the van, the range began to narrow until, at 09.09 the *Lion* opened fire with her forward 13·5-inch guns on the *Blücher*, the rear ship of Hipper's line. Not for another eleven minutes could any of the German ships reply; then only the *Derfflinger*'s 12-inch guns were able to reply at 20,000 yards range. In the meantime the *Blücher* had suffered her first hit on her forecastle.

At length the range dropped sufficiently for the *Seydlitz* and *Moltke*'s 11-inch guns to reply. All three German battle-cruisers concentrated on the *Lion*, leading Beatty's line, scoring a damaging but not crippling hit on her at the waterline. When the *Tiger* and *Princess Royal* were seen to pull out on to the *Lion*'s quarter to clear their field of fire, the *Moltke* shifted her fire to the *Tiger*, scoring a hit.

Both *Derfflinger* and *Seydlitz* continued to concentrate on the *Lion* which was now firing at the *Seydlitz* and had managed to hit her on the forecastle, though without inflicting crippling damage. The *Lion* was herself beginning to suffer; but suddenly the *Seydlitz* shuddered as a 13·5-inch plunged through the armoured wall of the barbette of her after-turret and exploded. Compartments all round were wrecked; but far worse, in the re-loading chamber a charge waiting to be fed into one of the 11-inch guns was ignited. Fire leapt upward into the turret and down into the ammunition chamber below: and as men tried desperately to flee into the adjoining barbette through a door normally kept closed, flames followed them to start a similar conflagration there. In this appalling inferno whence the flames shot mast high, the entire crew of both turrets – 165 men – died.

So certain was the gunnery officer that his ship must soon blow up that he ordered 'rapid fire' for the other two turrets to hurt the enemy as much as possible before the inevitable end. But the gallantry of a damage-control party was to save her. Though the control wheels of the magazine flooding valves were red hot, they seized and turned them to let the sea water in. And then, after this catastrophic occurrence, the gunnery

exchange turned in favour of the Germans.

The *Lion*, standing out clear of the clouds of black smoke streaming from the funnels of the British ships, was receiving all the German fire and was hit again and again, while the German ships, obscured by smoke from their destroyers, sustained no further damage. The poor *Blücher*, to be sure, her speed falling away, had to be abandoned to her fate and was battered to a wreck by Beatty's rear ships. But when, at 10.18, two of the *Derfflinger*'s 12-inch shells struck the *Lion* on the waterline simultaneously, wreaking heavy damage and causing her speed to fall away, a misunderstood signal led the remainder of the British force to give up the chase and concentrate on the already doomed cruiser. The *Blücher* sank; but Hipper's other ships escaped.

German gunnery in this Battle of the Dogger Bank had proved markedly superior to the British, the *Lion* being hit twelve times and the *Tiger* twice, as compared with two hits on the *Seydlitz* and one on the *Derfflinger*.

Admiral Franz Hipper (Baron von Hipper after the Battle of Jutland), commanded the Scouting Forces of the High Seas Fleet with his flag in the *Seydlitz* until the Dogger Bank Battle, 24 January 1915, when he shifted first to the *Moltke* and then to the newly completed *Lützow*, his flagship at Jutland.

Commodore Reginald Tyrwhitt (right) who commanded the Harwich Force of light cruisers and destroyers during the First World War. This force was the first to encounter the enemy in the Heligoland Bight skirmish in August 1914. He took part in the Battle of the Dogger Bank, but was held back in harbour by the Admiralty at the time of the Battle of Jutland.

Admiral Sir John (later Earl) Jellicoe, Commander-in-Chief of the Grand Fleet in the Battle of Jutland where, it is considered by many, his brilliant handling of his huge force in the early stages failed to bring decisive victory owing to his later excessive caution in the face of massed torpedo attack.

opposite
A detail from Turner's portrayal of the scene on the *Victory*'s deck after Nelson had been shot down by a musketeer from the *Redoutable*. Tate Gallery, London.

pages 62–63
The *Redoutable*, dismasted and in a sinking condition, surrenders to the *Victory*. From the painting by Mayer, Musée de la Marine, Paris.

And, appalling as the holocaust in the *Seydlitz*'s after-turrets had been, the disaster had exposed a defect in the system of ammunition handling: the lesson was learned and precautions taken to prevent a repetition which was to stand in good stead when the British and German fleets next clashed.

This was not, however, to be for more than sixteen months. The sight of the *Seydlitz*'s damage and the narrowness of his battle-cruisers' escape caused the Kaiser to ban any further sorties in the North Sea for the time being. Not until August 1915 were the *Seydlitz*'s repairs completed; and then, with the *Moltke* and *Von der Tann* she was transferred to the Baltic to give naval support to the military operations around the Gulf of Riga. Mines, and the little force of British submarines operating under Captain Max Horton were the main threat there. On 16 August, and again on the following day the battle-cruisers were intercepted by Horton's submarine *E9* but on each occasion at too great a distance for an attack. On the 19th, however, *E1* achieved a good position and launched a torpedo at the *Seydlitz*. The target's speed had been over-estimated; the torpedo passed ahead but streaked on to hit the *Moltke* stationed on the *Seydlitz*'s beam, causing serious but not fatal damage.

Soon afterwards Hipper took his ships back through the Kiel Canal to Wilhelmshaven; but the winter dragged by with the High Seas Fleet kept in harbour while German U-boats assumed the main role in the naval war. Then in February 1916 Admiral Reinhard Scheer, appointed Commander-in-Chief, inspired the High Command with a new offensive spirit. He was permitted to begin planning for another attempt to bring a portion of the Grand Fleet to action, this time with the collaboration of the naval Zeppelin airships to reconnoitre and U-boats to be deployed in ambush off the British naval bases.

Meanwhile, during March and April minor sorties were undertaken. No contact with British heavy ships were made; but on 24 April as the Scouting Forces set out on another raid to bombard Lowestoft the *Seydlitz*, flying the flag of Rear-Admiral Boedecker who had temporarily relieved Hipper, struck a British mine. A hole 900 square feet in extent was torn under the forecastle causing heavy flooding. Boedecker transferred to the newly commissioned *Lützow* and proceeded with the bombardment; *Seydlitz* limped back to base. Repairs were to take until 28 May, causing a postponement of Scheer's grand plan.

As always in naval affairs, the weather now took a hand. Day after day it was unsuitable for the Zeppelins; meanwhile, time was running out for the U-boats which had been in their allotted stations since 17 May. Scheer was forced to dispense with the air reconnaissance and the coded signal was made on the 30th to carry out the operation on the 31st. Hipper's Scouting Groups – *Lützow* (flagship), *Derfflinger*, *Seydlitz*, *Moltke* and *Von der Tann*, the light cruisers *Frankfurt* (flag of Rear-Admiral Boedecker), *Wiesbaden*, *Pillau* and *Elbing* and three flotillas of destroyers led by the light cruiser *Regensburg* sailed at 01.00 and steered northwards through the Heligoland Bight with the intention of letting themselves be 'discovered' off the Norwegian coast. This it was hoped would lure Beatty's battle-cruiser fleet out from Rosyth to be trapped by the main body of the High Seas Fleet following some forty miles astern of Hipper.

Unknown to Scheer, however, the operational signal had been intercepted by the British. They could not discover its exact meaning, but on the assumption that it ordered the High Seas Fleet to sea, the whole Grand Fleet had sailed on the evening of the 30th. Beatty's battle-cruiser fleet was to make rendezvous with Jellicoe's battle fleet off the Jutland Bank the following afternoon.

So it was that when Beatty on that clear afternoon with a gentle north-westerly breeze barely ruffling the surface of the sea, turned at 14.15 on to a northerly course for the rendezvous, his force of six battle-cruisers (*Lion*, *Princess Royal*, *Queen Mary*, *Tiger*, *New Zealand* and *Indefatigable*) and four modern, fast, 15-inch battleships of the 5th Battle Squadron, was steering roughly parallel with Hipper some forty miles apart. But it was not until scouting light cruisers on either side, *Galatea* and *Elbing*, investigating a neutral merchant ship, sighted one another and exchanged shots, that any inkling of this came to the two admirals. Turning to support their outriders, they came in sight of one another on the horizon.

With the advantage of the light, Hipper was the first at 15.20, to descry heavy ships coming up over the horizon. Reporting 'Enemy battle-fleet in sight', he recalled his light scouts and, at 15.30, seeing the enemy ships steering to cut him off from his battleship support, he swung round to a south-easterly course to draw them towards Scheer's approaching fleet. Beatty duly followed, steering at the same time to close the range and engage. With their bigger guns the British should have been able to do so sooner than the Germans; but their range-takers over-estimated the range, so that it was almost simultaneously that both sides opened fire at a range of 16,500 yards at 15.48. In the German ships the roar of heavy shells streaking overhead was heard and they splashed down a full mile beyond them. The Germans, with their stereoscopic range-finders were on their targets almost at once and the tall white splashes

above
After dismasting the British frigate *Guerrière*, the *Constitution* has luffed up across her bow and shattered her with raking broadsides. US Naval Academy Museum, Annapolis, Maryland.

Japanese artist's impression of the Battle of Tsushima with the *Mikasa* leading the Japanese battle-squadron across the front of the Russian formation where the *Oslyabya* and the flagship *Suvarov* are on fire, the former soon to capsize, the latter to be hammered to a sinking wreck.

could be seen straddling them. The *Lützow* engaging the *Lion*, the *Derfflinger* the *Princess Royal* and the *Moltke* the *Tiger*, all scored several hits in the first few minutes. The *Seydlitz*, engaged with the *Queen Mary*, was unlucky, when the British found the range, it was the *Seydlitz* that suffered the first damage as two 13·5-inch shells hit her. Once again her after-turret was penetrated; but the lessons learned in the Dogger Bank action prevented the same horrific calamity, though the turret was put out of action.

Elsewhere, the gunnery duel continued in favour of the Germans, partly owing to defects in the British armour-piercing shells which tended to explode before completing penetration. Thus, though the *Derfflinger* and *Lützow* were each hit by 13·5-inch shells, neither suffered serious damage at this time, whereas the *Lion* was hit six times. One shell, penetrating the midship turret set cordite ablaze and killed every member of the crew there. Only flooding the magazine saved her from the disaster which at 16.03 overwhelmed the rear ship *Indefatigable*, which blew up after being hit by a heavy salvo from the *Von der Tann*.

Beatty, confident in his superiority of one battle-cruiser over the enemy, had rushed into action without waiting for his battle-ships. He was now suffering for his impetuosity. Turning away, seeking a respite to make repairs and put out the fires raging in the *Lion*, he sent in his destroyers to distract the enemy. Before they could get across the *Lion*'s bow to close the German line, however, there came relief from another source: at 14.05 shell splashes taller than before rose

round the German ships. The 15-inch guns of Beatty's battleship squadron had at last got into action—and were firing with impressive accuracy. Almost at once the *Von der Tann* was heavily hit and only kept in action by heroic efforts. Then it was the *Moltke*'s turn to stagger under the impact of a 15-inch shell.

Meanwhile, the *Seydlitz* and *Derfflinger* were both engaging the *Queen Mary* who, in reply, had just hit the former, wrecking a 6-inch gun mounting. But for the over-sensitive British shells, disaster must have overwhelmed Hipper. Instead it was the *Queen Mary* which, hit by three shells of a salvo, followed by two more from the next, suffered the same catastrophe as the *Indefatigable*, blowing up and plunging to the bottom with all but a handful of her crew.

Nevertheless, damage was rapidly accumulating in the German battle-cruisers when, at last, came relief. Over the horizon ahead, rose the long line of mastheads of Scheer's battle squadrons; at 16.40 Beatty was forced to reverse course to escape and, in his turn to lure the Germans towards Jellicoe's approaching Grand Fleet. Hipper led his ships on to join Scheer. Meanwhile, between the opposing lines of battle-cruisers a destroyer battle had been raging as the boats of either side had advanced to attack with torpedoes.

As they clashed, two German boats, *V27* and *V29* were sunk by gunfire and the remainder had been forced to launch their torpedoes ineffectively at long range, though by forcing the 5th Battle Squadron to turn away they had brought some relief to Hipper. From amongst the British flotillas, the *Nomad* was disabled; but others had pressed on;

Admiral Reinhard Scheer, commanded the 3rd Battle Squadron of the High Seas Fleet until January 1916 when he became Commander-in-Chief and initiated the strategy which led to the Battle of Jutland.

The armoured cruiser *Blücher* capsized and sinking during the Battle of the Dogger Bank where she had been ill-advisedly included in the German battle-cruiser squadron.

From left to right, British battleships *Conqueror*, *Thunderer*, *Iron Duke* (fleet flagship), *Royal Oak* and *Superb* in line at the Battle of Jutland.

some managing to launch at less than 5,000 yards, forcing Hipper, too, to turn temporarily away, but at the cost of another of their number, the *Nestor*, brought to a stop. Others again, reaching a firing position later, sent a salvo of four torpedoes which reached Hipper's squadron as they were in the midst of their turn to take station ahead of Scheer. It was the unlucky *Seydlitz* which found herself in their path. Captain von Egidy's urgent helm orders swung her clear of three of them, but the fourth struck and exploded against the forward submerged torpedo flat—just where the mine damage had previously occurred. Once again the armoured torpedo bulkhead prevented it having a crippling effect. Though it added to the mounting damage in the hard-used ship it did not yet force her out of the line.

Now all forces on either side were speeding northwards. Beatty's battle-cruisers had drawn out of range, but the battleships of the 5th Battle Squadron, after suffering damage during their reversal of course, were hitting back hard. Their two leading ships, *Barham* and *Valiant*, were scoring heavily on the *Lützow*, *Derfflinger* and *Seydlitz*; *Warspite* and *Malaya* on the leading German dreadnoughts, *König*, *Grosser Kurfürst* and *Markgraf*. Soon, however, the greater speed of the British drew them all out of range and even out of sight in the growing haze and lingering clouds of funnel smoke. For a while the thunder of battle died away. On both sides damage-control parties strove to make good the damage. And all the while, unknown to the Germans, they were being drawn towards Jellicoe's huge fleet of twenty-four super-dreadnoughts and three battle-cruisers which

were hurrying south to be spread at the critical moment in an 'L'-shaped line forming a deadly trap.

By 17.30 Beatty's force was nearing the approaching Grand Fleet and he swung north-eastwards across Hipper's path, steering for his battle position in the van. Ten minutes later this brought Hipper's ships suddenly into sight at the killing range of only 14,000 yards. Unable, in the light conditions prevailing, to see their opponents, the German battle-cruisers were forced to submit to a hail of fire from the 5th Battle Squadron as well as the British battle-cruisers. All suffered severely; the *Seydlitz* repeatedly hit and set on fire, was down by the bow and listing to starboard. The *Lützow* was in an even worse case and would soon be forced to slow down and leave *Derfflinger* to lead the remainder.

Such punishment could not be borne for long. Hipper led away in a wide complete circle to fall back on the support of Scheer's battleships. By the time he had completed this, advanced scouts of the Grand Fleet had loomed in sight, the armoured cruisers *Defence* and *Warrior*. *Seydlitz*'s guns were turned on the former, flagship of Rear-Admiral Sir Robert Arbuthnot. In a violent explosion the cruiser disintegrated, leaving only a black column of evil smoke. The *Warrior*, taken under fire also, was shattered, but escaped for the time being under cover of the *Warspite* of the 5th Battle Squadron which, circling with a jammed helm, drew the fire of all the leading German ships. Both were forced to limp out of the battle and make for home, the *Warrior* having eventually to be abandoned and scuttled.

The moment of truth for the German fleet was now approaching. Across their path was spread a wall of steel, the van of the British battle fleet. Through the fog of war – the banks of smoke·from the hundreds of racing, coal-burning ships added to the haze natural to a North Sea summer evening – Rear-Admiral Boedecker's four light cruisers, *Frankfurt* (flag), *Wiesbaden*, *Pillau* and *Elbing*, ahead of Hipper, suddenly sighted the solitary British light cruiser *Chester*. As she turned to flee, damaged by their concentrated fire, they chased her, only in their turn to find themselves engaged by the 12-inch guns of Rear-Admiral Hood's three battle-cruisers, *Invincible* (flag), *Inflexible* and *Indomitable*. The *Wiesbaden* was hammered to a wreck, the

Pillau was heavily damaged, before they were lost to sight amidst smoke clouds. More confused fighting then as the Scouting Group's destroyers, advancing to attack Hood's squadron clashed with the latter's four destroyers, sinking the *Shark* and damaging the *Acasta* before launching their torpedoes, which were avoided. And finally Hipper's ships, the *Lützow* already lying low in the water, the others less, but still seriously damaged, found themselves under rapid and accurate fire from Hood's three battle-cruisers at a range of less than 11,000 yards.

Hipper turned away to a parallel course to bring all his guns to bear: a fierce duel ensued, with *Lützow* and *Derfflinger* concentrating on the *Invincible*, now savagely hammering

The amidships magazines of the battle-cruiser *Invincible* exploded after she was hit by a salvo of 12-inch shells from the *Derfflinger* during the Battle of Jutland. Only two officers and three ratings survived her sinking.

The *Seydlitz* severely damaged and on fire after the Battle of Jutland.

above
The *Seydlitz*, down by the bow and listing to port after numerous hits by heavy shell and one torpedo, steams for home after the Battle of Jutland. Drawing 43 feet forward she grounded near the Horns Reef and eventually reached harbour going astern and with the aid of salvage tugs.

right
The battered *Seydlitz* at Wilhelmshaven after the Battle of Jutland. Nearly 100 of her crew had been killed and 55 wounded. Repairs were to take four months to complete.

opposite, top
Admiral Sir David (later Earl) Beatty, who commanded the British Battle-Cruiser Fleet at the Battle of Jutland, on board HMS *Queen Elizabeth*. At the end of 1916 he became Commander-in-Chief of the Grand Fleet when Sir John Jellicoe left to become First Sea Lord.

Hipper's flagship. 'Keep at it as quickly as you can. Every shot is telling', called Hood up the voicepipe to his gunnery officer. But, in spite of repeated hits, ineffective British shells could not finish off the *Lützow*: in contrast hardly had the British Admiral spoken when a salvo of 12-inch shells fell upon his flagship. The same lack of protection against fire amongst the turret ammunition which had sealed the fate of the *Indefatigable* and *Queen Mary*, set off an explosion which tore her in half to plunge in a few seconds to the bottom. And as Admiral Scheer, realizing the trap into which he had steamed, signalled for an emergency reversal of course, his whole fleet, including Hipper's squadron, was able to fade back into the smoke haze; they were thus saved from destruction except for the *Lützow* which was at last slowed to a crawl and forced to limp away, eventually to be scuttled.

Once again the thunder of the guns ceased. And though the Grand Fleet turned in pursuit, it was not until Scheer turned back to try to force his way past to gain a clear route of escape that once more the head of his line and the four surviving battered German battle-cruisers ran into the devastating cannonade of Jellicoe's vast array. This time it would take more than a simple reversal of course to extricate himself. While he executed it, relief for his leading dreadnoughts must be obtained. So all available destroyers were ordered out to attack with torpedoes; to the battle-cruisers went the signal to 'charge' the enemy in what was to be remembered as their 'Death-Ride'.

A death-ride it should have been, indeed, as, led by the *Derfflinger* they swung gallantly round (in the *Seydlitz* the order was received with thunderous cheers) to face again the storm of shells in which they suffered further damage. But they were saved by the salvo of twenty-eight torpedoes launched by the German destroyers in the face of which Jellicoe felt constrained to turn his whole fleet away, running out of sight and out of

touch with the foe he had so brilliantly entrapped. The four German battle-cruisers, battered and weary, but, to the credit of their designers still partly battleworthy, turned to take up their proud position ahead of their battle line.

It was the climax of the Battle of Skagerrak as it was to be called by the Germans. The summer day was by now fading. Before Jellicoe was able to regain touch with his enemy it would be dusk and it was his firm policy not to seek a night action which always favoured the smaller, more compact fleet. Nevertheless, the German battle-cruisers were yet to suffer further damage as, shortly before dark they clashed once again with

their original antagonists, Beatty's squadron. With their targets showing up clearly against the sunset the British ships were able to avenge some of their earlier battering. Both *Derfflinger* and *Seydlitz* suffered further heavy damage before they turned away to escape. In the former 157 men had been killed. The *Seydlitz* had lost 98, with 55 more wounded.

When night fell Jellicoe gathered his fleet together and placed himself, as he believed, in position to bar Scheer's route of escape home. Scheer's decision was to steer relentlessly for the entrance to the swept channel through the German defensive minefields at the Horn's Reef Light Vessel, determined if necessary to

bludgeon his way, at any cost, through the Grand Fleet. Had Jellicoe been kept fully informed by the Admiralty of all the intelligence gleaned from radio interception, such a clash would no doubt have occurred. As it was, Scheer's route led him across the Grand Fleet's rear where Jellicoe had massed his numerous destroyer flotillas. One after the other, these encountered the German battle line. They attacked gallantly enough but failed either to deflect it or to inform their Commander-in-Chief of the situation. By dawn the High Seas Fleet was approaching Horn's Reef and, before they could again be brought to action, they reached the safety of their own protected waters.

For the *Seydlitz* the night had been perilous, indeed. Struck by twenty-one heavy and two medium shells, and one torpedo, she was almost in a sinking condition, her bow getting steadily lower in the water as a result of innumerable leaks. Much of her electrical equipment was destroyed making control of her surviving armament unreliable. She could no longer keep station and had to limp on alone. Thus, when, during the dark night massive black shapes were sighted ahead, Captain von Egidy knew that only wile and good luck could save him from being finally destroyed by the British battleships, against which he had stumbled. Fortunately the British challenge letters for the night had been discovered during a destroyer skirmish and promulgated to the German fleet. They were now flashed to and accepted by the British ships ahead; under cover of her own smoke the *Seydlitz* faded back into the night before circling round to pass across their wake.

Somehow, by heroic efforts and the endlessly repeated training in damage control undergone by her crew, she was kept uneasily afloat until, on the Horn's Reef, she grounded. There tugs and salvage vessels came to her rescue. Painfully, over the next two days she was brought into the Jade, finally to enter Wilhelmshaven dockyard for repairs which took four months to complete.

It was the end of a remarkable demonstration of stout ship construction as well as a saga of human courage and endurance. It was the end of the *Seydlitz*'s hard fighting career, too. She sortied with the High Seas Fleet again in April 1918 on an abortive attempt to intercept a merchant convoy between Norway and Scotland, but no encounter with the enemy developed. The next time she put to sea it was only to be surrendered, with the majority of the German fleet in accordance with the terms of the Armistice in November 1918 – under the guns of the ships she had fought so resolutely. Interned at Scapa Flow, she was scuttled by her skeleton crew on 21 June 1919. A sad end for a gallant ship.

above
21 November 1918. The High
Seas Fleet steams into the
Firth of Forth to surrender.

The *Seydlitz* with the interned
High Seas Fleet at Scapa Flow
where she was scuttled with
the remainder by their own
crews on 21 June 1919.

HMS WARSPITE

The first ship of the English Royal Navy to bear the name *Warspite*–or *Warspight* as it was more usually spelt at that time–was an Elizabethan fighting galleon launched in 1596. She took part in the capture of Cadiz that year under the command of Sir Walter Raleigh who was grimly gratified at having the opportunity to avenge the death of his friend Sir Richard Grenville and the loss of the *Revenge*, five years earlier. He destroyed two of the 'Apostle' class Spanish galleons which had then taken part–Alonzo de Bazan's flagship, the *San Felipe* and the *San Tomas*– and captured the *San Mattias* and *San Andreo*.

It was Charles II and Samuel Pepys, the first of the long line of Secretaries of the Navy which came recently to an end with the absorption of the Admiralty into the more prosaically named Ministry of Defence, who were responsible for the building in 1666 of the next *Warspite*, a 64-gun 3rd Rate of 898 tons. She played a distinguished part in the crushing defeat of the Dutch in the St James's Day fight in 1666 and, in a brilliant convoy defence on Christmas Day the same year, in which she helped to capture the entire Dutch attacking force. She was paid off prematurely with the rest of the fleet by the impecunious sovereign, but was fortunately laid up elsewhere than in the Medway when the Dutch made their devastating raid on the reserve fleet there in 1667. She was thus available to take part in the battles of the Third Dutch War and again in the war with France, notably the victory of Barfleur and La Hogue in 1692. Rebuilt at Rotherhithe in 1700 she took part in Rooke's capture of Gibraltar in 1704 and the Battle of Malaga which followed. She was finally paid off in 1712 after a career of forty-six years' service.

The third *Warspite* was a 74-gun ship-of-the-line which took part in Boscawen's victorious Battle of Lagos and Hawke's immortal annihilation of a French squadron in a gale of wind amidst the rocks and hazards of Quiberon Bay, both in the *annus mirabilis* of 1759.

Three other *Warspites* served with the Royal Navy over the next century and a half before the subject of this history was launched in the royal dockyard at Devonport on 26 November 1913. Designed under the aegis of Sir Eustace Tennyson d'Eyncourt, the Director of Naval Construction from 1912 to 1924, she was one of five of a revolutionary type of warship, prototypes of the fast battleships which were eventually to replace the ponderous mastodons which had formed the backbone of contemporary fleets. The fact that they mounted eight 15-inch guns, as compared to the ten 13·5-inch of the preceding 'super-dreadnoughts', followed the natural development of ever-increasing gunpower for each successive class of such ships. More of an innovation and in line with the precepts of that great reformer and creator of the Royal Navy of that era, Admiral Sir John Fisher, was their turbine machinery–double the horse-power of the preceding *Iron Duke* class, fed by steam from 24 boilers fired entirely, for the first time, by oil fuel. Driving four propeller shafts this gave them the unprecedented speed, for a battleship, of 25 knots. They were also, at 27,500 tons displacement, 5,000 tons heavier than the *Iron Dukes* and were 600 feet in length, a little over 90 feet in beam.

The First World War had been under way for eight months when the *Warspite*, under the command of Captain E. M. Philpotts, joined the Grand Fleet at Scapa Flow on 13 April 1915, being attached until the arrival of her sisters to the 2nd Battle Squadron. The action-filled career covering thirty years that was to follow did not open on a very promising note when, on 16 September 1915, as a result of 'a grave error of judgment' by captain and navigator, in the view of a subsequent court-martial, the ship grounded off Dunbar at fourteen knots. Repairs kept her in dockyard hands until 20 November when she joined her new sisters *Queen Elizabeth* and *Barham* to form the nucleus of the 5th Battle Squadron. A second mishap two weeks later when the *Warspite* and *Barham* collided during manœuvres fortunately caused only minor damage.

In March 1916, the 5th Battle Squadron was joined by the fifth and last of the class, the *Valiant*. But the *Queen Elizabeth* was temporarily detached when the squadron sailed on the evening of 30 May from Rosyth with Admiral Beatty's Battle-Cruiser Fleet; so that on that momentous occasion which was to develop into the Battle of Jutland, the 5th Battle Squadron was composed of the *Barham* (flagship of Rear-Admiral Hugh Evan-Thomas), *Valiant*, *Warspite* and *Malaya*.

The Admiralty's radio monitoring service had correctly deduced that some major operation by the German High Seas Fleet was planned for the 31st. In the hope of at last bringing their elusive enemy to action, therefore, the Grand Fleet, under Admiral Sir John Jellicoe, centred on its immense force of twenty-four super-dreadnoughts, had also put to sea. Through a calm, sunny, spring morning the Battle-Cruiser Fleet had steered eastwards across the North Sea, but had seen nothing of the enemy when at 14.15 it turned to make rendezvous with the Grand Fleet some sixty-five miles to the north.

Just as all concerned were deciding that yet another 'sweep' was to be fruitless, however, the situation was suddenly transformed by the electrifying signal, 'Enemy in sight!' from the *Galatea*, one of Beatty's light cruisers scouting to the eastward. Going to investigate a peaceful Danish merchantman, she had encountered and engaged the German light cruiser *Elbing* similarly reconnoitring for the German force of five battle-cruisers under Rear-Admiral Hipper. Both battle-cruiser forces turned to support their outriders and at 15.20 sighted one another.

Hipper altered course south-easterly to draw Beatty towards the main battle squadrons of the High Seas Fleet which, as yet unknown to the British, were coming out in full strength in the hope of catching a detached portion of the British fleet and defeating it before support could reach it. Beatty confidently turned to a course parallel to Hipper's and at 15.48 the former's six ships, *Lion*, *Princess Royal*, *Queen Mary*, *Tiger*, *New Zealand* and *Indefatigable* began a gun duel with Hipper's *Lützow*, *Derfflinger*, *Seydlitz*, *Moltke* and *Von der Tann*.

Although Beatty might be excused for feeling confident in his superiority of one ship over the enemy, it was nevertheless a grave mistake that in his impetuosity he had led off at twenty-four knots to the eastward without waiting to ensure that Evan-Thomas, stationed six miles to the north-west of him, had been able to take in the signal to conform, made by flag and obscured by the smoke of his coal-burning ships. By the time it had been passed by searchlight eight minutes had gone by: the splendid ships of the 5th Battle Squadron were thus left more than ten miles behind, working up to their maximum speed of twenty-five knots and cutting corners in an effort to catch up.

Before they could get into action Beatty had discovered that for reasons not apparent at the time, his superiority over Hipper was illusory. It was to emerge later that not only did the arrangements for handling ammunition in the British ships leave them liable to devastating magazine explosions should a turret be hit, but British armour-piercing shell fuses detonated their bursting charges before instead of after penetrating the enemy's armour. Consequently, before the 5th Battle Squadron at last, at 16.05, broke through the pall of smoke to sight and engage Hipper's battle-cruisers at a range of 19,000 yards, Beatty's rear ship *Indefatigable* had blown up and sunk, his flagship, *Lion*, had been heavily damaged as had the *Tiger* and *Princess Royal*, forcing Beatty to sheer away and open the range.

The enemy, too, had suffered hits but their damage was less than it would have been had the British shells been more efficient. Now the battleships turned parallel to them and opened up with their 15-inch guns, firing, as the German Commander-in-Chief, Admiral Scheer, was to record 'with extraordinary rapidity and accuracy', while Hipper was to write that 'only the poor quality of the British bursting charges saved us from disaster'. And though Beatty was to suffer another catastrophic blow when at 16.26 the *Queen Mary* met the same fate as the *Indefatigable*, the German battle-cruisers were themselves in danger of imminent destruction when the situation was dramatically transformed.

From the light cruiser *Southampton*, flagship of Commodore Goodenough's squadron scouting ahead, came the signal, 'Enemy battle fleet bearing S.E.' Beatty in danger of being lured into the arms of the overwhelming force of Scheer's battle squadrons, led his squadron round on to a reverse course to the north-west. Evan-Thomas, still some eight miles behind, held on to the south to cover the battle-cruisers' retirement and not until his squadron had raced past them on an opposite course did he, too, reverse course. Instead of doing so with all ships turning together, however, he led them round, as ordered by Beatty, in succession. This not only delayed the reversal, allowing the van of German battle squadrons to come within range, but it offered a fixed aiming point through which each of his ships had to pass and on which the German guns could concentrate. The *Barham*, *Warspite* and *Malaya* were all hit several times during the turn, only the *Valiant* escaping scot-free; but the design of these well-armoured ships proved sound, and soon after 17.00 all were steaming at full speed after Beatty's battle-cruisers, the *Barham* and *Valiant* continuing to deal out punishment to Hipper's ships. The *Warspite* and *Malaya* shifted their aim to the head of the

Admiral Sir John (later Lord) Fisher, the great innovator and reformer of the Royal Navy. He was responsible for revolutionary changes in the training of young officers, as well as the design and construction of the *Dreadnought* which made all previous battleships obsolete at a stroke.

German battle line, hitting the dreadnoughts *Grosser Kurfürst* and *Markgraf* until the greater speed of the British ships drew them out of range and fire was turned again on to Hipper's battle-cruisers. Though only fleeting glimpses of the latter could be had through the haze and smoke to the eastward, they suffered heavily from the 5th Battle Squadron's good shooting, particularly the flagship *Lützow* and the *Seydlitz*.

So the great concourse of ships steered northwards to where, unknown to the Germans, Jellicoe's greatly superior Grand Fleet was preparing a perfect tactical trap. Before this could be sprung, however, Jellicoe's advanced scouting forces, the battle-cruisers *Invincible*, *Inflexible* and *Indomitable* to the eastward, and ships of the First Cruiser Squadron on the western flank were suddenly confronted by the German capital ships looming out of the smother ahead. In a fierce exchange of fire between the opposing battle-cruisers, in which both sides scored heavily, the *Invincible* suffered the same catastrophe as had the *Indefatigable* and *Queen Mary*, disintegrating in a horrific explosion. On the other wing the cruiser *Defence*, overwhelmed by the fire of the leading German battleships, was similarly destroyed; the *Warrior*, almost as heavily damaged and badly on fire staggered away westwards, out of action, towards the 5th Battle Squadron which was steering to take up its station in the rear of the Grand Fleet battle line. But for a misfortune that now struck the *Warspite*, the stricken cruiser must also have gone down.

In the midst of a circling manœuvre as the *Warspite* was following the *Barham* and *Valiant* round, her helm jammed. As Captain Philpotts recorded: '*Warspite* shaved close under *Valiant*'s stern, and every attempt was made by helm and engines to bring her head back to port, with the dire result that she only closed the head of the enemy's battle fleet at decreasing speed. I then decided to go full speed ahead, and continued to turn to starboard. I am unable to give further details, except that I managed to get away to the northward after practically turning two circles under the concentrated fire of several of the enemy's battleships. During this time centralised control was impossible, but fire was kept up in local control. Closest range was estimated to be about 12,000 yards, and the ship was badly damaged by shell fire but not completely disabled.'

As one of the *Warspite*'s midshipmen stationed in the after torpedo control described it: 'We suddenly found ourselves hauling out of the line and rushing towards the German fleet . . . All that we knew was that we were in a hail of fire; in fact so much so that the salvoes falling short and over made such splashes that a lot of water came into the tower and we got quite wet . . . We thought that our own 6-inch guns were firing, but discovered later that it was the enemy's shell bursting on our armoured belt.'

The *Warspite*'s agony was the *Warrior*'s salvation – for the time being at least. The cruiser limped away and was later taken in tow, but all efforts to save her were finally in vain and she was scuttled by her crew on the following day. Nevertheless many lives were undoubtedly saved by the unwitting diversion staged by the *Warspite*. Severely damaged and limited to sixteen knots for fear of flooding her engine rooms at any higher speed, the

The *Warspite* at Jutland, circling with helm jammed under the concentrated fire of the German battleships, suffers damage which forces her out of the action; but she has drawn fire off the crippled armoured cruiser *Warrior*, enabling her to escape immediate destruction. National Maritime Museum, London.

battleship was ordered home and took no further part in the great battle.

The design of the *Warspite* had indeed been vindicated by the events of 31 May 1916. Though struck sixteen times by heavy shell she was still able to steam at sixteen knots and, when first-aid damage repairs had been made, several knots more; all her guns were fit for action though the central control system had been damaged; furthermore her stout armour and good design had limited her casualties to one officer and thirteen men killed, four officers and thirteen men wounded. By 22 July she had been repaired and was again with the Grand Fleet.

For the remainder of the First World War the *Warspite* continued to take part in the unspectacular, largely uneventful operations by which the Grand Fleet kept its iron grip on the North Sea penning the enemy in harbour and enforcing the blockade which played so important a part in wearing down the German will to fight. And on 21 November 1918 the reward for those weary years of watch and ward came as she sailed with the fleet to accept the surrender of the High Seas Fleet off Rosyth.

The years of peace which followed saw the reduction of the Royal Navy, by international agreements, to a fraction of its former size. By the early 1930s, in accordance with limitation treaties, all but the five *Queen Elizabeth* class, five of the later, but slower *Royal Sovereigns*, and three battle-cruisers, *Hood*, *Renown* and *Repulse* had been scrapped. Two battleships, *Nelson* and *Rodney*, had been added. All were outmoded in comparison with newer fast battleships being acquired by other navies using the improved ship-

building techniques which had been developed. The limitation treaties permitted modernization, however, and it was decided to give the *Queen Elizabeth* class such treatment, rather than replace them by new ships.

The first to be taken in hand in 1934 was the *Warspite* and for the next three years she was in dockyard hands at Portsmouth where she was as a start stripped down to her bare hull; her propelling machinery, her boilers and funnels and her 15-inch guns were all removed. New Parsons turbines replaced the old; in place of the 24 boilers which had provided their power were substituted only 6 of the latest design which permitted her original pair of funnels to be reduced to one, though of a larger size. The high-pressure steam system developed the same horsepower as before. Better protection against air attack and the plunging trajectory of shells in long-range action was provided by increasing the thickness of her deck armour. The 15-inch turrets were modified to increase the maximum elevation of the guns from 20 to 30 degrees giving them a range of 32,000 yards. New fire-control systems were fitted for the 6-inch guns as well as the main armament. The former were reduced in number from eight on each side to four; but, instead, an anti-aircraft armament was mounted which, at that date, seemed formidable—two 4-inch twin mountings abreast the single funnel, two eight-barrelled 2-pounder 'pom-poms' above them, and two four-barrelled 0·5-inch machine guns on top of the superimposed turrets. Finally a hangar for two Swordfish seaplanes was erected abaft the funnel, a catapult to launch them and a crane to hoist them back on board.

All this made the *Warspite* a much more formidable man-of-war; but in one vital respect she was to remain a battleship of an

HMS *Warspite* as she appeared during the First World War and prior to modernization in 1934.

The *Warspite* after modernization in 1934, when replacement of her original twenty-four boilers by six of the latest design permitted reduction of her funnels to one. At the same time increase in the maximum elevation of her 15-inch guns gave them a range of 16 nautical miles.

era that was passing. Her hull, with its external anti-torpedo 'bulges', which had been added in 1926, limited the top speed at which even her new engines could drive her to a little less than 24 knots during her trials in 1937. Battleships already being built for the British and other navies were to be capable of 30 knots, a speed essential for the aircraft-carrier-dominated fleets of the Second World War. And, indeed, similarly modernized dreadnoughts of the Italian navy were capable of 27 knots.

The outbreak of the Second World War found the *Warspite* serving as the flagship of Admiral Sir Andrew Cunningham, Commander-in-Chief in the Mediterranean; but when Mussolini delayed taking his country into war alongside Nazi Germany, she was transferred to the Home Fleet where, between 4 December 1939, when the battleship *Nelson* was damaged by a magnetic mine, and March 1940, she was

also the fleet flagship.

It was not, however, until the war in home waters erupted into activity with the German invasion of Norway on 9 April that she came into contact with the enemy. To what an extent the Admiralty was taken by surprise by this development may be judged from the fact that the *Warspite* had already sailed to return to the Mediterranean. She was recalled and rejoined the Home Fleet on the 10th. Inept handling of the situation by the Admiralty and the Commander-in-Chief had enabled the greatly inferior German fleet to carry out the occupation of Norway's principal ports early on the 9th without interference by the Home Fleet except for a brief skirmish off the Vestfiord in the far north between the battle-cruiser *Renown* and the German fast battleships *Scharnhorst* and *Gneisenau*. The German ships suffered quite severe damage, the *Renown* very little, before the former fled under cover of wild stormy weather and blanketing snow squalls.

Otherwise only the German squadron carrying troops for the occupation of the Norwegian capital had met with effective resistance in Oslofiord where the new heavy cruiser *Blücher* was sunk by guns and torpedoes of the shore defences. Nevertheless the German forces might yet be made to pay heavily for their temerity if action were quickly taken. This was especially true at Narvik, at the head of the Vestfiord, where a flotilla of ten large destroyers had delivered the occupying troops and had to refuel before they could start on their homeward journey. And there an officer with the necessary dash and determination to take advantage of the situation was present in Captain B. A. W. Warburton-Lee in the destroyer *Hardy*, accompanied by the *Hunter*, *Hostile*, *Havock* and *Hotspur*.

Ordered to Narvik to investigate a report that a single enemy ship had arrived there and landed a small force, he discovered from Norwegian pilots at the mouth of the fiord that at least six enemy ships more powerful than his own had preceded him. Without hesitation he decided to deliver a surprise attack at dawn in which two of the German destroyers, the *Wilhelm Heidkamp* and *Anton Schmitt* were sunk, as well as a number of enemy merchant ships, and two destroyers damaged. But, trapped at the last minute, as he steered to withdraw, Warburton-Lee found himself engaged by fresh enemy forces emerging from side fiords where they had been berthed. Though two more of the Germans were heavily damaged in this stage of the fight, the *Hardy* and *Hunter* were both destroyed, Warburton-Lee himself being amongst those killed.

The remainder of the British flotilla escaped leaving only four of the German ships fully seaworthy and all short of fuel and ammunition. Immediate action by other British forces in the vicinity could have completed the annihilation; but hesitation and indecision, replacing Warburton-Lee's gallant resolve, caused delay. So it was fortunate that the German flotilla commander was equally irresolute and did not risk attempting a breakout. His ships were still at Narvik when at 13.00 on the 13th the *Warspite*, commanded by Captain Victor Crutchley, as well known to the Navy for his luxurious beard–unfashionable at that period–as for the Victoria Cross he had earned in the Zeebrugge exploit of the First World War, nosed her way majestically up the fiord with nine destroyers, some screening her against attack by the submarines believed to be present, others with sweeps out against a suspected minefield. At the battleship's masthead fluttered the flag of Vice-Admiral Whitworth.

Aloft and scouting ahead was the battleship's Swordfish piloted by Petty Officer F. R. Price with Lieutenant-Commander W. L. M. Brown as his observer. They were to have a quick and unexpected success. Having reported that two enemy destroyers were moving seawards and that six more were in Narvik harbour, evidently hastily raising steam, they turned to examine another inlet, the Herjangsfiord running northwards off the main fiord. Lying fully surfaced at anchor and caught quite by surprise was *U.64*. It was a perfect target and Price made no mistake with his two anti-submarine bombs as he dived to release. A direct hit sent the U-boat to the bottom in half a minute.

Returning down the fiord, the airmen saw that one of the two destroyers under way had turned to hide herself in ambush in an inlet on the southern side. This was the *Erich Köllner*, one of the two damaged too badly in the previous battle for local repairs. Warned by the aircraft's report, the two leading British destroyers, *Bedouin* and *Eskimo*, were well prepared and the luckless *Köllner* was smothered and destroyed by gunfire and torpedo, the former including a salvo from the *Warspite*'s 15-inch guns.

The other enemy destroyer, the *Hermann Künne*, had turned back and joined three others, *Hans Lüdemann*, *Wolfgang Zenker* and *Bernd von Arnim*, which had got under way. A confused battle followed in visibility lowered by snow flurries, some natural, others induced by the thunderous blast of the *Warspite*'s guns shaking the snow off the steep sides of the fiord, as they occasionally found targets to engage. It is not clear from the records just what all these targets were; but one certainly was the destroyer *Diether von Roeder* which, too damaged to leave her berth at the Narvik wharf, opened fire with her 5-inch guns and was taken for a shore battery. She was nevertheless not silenced until the British *Cossack*

German destroyer *Georg Thiele* scuttled in Rombaksfiord after the Second Battle of Narvik in which the *Warspite* took part as flagship of the British force.

The Commander-in-Chief, Mediterranean, Admiral Sir Andrew Cunningham, inspecting the crew of his flagship, HMS *Warspite*.

opposite
Framed between the quarter deck and the 15-inch guns of the *Warspite*, the aircraft carrier *Formidable*, which took the place of the *Illustrious* after the latter had been crippled by German dive-bombers in January 1941. The *Formidable* was herself similarly put out of action four months later during the battle for Crete.

entered the harbour and engaged in a brief point-blank duel in which the latter was heavily damaged and ran aground. Soon afterwards the *Roeder*'s crew blew their ship up to prevent her capture.

The remaining German destroyers fought their hopeless battle with equal gallantry, the *Lüdemann*, *Zenker*, *Arnim* and *Georg Thiele* retiring up the eastern extremity of the fiord – the Rombaksfiord – where they were finally destroyed but not before they had damaged the *Punjabi* and the *Eskimo*, the latter having her bow blown off by a torpedo. The last of the enemy to get under way, the *Erich Giese*, was quickly smothered and sunk by the fire of six British destroyers.

So the second Battle of Narvik came to an end with the whole enemy's naval force destroyed. Had a military force accompanied the *Warspite*'s squadron, the port could have been captured that day; for the German troops, thoroughly demoralized, had fled inland, asking Norwegians they met for the way to Sweden. But the ineptitude which dogged British strategy at that time caused two days' delay during which the Germans recovered their morale and re-occupied the town.

A long siege followed, hampered by the deep snow for which the Allied troops were ill-equipped. Even a bombardment by the *Warspite* and other ships on 24 April failed to dislodge the enemy and it was not until the snows had melted that Narvik was finally taken on 24 May – only to be evacuated early in June when the news of the German advance into France made it clear that continued occupation even of northern Norway was beyond the Allies' resources.

Meanwhile the *Warspite*, now commanded by Captain D. B. Fisher, had returned to hoist Admiral Cunningham's flag in the Mediterranean in preparation for Italy's

entry into the war on Germany's side which took place on 11 June 1940. On the following day, in company with her unmodernized sister, the *Malaya*, and the veteran aircraft carrier *Eagle*, she led the Mediterranean Fleet out from its base at Alexandria for its first sweep of the central Mediterranean which was not challenged by the greatly superior Italian fleet or harassed by the Italian air force.

The next sortie was delayed by Admiral Cunningham's need to negotiate with the French Admiral Godfroy the neutralization of the French squadron at Alexandria following the capitulation of France on 22 June. Having finally achieved that, Cunningham took his fleet to sea again on 7 July to cover two small convoys to Malta and at the same time hoping to provoke an action with the Italians. On this occasion he made the old battleships *Royal Sovereign* and *Malaya*, with the *Eagle*, into a separate force, giving the *Warspite* her own screen of five destroyers so that she could operate to the advantage of her better gun-range and speed. His five 6-inch cruisers formed a third force.

As it happened, the Italian fleet, under Admiral Inigo Campioni, comprising the two old, but modernized and fast (27 knots) battleships *Giulio Cesare* and *Conte di Cavour*, accompanied by 16 cruisers of which six were heavy, 8-inch types, had put to sea on the 6th also to cover a convoy for Libya; this was not known to Cunningham until the afternoon of the 8th when a scouting submarine reported the Italian force in the central basin, north of Benghazi. The Mediterranean Fleet had meanwhile been under almost incessant high-level bombing attacks all day which, though delivered with remarkable accuracy, had achieved only a single hit on the bridge of the cruiser *Gloucester*, killing Captain Garside and seventeen others. Cunningham now had a chance of striking back if he could get between the Italian fleet and its base at Taranto and he at once steered to do so. The Italians were forewarned of this move, however, through their ability to decode certain British naval messages, and Campioni was ordered to avoid being brought to action before noon on the following day by which time he would be under the 'umbrella' of the Italian air force.

This he succeeded in doing, but no bombers had come to support him by the time the two fleets came in contact with one another at 15.00 on the 9th. Not that Campioni should have needed such assurance with his greatly superior cruiser strength and his two battleships – faster than any of their opponents and able to outrange all but the *Warspite*. And so long as the *Warspite*, far ahead of her consorts at first, circled and waited for them to join her, no action between the opposing battleships took place, while an unsuccessful attempt was made by the handful of Swordfish torpedo planes available from the *Eagle* to slow the Italians down.

But at 15.53, while the *Royal Sovereign* and *Malaya* were still trailing some way astern, from the *Warspite*'s fighting top the two enemy battleships came in sight at thirteen miles. On both sides the great guns, elevated at their maximum range, opened fire. Both achieved impressive accuracy, straddling their targets almost at once; but it was the *Warspite* which secured the first–and only–hit of the exchange at 16.00 when a great orange-coloured flash at the base of the *Giulio Cesare*'s funnels marked the explosion of a 15-inch shell. The enemy flagship suffered 115 casualties from this one hit; four boilers were put out of action and her speed was reduced temporarily to 18 knots. Under orders to take no risks with the Italian fleet, Campioni at once turned away under a smoke-screen. As Cunningham rightly suspected that this was part of a plan to lure him over a submarine ambush, he declined to follow into the murk and the battle petered out. Only now did the bombers of the Italian air force appear on the scene, attacking their own ships as readily as the enemy's to the fury of Admiral Campioni as could be judged from intercepted radio messages.

Nevertheless the Mediterranean Fleet's ordeal during the next three days was a daunting one. With only three biplane Gloster

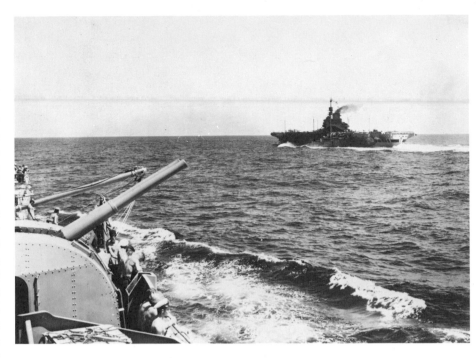

Gladiators from the *Eagle* as fighter defence, there was little to hinder the repeated massed attacks by shore-based bombers. During the forenoon of the 12th, for instance, salvoes of bombs fell close round the *Warspite* on twenty-two occasions–a total of 300 near or fairly near misses; the climax occurred when some three dozen bombs fell simultaneously, all within 200 yards. But the stout old veteran survived it all; nor was a single ship in the fleet hit, which seemed a miracle at the time, while the Gladiators fought back nobly,

The aircraft carrier *Illustrious*, which provided the air element of the Mediterranean Fleet from September 1940. From her deck, on the night of 11 November 1940, took off the Swordfish aircraft which crippled two Italian battleships and put a third permanently out of action in the harbour of Taranto. On 10 January 1941 the *Illustrious* was heavily damaged by a massed dive-bomber attack by German aircraft based on Sicily.

shooting down five of the enemy aircraft.

Over the next three months the *Warspite* was at sea on a number of occasions; to bombard Italian-held Bardia on 16 August when her 6-inch and 15-inch guns did heavy damage; at other times to cover convoys to and from Malta with one of which, at the end of that month, came welcome reinforcement in the shape of the *Warspite*'s sister ship *Valiant*, now also modernized, and the new aircraft carrier *Illustrious* operating, besides her 18 antiquated Swordfish torpedo-reconnaissance planes, a squadron of 15 Fairey Fulmar fighters – a great improvement upon the *Eagle*'s three Gladiators. In September it became clear that the Italian air force had learned how ineffective even their accurately delivered high-level bombing attacks were on ships free to manœuvre; they introduced, for the first time, torpedo planes, one of which sank the cruiser *Kent* on the 17th. Twelve days later the *Warspite*, at sea with the fleet, was narrowly missed by four air-dropped torpedoes.

In November a complex operation covering Malta convoys and meeting further reinforcements in the shape of the unmodernized *Barham*, two cruisers and six destroyers having been successfully completed, the famous night attack by Swordfish torpedo planes from the *Illustrious* was triumphantly delivered, leaving the Italian battleships *Littorio*, *Duilio* and *Cavour* all sunk at their moorings; the first two were to be out of action for the next six months, the third permanently.

The Mediterranean was once again dominated by the Royal Navy and in December Admiral Cunningham demonstrated the fact by taking the *Warspite* and *Valiant* into the Adriatic to deliver a surprise bombardment on the Albanian port and airfield of Valona which, since Mussolini's unprovoked attack on Greece in the previous October, had been the main supply port of the Italian invasion forces' On 2 January the *Warspite* again turned her 15-inch guns on shore targets – the port of Bardia once again, in support of General Wavell's advancing Army of the Nile.

But this favourable state of affairs was about to be dramatically reversed by the intervention of the Germans in the Mediterranean. Mussolini had over-reached himself with his attack on the Greeks who were fighting back successfully. The partial neutralization of his fleet at Taranto had enabled the British to cripple the convoy system supporting his Libyan armies which had suffered severe defeat. Hitler, to his annoyance, found himself forced to go to his ally's assistance. To the airfields of Sicily and Sardinia he deployed Fliegerkorps X, an independent, self-contained air unit totalling some 450 aircraft, the dive-bomber pilots of which had been given special training in shipping attacks.

By the beginning of January 1941 Fliegerkorps X was ready and when, on the 10th, the Mediterranean Fleet met an eastbound convoy for Malta and Greece south of Sicily, the Stuka dive-bombers swarmed into the sky. They made a dead set at the *Illustrious* whose little handful of Fulmar fighters could do little to protect her. She was hit six times and only her armoured flight deck saved her from destruction, enabling her to limp away to Malta for temporary repairs. From the *Warspite*'s bridge, Admiral Cunningham, watching, admitted that 'there was no doubt we were watching complete experts ... We could not but admire the skill and precision of it all.' The *Warspite* did not escape attack entirely, but the only bomb which hit her burst on her starboard anchor and did very little damage. This attack on the *Illustrious*, and others the next day which sank the cruiser *Southampton* and damaged the *Gloucester* off Malta, followed by incessant raids on Valetta's dockyards in a vain effort to finish off the carrier, were the opening moves of what was to develop into the first 'blitz' or effort to neutralize the island by air attack. It was to fail. The *Illustrious* was

The Italian battleship *Vittorio Veneto*, flagship of the Commander-in-Chief, Admiral Angelo Iachino, mounted eight 15-inch guns and had a speed of 30 knots. During the Battle of Matapan, 28 March 1941, she was torpedoed by a naval Swordfish plane from the *Formidable*. Her speed reduced for a time to 9 knots, she was enabled to escape engagement with the *Warspite* by the heroic efforts of her engineers who restored her speed to 20 knots. When Italy capitulated, she surrendered at Malta with the remainder of the fleet.

Modern sea warfare as seen by Japanese artists. *Top:* the Battle of Tsushima, 1905. A Russian battleship blown up and sinking. *Centre:* the surrender and sinking of a Russian warship during the Battle of Tsushima. The *Mikasa* can be seen through the smoke in the background. *Bottom:* Japanese crews firing broadside guns in one of their earliest warships.

An artist's impression of the Battle of Jutland. HMS *Warspite*, circling with damaged helm under fire from German battleships. The deployment of the Grand Fleet from cruising disposition to line of battle is incorrectly portrayed. The *Invincible* is shown blowing up in the middle background. Ministry of Defence.

able to get away to Alexandria *en route* for more complete repairs in the United States: Malta, in spite of its tiny force of Hurricane fighters, was still 'in business' when half of Fliegerkorps X had to be transferred to North Africa to support the defeated Italian army and the German Afrika Korps which Hitler had also been forced to deploy in aid of his incompetent ally. The full fury of the blitz died away.

Nevertheless, disaster impended for the British in North Africa, their strength depleted by transfers to the aid of Greece. Before these reversals of fortune, however, the Italian navy was to suffer another severe blow in the Battle of Matapan on 28 March 1941. In that action, into which the reluctant Italian fleet was goaded by their impatient German ally, the main credit for the British victory must go to the crews of the Albacore and Swordfish torpedo planes from the *Formidable*, which had taken the place of the *Illustrious* in the fleet. They first torpedoed the Italian *Vittorio Veneto* temporarily slowing her down, but not quite enough to permit Cunningham's battle squadron to bring her to action; they then immobilized the heavy cruiser *Pola*; and when the Italian Admiral Iachino sent her sister ships *Zara* and *Fiume* with four destroyers back to stand by her, he delivered all except two destroyers to destruction.

In the *Warspite*, Cunningham was leading the *Valiant* and *Barham* through the night towards the *Pola*, which had been located by the *Valiant*'s radar, when the *Zara*, *Fiume* and their destroyers were sighted crossing the bow. The enemy were quite unaware of their impending doom as, with the perfect drill of often-practised night action, the battleships' big guns trained round and the sights settled down on the cruisers barely 3,000 yards away. From the destroyer *Greyhound* on the screen, a searchlight beam stabbed out illuminating the target: fifteen seconds later, at 22.28 there came the blinding flash and thunder of the *Warspite*'s first 15-inch broadside, followed another ten seconds after by the first salvo of 6-inch. The result was spectacular. The cruiser aimed at burst immediately into flames: one of her turrets was seen to fly bodily into the air: within fifty seconds the *Warspite*'s guns were able to shift to the next cruiser, with the same devastating effect, leaving the first target to be finished off by the *Valiant*. Two of the Italian destroyers managed to escape but two were sunk by Cunningham's destroyers; the *Pola* was later sunk at leisure after her crew had been taken off by other British destroyers.

So ended the Battle of Matapan – tactically, perhaps, a mere skirmish; but strategically it was to have the effect of deterring Italian naval intervention in the daunting days to come when the Mediterranean Fleet, with virtually no air cover, was to suffer heavily as its ships fought, first to cover the evacuation

Some of the Eastern Fleet hastily gathered to defend the Indian Ocean against the Japanese at the beginning of 1942 – *Warspite* (flagship), *Formidable* and two of the unmodernized veterans of the First World War, *Resolution* and *Royal Sovereign*. Efforts to bring to action the greatly superior Japanese Fast Carrier Striking Force off Ceylon in April 1942 fortunately failed.

opposite, top
Admiral Hipper's battle-cruisers at Jutland, 1916. On the left, the *Lützow*. From the painting by Claus Bergen in the National Maritime Museum, London. (On loan to the Royal Hospital School, Holbrook.)

opposite, bottom
Windy Corner by D. Wales Smith. The 5th Battle Squadron engaging the van of the High Seas Fleet as they steer to join the Grand Fleet battle line. Shortly after this the *Warspite*'s helm jammed during a turn; she suffered crippling damage as she circled under concentrated fire and was driven out of action. National Maritime Museum, London.

The *Warspite* (right) and the *Valiant*, her sister ship, in the Ionian Sea before the invasion of Sicily.

of our army from Greece, between 24 and 30 April, then in defence of Crete from 20 to 27 May, and finally in the evacuation from that island, too, all within a few minutes' flight from enemy airfields.

The battle for and evacuation from Crete was to cost the fleet three cruisers and two destroyers sunk, two battleships, an aircraft carrier, two cruisers and two destroyers damaged beyond local resources' ability to repair. One of the battleships damaged was the *Warspite*. With the *Valiant* and ten destroyers she was operating to the west of Crete in support of light cruisers and destroyers which had been repelling invasion flotillas approaching from Greece, when, at 13.30 on the 22nd a swarm of fighter-bombers swooped. Diving through a curtain of shell-bursts, three of them aimed at the *Warspite*; two narrowly missed with their 500-pound bombs, but the third dropped his on the forecastle deck where it burst on one of the forward 4-inch AA guns, blowing one of the twin mountings over the side and blasting a hole through the deck to start fires in the 6-inch battery. Amidst gruesome scenes of carnage and burned men, the Executive Officer, Commander Sir Charles Madden, led damage-control and fire parties and others to tend to their wounded comrades. Fires were extinguished and temporary repairs made and, horrifying as the casualties were, the *Warspite* was luckier than the cruisers *Gloucester* and *Fiji* and the destroyer *Greyhound*, all of whom were sent to the bottom within sight of her that afternoon. Soon afterwards the *Warspite* was detached to return to Alexandria where she arrived on the 24th to land

her wounded. After further temporary repairs she was sailed via the Suez Canal to make the long passage across the Indian and Pacific Oceans to Seattle where she was taken in hand in the Bremerton Naval Yard.

Repaired and again battleworthy, she was re-commissioned there on 28 December 1941. Three weeks earlier, hard-pressed Britain had found herself joined by the United States in her struggle, but with a new, powerful naval opponent in the shape of Japan. Against the Japanese aggression she had few resources to pit, especially since the loss of the modern battleship *Prince of Wales* and the old battle-cruiser *Repulse* to Japanese naval air attack in the first few days of the new campaign. Other warships which had been in the Far East at the outset had been overwhelmed during or after the Battle of the Java Sea at the beginning of March 1942. A new Eastern Fleet was, therefore, being scraped together to try to defend the Indian Ocean, its backbone–if it can be so called–being the four ancient, slow, unmodernized battleships of the *Royal Sovereign* class.

Arriving from England in the carrier *Formidable* to take command of this force at Colombo was Admiral Sir James Somerville, the former commander of Force H in the Mediterranean. Together with the *Indomitable*, also allocated to it, the Eastern Fleet might have been a force of some effectiveness if these carriers had had aircraft better than the slow, lumbering Albacore biplane torpedo planes and the low-performance Fulmar fighters which, apart from a few American 'Wildcats' were the best that could be provided for the Fleet Air Arm at that time. However,

cluded that the information of the enemy's approach had been false and, having sent away two of his cruisers, *Dorsetshire* and *Cornwall*, to Colombo to resume their previous occupations and the little carrier *Hermes* to Trincomalee, he steered with the remainder for Addu Atoll, 300 miles to the west.

Hardly had he arrived on the 4th when the Japanese were located 360 miles south-east of Dondra Head. He had been caught embarrassingly 'on the wrong foot'; but now that the quality of the Japanese carrier force is known this apparent strategic blunder can only be looked upon as a blessing in disguise. While Force A, which sailed as soon as refuelled, was pounding eastwards, Colombo harbour was attacked, the *Dorsetshire* and *Cornwall*, hurrying to rejoin, were pounced upon by Japanese dive-bombers and sent to the bottom in a few minutes–an example of what must have happened to others of the Eastern Fleet had the Japanese force been encountered. Fortunately, though Somerville searched for his opponent, Nagumo had turned away south-east in preparation for his further

The *Warspite*, severely damaged by a radio-guided bomb off Salerno on 16 September 1943, is towed back to Malta by a flotilla of salvage tugs.

to be the centre of some sort of a fast carrier squadron, the *Warspite* was also allocated and since 22 January had been on passage from Seattle, via Sydney, N.S.W. On 23 March she arrived at Trincomalee where Admiral Somerville hoisted his flag as Commander-in-Chief Eastern Fleet a week later, and Captain F. E. P. Hutton relieved Captain Fisher. Commander Sir Charles Madden remained as Executive Officer. Information of a Japanese attack on Ceylon impending on 1 April had already come in and by 30 March Somerville had collected his scattered fleet, some from the secret base of Addu Atoll in the Maldive Islands, others from Colombo and Trincomalee, at a rendezvous south of Dondra Head. He divided them into a fast Force A composed of *Warspite*, the two fleet carriers, four cruisers and six destroyers, and a slow Force B, his four R class battleships and some equally old light cruisers and destroyers.

Although Somerville had no full information on the overwhelming strength of the Japanese force under Vice-Admiral Nagumo coming against him–five fleet carriers equipped with some of the best fighter and strike planes in the world, supported by four fast battleships, three cruisers and eight destroyers–he knew that his own motley collection of ships was sure to be totally outclassed. All he could hope was that an opportunity might be given for his Albacores to press home a night torpedo attack. His main policy could only be one of keeping his fleet 'in being' and avoiding decisive action. However, when no sign of the enemy had appeared by 2 April and his ancient battleships were already requiring fresh water and more fuel, he con-

The *Warspite* bombarding German strong points during the invasion of Europe. Off Normandy, 6 June 1944.

attack on Trincomalee on the 9th, and no contact was made. Without means of replenishment at sea, there was nothing Somerville could do but retire to Addu Atoll again, subsequently sending his slow squadron away to Mombasa for much-needed training, while he took Force A to Bombay.

It was a black and shaming experience both for the Admiral and the *Warspite* to have to avoid being brought to action–though, in fact, following the attack on Trincomalee the Japanese fleet left the Indian Ocean, never to return. Nevertheless, only a defensive posture was feasible for the Eastern Fleet of which the *Warspite* remained flagship for the next eleven months, finally leaving for home in March 1943. Indeed, the splendid old ship had been overtaken by the slow march of time and history which had relegated battleships to the subsidiary roles of bombardment and, if fast enough, of escort for the new queens of sea battle, the aircraft carriers. Fleet actions had become long-distance affairs with missiles carried hundreds of miles by aircraft launched from ships which would never come within sight of their opponents. Only once again, up in the storm-filled darkness of the Arctic night, on 26 December 1943, would battleship fight battleship when the *Duke of York* crippled the *Scharnhorst* with radar-directed 14-inch guns and delivered her to final destruction by the torpedoes of cruisers and destroyers.

Nevertheless, the *Warspite* was yet to play the lead on several occasions. The first of these was when, during the invasion of Sicily she led her sister, the *Valiant*, to bombard Catania in support of the held-up Eighth Army on 17 July 1943; and to clear the way for the crossing of the Straits of Messina by shattering the enemy gun batteries near Reggio. In September she was with Force H supporting

the Salerno landings when there occurred a dramatic occasion worthy of such a historic ship, as she met the surrendering Italian battle fleet and led them into captivity under the guns of the fortress of Malta.

This should have been her last duty before returning to England; and, indeed, she had already sailed westwards from Malta when the crisis in the Salerno operations caused her to be recalled, once again to bring her guns to the aid of hard-pressed soldiery. How effective she was can be gauged from the enemy's War Diary for 16 September: 'Our attack had to stop . . . because of the great effect of the enemy sea bombardment and continuous air attacks.' Or as Admiral Cunningham's despatch puts it: 'the Naval gunfire incessant in effect, held the ring when there was danger of the enemy breaking through to the beaches'.

The Germans were now to have their revenge, however. They had evolved the combination of a new, very fast, high-flying Dornier 217 bomber and the FX 1400 guided, armour-piercing bomb. The surrendering Italian battleship *Roma* had already been sent to the bottom by this new device. Now it was the *Warspite*'s turn to suffer. On the afternoon of the 16th, a few minutes after she had successfully beaten off an attack by a dozen fighter-bombers, three FX bombs were accurately directed on to her. Two narrowly missed, but the third plunged through into a boiler room where it burst, bringing the ship to a stop with no steam, and putting her armaments out of action. The casualties, astonishingly, were limited to nine killed and fourteen wounded.

But the old ship was totally crippled and only through the efforts of a little flotilla of salvage tugs was she towed back to Malta and on to Gibraltar where she was made fit to limp home as part of a convoy in March 1944.

Already the time had come when it was no longer economical to restore her to her full status as a battleship 'of the line'. This time no repairs to the shattered boiler room were made, and only three of her four turrets were made serviceable. Thus, although she could still make twenty-one knots at full power, it was virtually as a monitor that she was re-commissioned in time to form part of the bombardment force during the Normandy landings on 6 and 7 June 1944; in August to turn her great guns again on enemy batteries holding up American troops in Brittany; at Le Havre in September; and finally on 1 November 1944, during the storming of Walcheren Island, her bombardment of the numerous enemy batteries did much to reduce the number of casualties suffered by British landing-craft crews and the Royal Marine Commandos they took in to the assault.

When 'Cease Fire' was sounded at the end of that day on board the *Warspite*, it marked the end of a remarkable fighting career. She was steamed back to Portsmouth where on 26 July 1945 she was paid off and put up for disposal as scrap, 30 years, 4 months and 18 days since she was first commissioned.

But the old lady had no intention of going quietly and submissively to such an unhonoured end. While in tow from Portsmouth for the Clyde in March 1947, she parted the tow in heavy water and cast herself on the rocks of Mount's Bay. And there she was slowly, over the next nine years, dismantled.

A commemorative relic of the seventh *Warspite* lives on, however, in the shape of her battle ensign hanging in St Giles' Cathedral, Edinburgh, where it was laid up by Admiral of the Fleet Sir Andrew Cunningham at the time of his installation as a Knight of the Thistle on 27 September 1945 – a tribute to the flagship which had served him so well.

The 30-year-old veteran *Warspite* lies in Portsmouth Harbour awaiting her last voyage – to a breaker's yard. On passage she was to part the tow in heavy weather and cast herself on the rocks in Mount's Bay, where she would be finally dismantled.

89

USS WASHINGTON

Between 1922 and 1936 the major naval powers enjoyed a partial ship-building 'holiday' in respect of battleships in accordance with the terms of the Washington Treaty for the limitation of armaments signed by the United States, Great Britain, Japan, France and Italy. This had restricted the total tonnage of battleships each navy might have in being, though it had allowed certain ships under construction at the time to be completed, provided others were scrapped in their place when they commissioned. It had also restricted the size of individual ships built on those terms to 35,000 tons displacement. Thus Great Britain had completed the *Nelson* and *Rodney* mounting nine 16-inch guns; the United States had done the same with the *Colorado* and *West Virginia* with eight 16-inch guns.

The Washington Treaty was due to terminate at the end of 1936; but in the hope of renewing it, a conference was called in 1935 in London. Chances of success were never high and, in fact, two of the signatories, Japan and Italy, were already secretly violating the terms of the original treaty, the former in respect of the size of cruisers they were building, giving out their displacements to be 10,000 tons as prescribed, whereas they were several thousand more. The Italians, in 1934, had laid down the battleships *Littorio* and *Vittorio Veneto* with a displacement of 41,167 tons, though given out to be only 35,000 tons, an armament of nine 15-inch guns and a speed of more than thirty knots. In reply the French laid down in the following year the 35,000 ton ships *Richelieu* and *Jean Bart*, mounting eight 15-inch guns and with a speed of thirty knots.

Nevertheless from the London Conference emerged the 1936 London Naval Treaty which, while it abolished all quantitative limits, would have restricted individual battleships to 35,000 tons displacement and 14-inch guns. Ostensibly this only awaited ratification by the Japanese to come into force at the end of the year. The United States accordingly waited before finalizing designs for the two new battleships approved by Congress in June 1936 to replace their two oldest dreadnoughts. Ratification was witheld by Japan and the London Naval Treaty collapsed.

So it was not until October 1937 and June 1938, respectively, that the United States laid down the *North Carolina* and her sister, the *Washington*. As Japanese building plans were kept a close secret, it was assumed that they would include a main armament of 16-inch guns for their new battleships. Nothing less would do for the American ships, therefore.

During the years since the last American battleships had been completed, a technical revolution in the design of such ships had taken place. Applied even to the modernization of older types such as the Italian *Cavour* class and a number of Japanese capital ships of the First World War era, this had increased the maximum elevation–and so the range–of their big guns, improved their propulsion machinery and increased their speed by as much as five knots in some cases. They thus became early examples of a new capital ship– the fast battleship. Meanwhile, as mentioned above, new ships were emerging with unprecedented speeds of more than thirty knots and, on very large displacements, able to carry very heavy armour and sacrifice nothing in gunpower. In addition to the two new Italian ships, the Germans, too, had laid down in 1936, the *Bismarck* and *Tirpitz*. Ostensibly of 35,000 tons, they actually displaced 42,000 which permitted them to mount eight 15-inch guns, to have a top speed of thirty knots and to enjoy an armoured belt of $12\frac{1}{2}$ inches as well as a 4-inch armoured deck. In 1937 the Japanese were to achieve the ultimate in battleships with the *Yamato* and *Musashi* of 64,170 tons displacement and nine 18·1-inch guns.

The *Washington*, therefore, of 35,000 tons was a comparatively modest project for the time of her inception: to mount her main armament of nine 16-inch guns and to have reasonable armour protection and top speed, great ingenuity had to be employed, particularly in saving weight. In place of the time-honoured system of riveting the plates of her hull and armour together, 35 per cent of the process was done by electric welding. Further weight was saved by rearrangement of the propulsion machinery to concentrate it in a reduced space.

By these means it was possible to give the *Washington* a narrow armour belt covering her machinery spaces, magazines and turret barbettes with a maximum thickness of 12 inches, tapering to 6½ inches below the water-line. Special protection for her propellers and steering gear was provided in addition to the armoured deck by an armoured box 6 inches thick on top, 11·8-inch sides and 11-inch bulk-heads fore and aft. An anti-torpedo bulkhead and 'bulges' gave her virtually a triple hull below the waterline. The maximum speed reached on trials was twenty-eight and a half knots. In addition to her three triple 16-inch turrets and ten twin 5-inch dual purpose (H/A L/A) guns her plans included sixteen 28-mm anti-aircraft guns, but by the time she entered service in May 1941 the inadequacy of this in the face of dive-bombing attacks had been learned and the number was increased to forty.

Such was the splendid ship which in March 1942 crossed the Atlantic to begin her war-time career as flagship of Rear-Admiral R. C. Giffen's Task Force 99 alongside her British allies of the Home Fleet based on Scapa Flow. Their main task was that of covering the convoys to Russia, sailing through the Arctic for Murmansk against the threat of the huge and powerful *Tirpitz*. Interesting comparisons were able to be made with HMS *Duke of York*, the fleet flagship, one of the first class of fast battleships of the Royal Navy. British strategy in connection with these convoys has been and will, perhaps, always remain a controversial issue. It will probably be agreed that with a strong force of German bombers and torpedo planes deployed on the airfields of northern Norway within an hour's flight of the convoy routes, as well as the *Tirpitz* and other heavy ships lying in ambush in Kaafiord, near the North Cape, in the words of the British First Sea Lord, writing to his American counterpart, Admiral King, 'the whole thing was a most unsound operation with the dice loaded against us in every direction'. Under such conditions it was not felt right to risk battleships inside the Barents Sea where they must be exposed to massed air attack with almost no fighter cover.

For political reasons, however – specifically to encourage our hard-pressed Russian ally – the convoys were to continue through the mid-summer period of constant daylight so favour-able to the enemy air force. The heavy units of the Home Fleet, including the *Washington*, were therefore deployed as distant cover. Between 26 April and 7 May 1942 they were at sea in support of two convoys which, though harassed by enemy light naval forces, torpedo planes and U-boats, were not directly threatened by heavy units. While at Scapa in June the *Washington* was visited by King George VI, always keenly interested in naval matters. Then in July came the disastrous episode of Convoy PQ17 which, having been

The United States battleship *Washington* nearing completion of fitting-out at the Philadelphia Navy Yard at the beginning of 1941.

USS *Washington* in 1941. She and her sister, the *North Carolina*, were the first of the new American fast battleships whose design was unrestricted by Treaty limitations. Much smaller than their foreign contemporaries, the German *Tirpitz* and *Bismarck* or the Japanese *Yamato* and *Musashi*, they nevertheless, on 35,000 tons displacement, mounted nine 16-inch guns and had a speed of 28½ knots.

successfully protected to beyond Bear Island by its close escort against massive air and submarine attack, was ordered by the Admiralty, over the Commander-in-Chief's head, to scatter at the threat of a sortie by the *Tirpitz*, the pocket battleships *Admiral Scheer* and *Lützow* and the heavy cruiser *Hipper*. It had thus been delivered up to destruction piecemeal by U-boats and bombers. Twenty-three merchantmen, the majority of them American, were sunk. The *Washington* was with the Commander-in-Chief's distant covering force and must have shared in the feeling of dismay with more than a hint of shame which spread through the fleet at the apparent betrayal of the merchantmen.

Convoys to Russia were stopped after this until the shorter days of September; so in August the *Washington* returned home. She was urgently needed in the south Pacific where the naval campaign in support of the struggle for the Solomons Island of Guadalcanal was raging. It had opened on 9 August with the disastrous Battle of Savo Island in which the Japanese demonstrated their great superiority in night action in spite of their having no radar. The Australian cruiser *Canberra* and the American cruisers *Vincennes*, *Astoria* and *Quincey* had all been sunk without loss to their opponents.

Over the next six months the Japanese were to retain this superiority by night, inflicting some painful defeats; one notable exception, as will be told later, was to be the action in which the *Washington* played the principal part.

By day, on the other hand, American naval air power, shore-based on Henderson Field, Guadalcanal and ship-borne in the carrier Task Forces, were able to dominate the sea approaches to the island and ensure the supply of the troops on it. On 15 August 1942, the *Washington* sailed from the American East Coast via the Panama Canal to join this fierce fighting.

Her arrival on the scene was timely indeed; her sister ship *North Carolina*, had preceded her, but on 15 September she was torpedoed by a Japanese submarine and was forced to limp back to Pearl Harbor for repairs. This left the *Washington*, for the time being, the only battleship operating with the South Pacific Command. Flying the flag of Rear-Admiral Willis A. Lee, she at first led Task Force 64 which included three cruisers and six destroyers operating as cover for the supply and reinforcement convoys for the troops on Guadalcanal against the greatly superior Japanese battle squadron poised threatingly at Truk.

The German battleship *Tirpitz*, contemporary with the USS *Washington*, displaced 42,000 tons, mounted eight 15-inch guns and had a speed of 30 knots.

But the nature of naval warfare as waged in the Pacific had made encounters between large surface forces by day almost impossible. Such battles as developed were fought at ranges of several hundred miles by aircraft taking off from the opposing carrier forces. It soon became apparent that groups such as Task Force 64 had no independent role to play –at least by day. During the carrier Battle of Santa Cruz Islands on 26 October, it operated separately. It took no active part but, hovering in the background, offered itself as a tempting target to Japanese submarines

which twice narrowly failed to torpedo the battleship. Had it been with the American Carrier Task Force it is possible that its massed anti-aircraft gunfire, particularly the *Washington*'s twenty 5-inch, might have prevented the loss of the *Hornet*, sunk by dive-bombers and torpedo planes, and damage to the *Enterprise*'s flight deck and forward elevator.

Following this battle, therefore, Task Force 64, now strengthened by the addition of the battleship *South Dakota*, was incorporated in Task Force 16, centred on the carrier *Enterprise*. Early in November it became clear that

The French fast battleship *Richelieu*, laid down three years earlier than the *Washington*, on a displacement of 35,000 tons, mounted eight 15-inch guns in two quadruple turrets forward, and had a speed of 30 knots.

the Japanese were preparing an all-out effort to run reinforcements and supplies to their troops holding the western end of Guadalcanal and, at the same time, to smother Henderson Field and the troop positions round it with massive naval bombardments under cover of darkness. The Americans had also prepared a convoy of seven large transports carrying troops and supplies to the island, and these arrived safely on 11 November under escort by a force of cruisers and destroyers, under Rear-Admiral David Callaghan. Unloading began at once and continued during the next day undeterred by Japanese air attack. But when information came in of strong Japanese surface forces, including two battleships, heading for Guadalcanal to arrive during the night of the 12th, the transports were withdrawn.

The problem remained how to beat off the impending onslaught on the airfield and the soldiers defending it. From the South Pacific Fleet base at Noumea, Task Force 16, with the *Enterprise* still under repair, was hurried forward. But it could not be in the area until the 13th: into the breach was moved Callaghan's force to meet the Japanese bombardment squadron composed of the battleships *Hiei* and *Kirishima*, each mounting a main armament of eight 14-inch guns, the light cruiser *Nagara* and 14 destroyers. For a night engagement, Callaghan's two heavy cruisers, *San Francisco* and *Portland*, each mounting nine 8-inch guns and the light

USS *Washington* (foreground) flagship of Rear-Admiral R. C. Griffen's Task Force 99, operating with HMS *Duke of York*, Home Fleet flagship of Admiral Tovey, as covering force for Allied convoys to north Russia in the spring and summer of 1942.

above
A bomb explodes amongst an
Allied convoy to north Russia.

In July 1942, Convoy PQ 17 to
north Russia was ordered by
the Admiralty to scatter and its
escort withdrawn at a threat of
attack by the *Tirpitz* and other
German capital ships. Twenty-
three merchant ships were sunk
by air or submarine attack, like
the one seen here, as a result
of this much criticized decision.
The USS *Washington* was part
of the distant covering force
during this operation.

cruisers *Helena* (fifteen 6-inch), *Juneau* and *Atlanta* (sixteen 5-inch) and eight destroyers, enjoying the advantage of radar, which the Japanese did not have, might appear, on paper, to have been not inferior to the Japanese force, particularly as the enemy battleships had been supplied with thin-shelled, impact-fused bombardment projectiles.

On the other hand the Japanese were highly trained for night action; they had the advantage of flash-less powder for their guns; above all, and unknown to their opponents, they were equipped with the deadly effective, long-range, liquid oxygen-fuelled torpedoes known as Long Lances.

Thus it was that in the battle which ensued during the night of 12 November, the cruisers *Portland*, *Juneau* and *Atlanta* were quickly disabled – the *Atlanta* having later to be scuttled; Callaghan's flagship *San Francisco* was savagely mauled, the Admiral and his staff being killed, four American destroyers were sunk and another disabled. In reply two Japanese destroyers were sunk and the *Hiei* so damaged that she was only able to limp away slowly, leaving her a prey to American aircraft at daylight.

Task Force 16 had by that time arrived within striking distance and it was aircraft from the partially repaired *Enterprise* which brought the damaged battleship to a halt. Hammered all day by bombers, the *Hiei* was finally scuttled, her survivors being taken off by Japanese destroyers. Her destruction had been achieved at a painful cost to the Americans – a cost increased when the *Juneau*

was torpedoed and sunk with heavy loss of life by a Japanese submarine as the remnants of Callaghan's force retired. Henderson Field had been saved from bombardment, to be sure; but the Japanese had another force of four heavy cruisers – *Chokai*, *Kinugasa*, *Suzuya* and *Maya*, two light cruisers and six destroyers – on its way to cannonade on the following night, 13 November. To oppose them, Rear-Admiral Thomas Kinkaid, commanding Task Force 16 was ordered to detach Task Force 64 – the *Washington* and *South Dakota* and the destroyers *Walke*, *Benham*, *Preston* and *Gwin*; but the order reached him, where he was operating 350 miles south of Guadalcanal, too late, and the Japanese were unchallenged as they hurled a storm of 8-inch and smaller shells amongst the aircraft on Henderson Field. They were made to pay heavily for this during the 14th, however, when planes from the airfield and from the *Enterprise* sank the *Kinugasa* and damaged the *Chokai*, the *Maya* and the light cruiser *Isuzo*. The aircraft went on to harry the Japanese troops and supply convoy of eleven transports making for Guadalcanal, sinking or crippling seven of them before darkness brought the incessant attacks to an end.

The Japanese effort was not expended yet, however. The four remaining transports and their escorts pressed on through the night. At the same time the Japanese fleet commander, Admiral Kondo, was steering to renew the bombardment with a force composed of the heavy cruisers *Atago* (flagship) and *Takao*, the battleship *Kirishima*, two

Henderson Field, Guadalcanal, just after the American victory. The runway is almost complete, and the circular dispersal area can be seen. US air photograph. The *Washington* played a crucial part in its defence against Japanese bombardment in the night Battle of Guadalcanal 13/14 November 1942, when she destroyed the Japanese battleship *Kirishima*.

light cruisers and nine destroyers. To oppose this threat, Rear-Admiral Lee advanced with Task Force 64, past the western point of Guadalcanal and onwards to start to circle the steep-sided cone of Savo Island some ten miles to the north at 01.00. As he did so, Kondo's force was coming south, leaving Santa Isabel Island to starboard. A gentle breeze was barely ruffling the black waters; under a quarter moon, due to set at 01.00, visibility was some seven miles for experienced look-outs.

Once again an American and a Japanese force not greatly unequal in material strength were to clash in night action. Once again the former was to have the advantage of radar –but the disadvantage of being a hastily gathered group of ships inexperienced individually and as a team. But the *Washington*, at least, under the command of Captain Glenn B. Davis and his team of senior officers: Executive Officer–Cdr. Harvey T. Walshe Navigating Officer–Cdr. Edwin S. Schanze Engineer Officer–Cdr. John A. Strother Gunnery Officer–Lieut.-Cdr. Edwin B. Hooper and guided by the tactical and technical know-how of Admiral Lee who had been Director of Fleet Training until three months ago, was trained to a hair.

Nevertheless keen Japanese eyes first detected the presence of an enemy before radar provided any warning to their opponents. Kondo had pushed forward ahead of his main body a scouting screen, the light cruiser *Sendai*, flying the flag of Rear-Admiral Hashimoto, and three destroyers. The American force was to the east of Savo Island, steering south in line ahead with the four destroyers leading when, at 22.10, from the *Sendai*, some nine miles astern of them, they were sighted against the light of the moon. Hashimoto detached two of his destroyers, *Ayanami* and *Uranami*, to circle Savo to the west and south while he continued to shadow from astern with his other destroyer.

On receiving Hashimoto's warning, Kondo sent the light cruiser *Nagara* and four destroyers ahead on a similar route to the west and south of Savo, retaining only two destroyers with his group of heavy ships. Not until 23.00, when Lee had altered course to west to pass south of Savo Island, did the *Washington*'s radar reveal to him that he had a 'tail'. For the next twelve minutes the contact was held as the range fell from nine miles to seven, at which point the *Sendai* came into view of the main gun director sights of the two battleships. In both ships the triple 16-inch gun turrets swivelled silently round and the gun barrels were elevated. Inside the armoured gun houses, massive machinery slid silkily to bring up the huge shells and the cordite propellant charges from shell rooms and magazines and thrust them into the open breaches; with a dull thud the breech-blocks closed and locked. 'Gun-ready' lamps flicked on. Only the pull of a trigger was now needed to blast the shells on their way. At 23.16 the Admiral gave the order, 'Commence firing when ready.' With a blinding flash and a head-splitting concussion the great guns erupted.

US carrier *Wasp* on fire and about to sink after being torpedoed by the Japanese submarine I-19 in the Coral Sea on 15 September 1942.

Japanese twin-engined 'Betty' torpedo planes from Rabaul attack the Allied invasion fleet off Guadalcanal.

As the towering shell splashes leapt upwards around his ship, Hashimoto turned hastily away behind a smoke-screen; but as he ran out of radar range and the firing died away, he swung back to follow again. And now the head of Lee's line came into action as, at 23.22 the destroyers *Walke*, *Benham* and *Preston* sighted the *Ayanami* and *Uranami* on the opposite course south of Savo and opened fire. A few minutes later the *Gwin* made contact with the *Nagara*'s flotilla and engaged. The superior Japanese night-fighting technique soon made itself felt and the *Walke*, *Preston* and *Gwin*, though they succeeded in crippling the *Ayanami*, were themselves so heavily damaged as to be knocked out of action; at the same time the *Ayanami* and *Uranami* launched a flight of Long Lances and at 23.38 both *Walke* and *Benham* were hit, the former being sunk, the latter's forecastle being blown off leaving her barely able to limp away southwards, eventually to be scuttled.

The American battleships had meanwhile come into action with their 5-inch batteries; but hardly had they done so than the *South Dakota* suffered a total electrical failure, silencing her guns and leaving her virtually blind, with no radar. Sheering out of line to starboard to avoid the crippled destroyers, she lost touch with the *Washington* and blundered on into view of the *Nagara* and her four destroyers. No less than thirty-four Long Lances were launched at her; but for once the Japanese aim was faulty and not one hit its target. The *South Dakota* was to suffer grievously for her wayward behaviour, nevertheless. For arriving on the scene was Kondo's main body, the destroyers of which now illuminated her with the blinding glare of their searchlight beams.

A storm of shells, 14-inch and 8-inch smashed into her superstructure. Destruction seemed inevitable; but rescue was, in fact, at hand. The *Washington*, her radar and control systems functioning smoothly, drawing clear of the mêlée south of Savo, was able to identify individual ships on her radar screen and had picked for her target the largest. In the nick of time her full gun-power, 16-inch and 5-inch, opened up a devastating fire on the *Kirishima* at the point-blank range of 8,400 yards. In seven searing minutes the Japanese battleship was reduced to a blazing wreck, hit nine times by 16-inch and forty by 5-inch shells.

The *South Dakota* seized the opportunity to withdraw southwards to lick her wounds. Kondo, too, had had enough, both of his cruisers having taken several hits; leaving the *Sendai* and four destroyers to stand by the *Kirishima* and pick up her crew and that of the *Ayanami*, both of which were scuttled, he turned away in retreat. For a while the *Washington* followed, alone of Lee's squadron still in action, but soon turned back to gather his survivors together. It was a fortunate move. From the Japanese transport convoy, still advancing to unload its troops and supplies, two escorting destroyers had been sent forward. Sighting the battleship, they had launched torpedoes which must otherwise have hit; as it was, several exploded in the *Washington*'s wake.

So ended the second Battle of Guadalcanal. It had come close to being a catastrophe for the American squadron, turned into victory only by the splendid performance of the *Washington*'s well-trained crew. The threatened bombardment of Henderson Field had been repulsed. And at daylight naval aircraft from it were able to destroy the last four Japanese transports where they lay beached. Though the Japanese were to hold on doggedly to their foothold in the western part of Guadalcanal for another ten weeks, suffering growing starvation, disease and shortage of ammunition, the fate of the island had been decided. In retrospect it can be seen to mark the great turning point in the Pacific War when the Americans and their Australian and New Zealand allies were able to go over to the offensive after the year-long defence forced on them by the lightning strokes of the Japanese at Pearl Harbor, Malaya and the Philippines.

The Japanese battleship *Kirishima* was destroyed by the radar-controlled fire of the *Washington*'s 16-inch guns during the night Battle of Guadalcanal on 13/14 November 1942.

The Battle of Guadalcanal was the only occasion when any of the American fast battleships came into direct action with Japanese capital ships–or with any warships, indeed. As noted earlier, the time was over in which fleet actions by day would be decided by the exchange of gunfire. Rival fleets would always be kept far beyond the range of guns by the strike aircraft taking off from the decks of carriers.

It was to provide gun defence for the carriers against such of these aircraft as broke through the fighter defences that had become fast battleships' principal role, a secondary one being to use their big guns to 'soften up' enemy positions ashore during amphibious operations. Thus we find the *Washington* forming part of carrier Task Forces in the Pacific usually with Admiral Lee's flag at her masthead, on virtually every operation of importance in the campaign continuing almost to the end of the war in which the Japanese were evicted successively from the Solomon Islands, New Guinea, the Gilberts, the Marshall Islands, the Marianas, the Philippines, the Bonins and Okinawa. In the great carrier Battle of the Philippine Sea, she was Lee's flagship in the battle line with the battleships *North Carolina*, *Iowa*, *New Jersey*, *South Dakota*, *Alabama* and *Indiana*, four cruisers and 13 destroyers, thrown forward to oppose any thrust by the enemy battleships–an unlikely contingency and one which did not take place.

During the vast Battle for Leyte Gulf, the same ships were again organized for surface action, being withdrawn from the Carrier Groups to which they had been attached to form a battle force. Had this Task Force 64 been left to protect the American amphibious Seventh Fleet operating off Leyte when the carrier fleet raced away northwards to attack the Japanese carriers, it must have met the Japanese battle squadron led by the huge battleship *Yamato*, mounting nine 18·1-inch guns as it debouched from the San Bernardino Strait on the morning of 25 October 1944 and the world would have seen one final,

cataclysmic clash between the steel leviathans. But it was not to be; the battle remained dominated by the aircraft of the American fleet. The Japanese battle squadron surprised the force of escort carriers of the Seventh Fleet; but, after sinking one of these almost unarmed and slow ships, it was driven off by the gallant attacks of the American destroyer escorts and the aircraft from the escort carriers. By the time a portion of Task Force 64 had returned, the Japanese had retreated through the San Bernardino Strait.

The *Washington* continued with the Pacific Fleet playing her part in repelling the massed *Kamikaze* suicide attacks which came near to forcing a withdrawal of the fleet. But in June 1945 her need for a refit took her back to the Puget Sound Navy Yard for a refit; and before that was completed in October, the end of the war, marked by the Japanese surrender on 16 August, had also brought the *Washington*'s fighting career to an end, though she was not finally de-commissioned until 27 June 1947. In 1960 she was sold for breaking up.

A direct hit from a US warship on a Japanese torpedo plane at Guadalcanal. The plane explodes and the torpedo falls harmlessly into the sea.

SCHARNHORST

By the naval terms of the Treaty of Versailles which brought the First World War to an end, Germany was not allowed to build any warship exceeding 10,000 tons standard displacement. Resentment of such humiliating restrictions was widespread, however, and one of the evasions perpetrated was in the design of the so-called pocket battleships, the first of which, the *Deutschland*, was launched in 1931. The world was amazed to learn that on a standard displacement of only 10,000 tons she was able to mount six 11-inch guns and eight 5·9-inch, to have armour protection 4 inches thick and, powered by diesel engines, a top speed of twenty-six knots as well as great endurance. She had, in fact, a standard displacement of nearly 12,000 tons; but even so, she was a brilliant achievement by German naval designers.

When, in 1935, the German government, by this time led by Adolf Hitler, having denounced the Versailles Treaty and negotiated a naval agreement with Great Britain which permitted Germany to build up to 35 per cent of the strength of the Royal Navy, a similar deception was employed. The first two battleships of this building programme, laid down that year and to be named *Scharnhorst* and *Gneisenau*, were given out to have a standard displacement of 26,000 tons whereas in reality it was to be nearly 32,000.

Even at this increased tonnage, however, sacrifices had to be made in one of the three main characteristics of a battleship–armament, armour protection and speed. In the case of these two ships it was the armament. A 12-inch armoured belt, two armoured decks of 4.3 inches and 2·4 inches and turret armour of 13·8 inches gave massive protection. The latest–and indeed, still experimental–high-pressure steam boilers driving turbines with super-heated steam gave them a maximum speed of over thirty-one knots. But in compensation the main armament was limited to nine 11-inch guns in three triple turrets with a secondary armament of twelve 5·9-inch and fourteen (AA) 4·1-inch. The *Scharnhorst* and her sister were insufficiently armed to engage French or British battleships or battle-cruisers, armed as they were with 13-inch, 15-inch or 16-inch guns. Unless they encountered the veteran British *Hood*, *Repulse* and *Renown*, and the French *Dunkerque* and *Strasbourg*, they would use their high speed to avoid action.

Their function, therefore, if and when the renewal of war with Britain and France should come, was commerce raiding–to harass the merchant convoys upon which the Allied war effort depended. Not until the intended 'Z' plan of naval ship-building matured in 1942–a plan which included six fast new battleships of 56,000 tons armed with eight 16-inch guns and three battle-cruisers with eight 15-inch and a speed of thirty-four knots–would a confrontation with the Allied or even the British fleet be feasible.

Hitler, however, began the Second World War in September 1939, when the *Scharnhorst* and *Gneisenau* were the only two German capital ships in service; and even then, though she had been in commission since January, the *Scharnhorst* was still undergoing trials, rectifying defects in her machinery, and shaking down her inexperienced crew in the Heligoland Bight. Her first wartime move was through the Kaiser Wilhelm Canal to Kiel to be fitted with a gunnery and surface-warning radar set–something which no British man-of-war was to enjoy for more than a year. Captain Curt Caesar Hoffman relieved Captain Ciliax who had gone sick and under her new commander she returned to Wilhelmshaven to join the *Gneisenau* in which flew the flag of Admiral Marschall, Commander-in-Chief of the fleet.

By the middle of November the two ships were considered ready for operations against the enemy; operations ideally suited to their designed capabilites, namely a surprise sweep of the sea area between Iceland and the Faeroes to disrupt the patrol line of British light cruisers and armed merchant cruisers which were enforcing the blockade of Germany by preventing her merchant ships breaking into or out of the North Sea. On 21 November they sailed and on the afternoon of the 23rd, some 150 miles to the westward of the Faeroes they came across the armed merchant cruiser *Rawalpindi*, a P. & O. liner converted to her wartime role by the mounting of seven 6-inch guns – no match for such powerful adversaries and, with a top speed of only seventeen knots, unable to escape. It took only a few salvoes from the *Scharnhorst* to reduce her to a stationary wreck which soon afterwards sank taking with her 270 officers and men. The German ship proceeded to pick up survivors and had taken a boatload of twenty-one on board when, from the flagship, came the order to get under way at once – an enemy warship had come on the scene.

This was the light cruiser *Newcastle*, armed with nothing bigger than 6-inch guns. But Admiral Marschall had no wish to get embroiled in a night action with the unidentified ship. He had done enough to disrupt the British naval dispositions and to give his new ships a shake-down cruise which had revealed machinery defects and a liability to damage in heavy weather. It was time to return home. The Allied naval forces had been stirred up like an ants' nest. Shaking off the *Newcastle*, Marschall steered north-east up into the Arctic where he waited until the onset of thick and stormy weather enabled him to make his way undetected through a patrol line of enemy cruisers and destroyers spread between Norway and the Shetlands. On the afternoon of 27 November, the battleships re-entered Wilhelmshaven, there to make good the various defects revealed by their first cruise.

These kept them in the dockyard until the middle of January when they both moved through the Kiel Canal to the Baltic for further training. This was much hampered by the severe icing conditions of that bitter winter and, except for a brief and abortive sortie from 18 to 20 February 1940, in an attempt to intercept the iron-ore convoys running between Norway and Britain, it continued until the beginning of April.

Meanwhile, in the greatest secrecy, preparations had been going on for an operation which was to involve the entire German navy – the invasion of Denmark and Norway. The plans called for the delivery simultaneously at dawn on 9 April of amphibious assaults at the Norwegian ports of Oslo, Kristiansand, Bergen, Trondheim and Narvik and the cable-station at Egersund. The two German battle-ships were brought back through the Kiel Canal in time to sail with the first two Groups – ten destroyers comprising Group 1 for Narvik, and the heavy cruiser *Admiral Hipper* and four destroyers of Group 2 for Trondheim, during the night of 6 April. In place of Admiral Marschall who was ill, Vice-Admiral Lütjens hoisted his flag in the *Gneisenau*. The battle-ships' task was to act firstly as cover for Groups 1 and 2 as they steamed north up the Norwegian coast, then to carry on into the Arctic to wait until it was time to give the same cover to them on their return journey from delivering the assault troops at the two northern ports.

It was a bold plan, indeed; even foolhardy, relying as it did upon the maintenance of secrecy to prevent a confrontation with the greatly superior British naval forces in home waters. And secrecy was broken as early as the afternoon of 7 April when, following a sighting by a British aircraft on reconnaissance, a force of twelve from RAF Bomber Command unsuccessfully attacked Groups 1 and 2 off the entrance to the Skagerrak. Ineptitude on the part of the British delayed the sailing of the Home Fleet until late that evening, and when it did sail it was deployed far out from the Norwegian coast, as to intercept any German warships attempting to break out into the Atlantic.

So the way north was left clear for German Groups 1 and 2 and only by chance was there a brief encounter in the early morning of the 8th. In heavy seas the German destroyers had become scattered as they strove to keep up with the battleships and the *Hipper*. In a break between the almost incessant rain squalls one of them, the *Bernd von Arnim*, suddenly sighted an enemy ship. It was the destroyer *Glowworm*. She had been one of the screen attached to the battle-cruiser

A model of the battleship *Scharnhorst* in the National Maritime Museum, Greenwich.

Admiral Günther Lütjens, who flew his flag in the *Gneisenau* during the Norwegian campaign and during the Atlantic sortie of *Scharnhorst* and *Gneisenau* in February 1941. He went down with the *Bismarck* when that ship was destroyed on 27 May 1941.

Renown which was covering a flotilla of minelaying destroyers laying a field off the entrance to the Vestfiord. A man had been swept overboard; the *Glowworm* had turned back to try to rescue him; in doing so she had lost touch and was now steering to rejoin.

From the two ships, rolling and pitching wildly, the guns barked out, though ineffectively. At the same time each sent an enemy report crackling over the radio waves. The *Arnim*'s signal brought the *Hipper* to her aid and the little *Glowworm*'s fate was sealed, though before she was sent to the bottom she succeeded in ramming and damaging the cruiser. Except for this chance encounter the programme for Groups 1 and 2 proceeded as planned. At noon on the 8th, the *Hipper* and her destroyers parted company and steered for Trondheim and that evening the ten destroyers for Narvik were also sent on their way. The *Gneisenau* led the *Scharnhorst* onward towards the Arctic.

At dawn on the 9th, while the Norwegian ports, taken by surprise, were falling into German hands with hardly a blow struck in defence, except in Oslofiord where the brand-new cruiser *Blücher* was sunk, the two battleships were punching their way into a north-westerly gale to the westward of the Lofoten Islands. Green seas tumbled along their decks. A succession of snow squalls swept over them; but there were brief breaks during which the sky cleared and a few stars gleamed. On the *Scharnhorst*'s bridge Kovettenkapitän Helmuth Giessler, the navigating officer, raised his sextant and squinted through its telescope at the western horizon to take a star sight. Instead of the star, he saw a rippling flash which could only be from gunfire; and then dimly on the horizon he made out the shape of a large warship.

It was the *Renown*, from whose 15-inch guns the flashes had come and round the *Gneisenau* rose the tall splashes of her shells. The German flagship and the British battle-cruiser had, in fact, been in sight of one another for some fifteen minutes. The *Renown* had manœuvred at once to get into range and at 19,000 yards had opened fire. Though it was not for several minutes that the German ships were able to reply, it was the *Gneisenau*, aided no doubt by her gunnery radar, which scored the first hit. This did little damage, however, and, in reply, a 15-inch shell wrecked the *Gneisenau*'s fire-control system and soon afterwards a second hit put her after-turret out of action.

It was no part of Admiral Lütjen's assigned task to get closely involved at this stage of the operations with an enemy capital ship, even a single unit against his two. At their full speed and accepting the resultant damage and flooding of their forward turrets, his two ships headed into the teeth of the storm, drawing out of range of the *Renown*, and out of sight amongst the snow squalls. Having shaken off the pursuit, Lütjens turned west towards the lonely Arctic island of Jan Mayen, far to the north of Iceland. There he remained undetected and, having catapulted off the *Scharnhorst*'s Arado float plane for Trondheim with a message arranging a rendezvous with the *Hipper* for 08.30 on the 12th, he began his return journey on the evening of the 11th. Though the three ships were sighted off the south-western tip of Norway early on the 12th, a bomber force sent against them failed to find them and they arrived without further incident at Wilhelmshaven that evening.

Once again, however, Germany's only two battleships had to be taken in hand for repairs which were to keep them out of service for the whole of May. This was particularly serious as the sea-borne assault on Norway, successful though it had been, had exacted a heavy toll from German naval strength. The cruiser *Blücher* had been sunk by the coast defences; the ten destroyers of Group 1 had been trapped and sunk at Narvik; the light cruiser *Königsberg* had been destroyed at Bergen by naval dive-bombers; British submarines had sunk the *Karlsruhe* and so damaged the pocket battleship *Lützow* (ex-*Deutschland*) that she would be out of action for nearly a year. This had left insufficient forces to harass the Allied troop and supply convoys supporting the operations which led to the re-capture of Narvik on 27 May.

So, as soon as the two battleships were repaired, Operation Juno was planned to deliver a surprise attack on the Allied shipping in the anchorages near Narvik. Sailing from Kiel after dark on 4 June, the *Gneisenau*, flying the flag of Admiral Marschall, *Scharnhorst*, *Hipper* and four destroyers slipped unseen through the Great Belt out into the North Sea and by the 6th had made rendezvous in the far north with an oil tanker from which the destroyers refuelled. The squadron was now ready for its planned descent on the Narvik area.

Unknown to the Germans, however, the decision to evacuate northern Norway had been taken by the Allies even before Narvik had fallen and the withdrawal was now in progress. The first troop convoy was already at sea and during the 7th, aerial reconnaissance reported it to Admiral Marschall. When reports of another large group of transports reached him the next day—as well as the contents of various British naval messages which had been deciphered—he correctly read the situation and decided to lie in wait—a decision which was strongly criticized by the German High Command where the signs had not been read aright.

Thus it was that during the 8th, ignoring renewed orders to make for Narvik, Marschall's squadron came first upon the tanker *Oil Pioneer* straggling from her convoy and escorted by the trawler *Juniper*. Both were sent to the bottom by the *Hipper*. Meanwhile, the *Scharnhorst*'s and *Hipper*'s planes had been catapulted off to search and the former discovered two large ships – the hospital ship *Atlantis* which, as she obeyed the rules of war and made no attempt to radio a warning, was allowed to proceed unharmed, and the liner *Orama*, a troopship, fortunately returning to England empty, which was quickly sunk by the *Hipper*'s 8-inch guns.

The Norwegian sea was becoming a busy area. Marschall's destroyers were again running short of fuel, but it was no time for a second refuelling operation. In company with the *Hipper* they were, therefore, sent away to Trondheim, leaving the two battleships in position to fall upon the troop convoy known to be on its way.

Fate now intervened, however, on the one hand to save the vulnerable troopships from possible destruction, on the other to provide the German battleships with a victim whose loss the Royal Navy could ill afford. At 15.45 that afternoon a warship's masthead was sighted from the *Scharnhorst* on the eastern horizon. Course was altered towards it, full speed rung on the engine-room telegraphs and very soon the silhouette of an aircraft carrier could be made out. Accompanying it were two destroyers. The carrier was the *Glorious*, one of the small number of ageing ships of that type available to provide the Royal Navy with air support until newer ships of the *Formidable* class under construction could be completed. She was all the more valuable in that her sister, *Courageous*, had been sunk by a U-boat's torpedoes a few months earlier. Now she had blundered into a trap while in no shape to defend herself. She was short of fuel and had steam only for moderate speed immediately available. Her hangars were cluttered with RAF Hurricane and Gladiator fighters which had been skilfully and gallantly landed – in spite of no arrester hooks – by pilots without any carrier training. No doubt on account of these various factors, no scouting aircraft had been sent up. Surprise was thus complete.

The destroyers *Acasta* and *Ardent* tried to screen the carrier with smoke as she turned away to escape but to no avail. The *Scharnhorst* opened fire at a range of 28,000 yards – far outside the range of the 4·7-inch guns in the *Glorious* and the destroyers – and it took only a couple of salvoes to score a first hit

HMS *Glowworm* under fire and steering to ram the cruiser *Admiral Hipper* before being destroyed off the Norwegian coast on 8 April 1940.

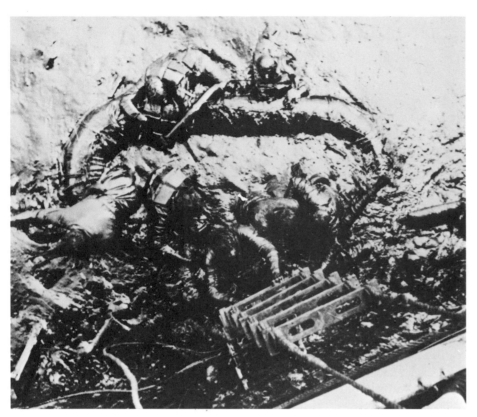

Survivors from the *Glowworm* being picked up from the oil-covered sea by the German cruiser *Admiral Hipper* on 8 April 1940.

airfield, suffered heavy losses. One bomb did, indeed, land on the *Scharnhorst*'s deck, but failed to explode.

By 20 June the *Scharnhorst*, with two engines functioning to give her a speed of twenty-five knots, set out for Germany. She was detected by air reconnaissance, but the first bombers sent out from Britain failed to find her; a puny force of six naval Swordfish planes attacked but their torpedoes were avoided and two of them shot down by the battleship's guns; nine RAF Beauforts took up the attack with bombs but failed to score any hits; and after taking shelter for a while in Stavanger fiord, on receiving news that the British Home Fleet was after her, the battleship reached Kiel at last and was taken in hand for full repairs.

These, including repairs to the *Gneisenau* which had been torpedoed by a British submarine, took until the end of the year and it was not until 23 January 1941 that the two battleships with Vice-Admiral Lütjen's flag in the *Gneisenau*, set out on their next adventure. In the meanwhile France had capitulated. Her Atlantic ports–Brest, Lorient and St Nazaire–were in German hands. Advantage was to be taken of this to deploy all available heavy ships in the Atlantic to harass the Allied merchant shipping. The *Admiral Scheer* and *Admiral Hipper* were already there; now the *Scharnhorst* and *Gneisenau* were to break out past Iceland to join the campaign. Tankers from which they could refuel were stationed in remote areas of the ocean.

During the night of 27 January Lütjens steered to pass between Iceland and the Faeroes, hoping to pass through undetected. But in the grey winter morning he was briefly sighted by the cruiser *Naiad* on patrol. He at once turned back at high speed, shaking off the shadower, and retreated into the Arctic wastes to refuel and await a further opportunity. This came on the night of 3 February when his two ships slipped through the Denmark Strait between Iceland and frozen Greenland waters, evading, with the help of radar, the British cruiser on patrol. By daylight they were clear out into the Atlantic.

At a rendezvous south of Greenland's Cape Farewell, the tanker *Schlettstadt* was met and the two ships refuelled again before setting off to intercept the westbound convoy HX 106 reported to the southward. Sure enough, dawn on the 8th revealed a forest of masts on the horizon. Lütjens divided his force, sending the *Scharnhorst* to attack from the north, *Gneisenau* from the south. As they drew nearer, however, amongst the pole-masts of the merchant ships was seen the fighting top of the battleship *Ramillies*–old and slow but armed with eight 15-inch guns. Captain Hoffman took the *Scharnhorst* within

which penetrated to the hangars and set aircraft ablaze. Others followed to reduce her to a flaming wreck and at 17.40 she finally rolled over and sank. The two destroyers had meanwhile advanced through a storm of fire to attack with torpedoes. The *Ardent* was the first to launch, forcing the battleships to sheer temporarily away, before she was overwhelmed and sunk by their gunfire. The *Acasta* suffered the same fate; but in her case one of her torpedoes hit the *Scharnhorst* below her after-turret, which was put out of action. Two officers and forty-six ratings were killed. About 2,500 tons of water taken in flooded her centre and starboard engine rooms, reducing her speed to twenty knots.

Marschall had no choice but to head with both ships for Trondheim where they arrived the following day. The Allied troop convoys reached home unmolested. With the aid of a repair ship, temporary repairs on the *Scharnhorst* were put in hand. A scouting Blenheim aircraft of the RAF located her on the 10th; and on the next morning twelve Hudson bombers attacked with armour-piercing bombs from 15,000 feet. It was a scaring experience for the German crew as thirty-six bombs fell all round their immobilized ship. But as was to be the case so often during the Second World War with high-level bombing at ships, not a single direct hit was scored. More to be feared were the Royal Navy's Skua dive-bombers from the carrier *Ark Royal* which next took up the attack; but, as recounted in the history of that ship elsewhere in this book, the surprise necessary for success was lost and the Skuas, set upon by German fighters from the nearby Vaernes

25,000 yards of the *Ramillies* before turning away, with the object of luring the British battleship, leaving the *Gneisenau* to attack the merchant ships. But Lütjens' orders strictly debarred him from getting involved with such a ship. He not only recalled the *Scharnhorst* and withdrew, but censured Hoffman for his initiative. Hoffman resented this keenly and his action was supported by the High Command when they later received Lütjens' report.

For the next two weeks the battleships searched in vain for victims. They endured several days of furious Atlantic tempests and for all their beauty and many excellent battle features they again revealed an inability to surmount such weather undamaged and the *Scharnhorst*'s machinery gave constant trouble. At last on 22 February a group of ships was sighted—five westbound, empty merchantmen which had recently been dispersed from a convoy and so were without escort. One after the other they were sunk by gunfire—a total of 25,784 tons. In spite of attempts to jam their signals, some succeeded in getting the alarm through to the shore; 180 survivors were picked up (11 had been killed). For this rather meagre prize, Lütjens' position had been given away. He decided to shift his ground and make for the Sierra Leone–UK convoy route on the other side of the Atlantic; and there he arrived on 3 March.

Once again the British convoy system, gathering all shipping into a few groups, tiny oases in the otherwise empty ocean spaces, frustrated Lütjens' search. And when, on the 7th, a convoy was at last discovered, attack was again barred by the presence of a 15-inch gun battleship, the *Malaya*. Lütjens was able, however, to direct two U-boats to this convoy which sank seven of its ships, during the night of 8 March. The following day he made his only victim in those waters when the *Scharnhorst* sighted the Greek ship *Marathon* sailing alone and sank her. Various orders had, meanwhile, come in from the High Command, the sum of which added up to instructions to do what damage he could on the convoy routes up to 17 March, and then make for Brest to prepare for joint operations with the huge,

The *Scharnhorst* heads into Arctic seas. Ice is coating the guns and rigging. She and her sister *Gneisenau* repeatedly suffered damage and flooding of the forward turret from heavy seas.

The cruiser *Admiral Hipper* in dock at Brest in February 1941, swathed in camouflage against the air-raids by which she was narrowly missed on several occasions.

new battleship *Bismarck* and the heavy cruiser *Prinz Eugen* which would break out into the Atlantic at the end of April.

North-westward, therefore, the *Scharnhorst* and *Gneisenau* steamed, away from the breathless heat of calm tropical seas towards the restless North Atlantic. In company with them were two of their supply ships, the *Uckermark* and the *Ermland*. To widen the scope of his sweep, Lütjens spread the four ships at double visibility distance apart – 30 miles by day, making a front of 120 miles. These methods brought a brief but bountiful harvest during 15 and 16 March as this gigantic rake gathered in no less than 16 ships all from a recently dispersed westbound convoy. The freighters were sunk, three tankers being sent off to the Gironde with prize crews, though two were to be intercepted *en route* and scuttled. The massacre was brought to an end on the evening of the 16th when the battleship *Rodney* came on the scene whereupon Lütjens ordered retirement at high speed, so evading the 16-inch guns of the slow newcomer.

All this had stirred up a hornet's nest of British warships trying to locate the *Scharnhorst* and *Gneisenau* and the *Hipper* and *Scheer*; the two latter were at the time steering to break back through the Denmark Strait to Germany. After refuelling at a mid-ocean rendezvous on the 18th, therefore, Lütjens shaped course for Brest. It was high time: for coming up from the south were the carrier *Ark Royal* and the battle-cruiser *Renown* of Admiral Somerville's Force H – the squadron which, ten weeks later, was to deliver the blow which sent the *Bismarck* to destruction by the Home Fleet. And it was an aircraft from the *Ark Royal* which now located the *Scharnhorst* and *Gneisenau* on the evening of 20

March. Lütjens was luckier on this occasion: for a combination of communications failures and the onset of thick weather caused contact to be lost and prevented the launching of *Ark Royal*'s torpedo squadrons; and by the following afternoon he was under cover of his own shore-based aircraft. Dawn on 22 March saw the German battleships being escorted into Brest by minesweepers. So ended the only successful operation by battleships against the vital Atlantic merchant traffic.

The satisfaction felt by the German crew, outwardly expressed by the ten large battle ensigns flown at the mastheads and yardarms of the two ships must, however, be seen as mistaken when their situation is examined. Both ships had numerous defects to remedy, the *Scharnhorst*'s being chiefly in the boiler super-heaters which had given constant trouble throughout the cruise. Repairs would take many weeks even if allowed to proceed unhampered. But eight days after arrival came the first of a succession of air raids. They were to continue incessantly at brief intervals.

At first they were ineffective, the bombs falling mainly on the town. But on the night of 4 April came evidence of improving performance by the bombers of the RAF when a 500-pound armour-piercing bomb landed alongside the *Gneisenau* where she was berthed in the partly filled dry-dock. It failed to explode, but the *Gneisenau* was moved out to the Roads; and there, on the morning of the 6th, Flying Officer K. Campbell flew with superb gallantry through a storm of gunfire to launch a torpedo before being shot down and killed. The *Gneisenau* was struck on her starboard side, the explosion wreaking damage which would take at least six months to repair. Taken back into dry-dock, the unlucky ship

was hit again four days later by a bomb which killed fifty of her crew, wounded ninety more and started a fierce fire.

For the next two months, frustrated by extensive camouflage and a system of smoke generators to shroud the whole area at the first alarm, repeated air raids had no further success. In the meantime, during the last week of May the Germans were elated by the news of the *Bismarck*'s break-out into the Atlantic in company with the *Prinz Eugen*, and their destruction of the British battleship *Hood*, only to be cast back into gloom by the sinking of the *Bismarck*, taking with her Admiral Lütjens and all but a handful of her crew. On 1 June the *Prinz Eugen* arrived at Brest, having achieved nothing. A month later she, too, became a victim of British bombers, suffering damage that put her out of action for three months and casualties amounting to fifty killed and thirty-two wounded.

Not until 23 July was the *Scharnhorst* at last fit to run trials. Captain Hoffman took her down the coast to La Pallice. Trials went with hardly a hitch; a speed of thirty knots had been recorded and the ship had returned to the Roads of La Pallice for minor adjustments. But once again it was to be demonstrated that naval operations could no longer be conducted without the co-operation of an air arm. The British had been warned of the ship's departure by the heroic little band of French secret agents operating in Brest under Lieutenant (later Vice-Admiral) Philippon. Air reconnaissance located her and a bombing operation was quickly mounted against her where she lay at anchor. Fifteen high-flying Halifax bombers achieved five direct hits. Only two bombs exploded and these did comparatively little damage. Three heavy armour-

piercing bombs plunged through the battleship's armoured deck and out through the hull without exploding.

The *Scharnhorst* could be said to have lived up to her reputation of being a lucky ship—certainly as compared to the ill-starred *Gneisenau*. Nevertheless, the three armour-piercing bombs had torn huge holes and no less than 3,000 tons of water had flooded in. Lying very low in the water she hurried back through the night to Brest for repairs; she was out of action again for four months.

The conclusion that the German squadron at Brest would be unlikely ever to escape the attentions of the RAF long enough to become battleworthy was at last reached by the German High Command. Conferences at Hitler's headquarters, attended by Vice-Admiral Ciliax, the *Scharnhorst*'s first captain, who had now hoisted his flag in her following Lütjen's death, heard the Führer demanding that they be got back to Germany for deployment in Norwegian waters. He was convinced that Britain was planning a landing in the north. He now proposed that rather than risk a confrontation with the British Home Fleet they should be brought back through the English Channel.

Alone amongst his naval advisers, Ciliax agreed that such a seemingly suicidal plan was feasible on three conditions. The operation must be launched with great secrecy and with no preliminary sortie. The ships must leave Brest after dark, which meant that they would have to pass through the Straits of Dover in daylight. And continuous fighter cover throughout daylight hours must be provided by the Luftwaffe.

The precarious position of the German ships at Brest was emphasized when the

The veteran battleship HMS *Malaya* which was used as convoy escort during 1941. It was her presence with a Sierra Leone convoy which deterred the *Scharnhorst* and *Gneisenau* from attacking on 7 March 1941.

Flying-Officer Kenneth Campbell, who was posthumously awarded the Victoria Cross for his gallant aerial torpedo attack which seriously damaged the *Gneisenau* at Brest on 6 April 1941, putting her out of action for six months.

Gneisenau was again damaged by a bomb on 6 January, entailing two or three weeks of repair. As Hitler succinctly put it, their situation was like that of a man with cancer. Although there was danger in an operation, it offered the only chance of survival. And so Operation Cerberus was decided upon. The ships would leave on 11 February 1942–a moonless night. Channels through the minefields sown by the British off the French and Dutch coasts would be swept and carefully marked. Daylight would find the squadron off Cherbourg after which the Luftwaffe was to provide a continuous fighter 'umbrella' of never less than sixteen fighters.

In spite of extensive security precautions, Philippon's organization was able to warn the British on 1 February that a break-out was impending, though not that a route through the Channel was to be taken. Nevertheless on the 3rd the orders were given to put into force Operation Fuller–planned to counter just such a move. This was not primarily a naval responsibility. Aerial dogma contended that no large warships could operate in the Channel unless they enjoyed the support of clear air superiority. This was no doubt true if the enemy's air striking force was effective, and it was accepted by the Admiralty to the extent that Operation Fuller called for only minor naval forces in the south–a handful of motor torpedo-boats based on Dover and Margate and a flotilla of six old destroyers at Harwich. In addition and, in the event, the Admiralty's most valuable contribution, was their arrangement whereby a fresh field of magnetic mines was laid off the Frisian Islands by aircraft of RAF Bomber Command. Opposition to any appearance of the German heavy ships in the Channel would otherwise be supplied mainly by three squadrons of torpedo bombers of RAF Coastal Command and more than 300 bombers of Bomber Command. The only naval aircraft involved were six of the slow and vulnerable biplane Swordfish with which the Royal Navy had still to make do as torpedo aircraft. Similarly, warning of any foray by the Germans depended upon three radar-equipped aircraft of Coastal Command kept during dark hours, one over Brest, one between Ushant and Île de Brehat on the north Brittany coast and one between Le Havre and Boulogne.

The German plan was a bold one: for success it relied upon good luck and an ineffective British maritime air force. It was to enjoy both in full measure. On the night of 11 February, departure of the German squadron was delayed for nearly two hours by a false air-raid alarm. As a result the submarine *Sealion* operating off the entrance to the harbour and which must otherwise have seen them leave, had withdrawn. Then the aircraft patrolling that area had suffered a radar breakdown and returned to base for repair. Thus by midnight the three heavy ships and their escort of six destroyers were rounding Ushant undetected; but they should now have been coming under the radar eye of the second air patrol. That, too, however, had been withdrawn owing to a radar defect. The third patrol was withdrawn at dawn before the squadron had come within range of its radar. They were already approaching the Narrows, their air umbrella circling overhead and their surface escort increased by the addition of ten torpedo-boats and a number of motor torpedo gun boats before, at 10.42 they were at last seen and identified by the pilot of a Spitfire out on a fighter sweep which became involved in a dog-fight with their air escort. But it was not until he landed at 11.09 that he was able to make a report.

So much for the good luck which Operation Cerberus needed for success. Now the defects in British defence organization were to reveal themselves. Operation Fuller relied upon the co-operation of four separate and independent commands–RAF Coastal, Bomber and Fighter Commands and the naval Dover Command. The thirty-three Beaufort torpedo planes of Coastal Command were dispersed between Thorney Island on the Sussex coast, Leuchars in Fife and St Eval in Cornwall. Of the seven stationed at Thorney Island only four were immediately available and at 13.40 they were the first to take off. Becoming scattered *en route*, they attacked, unsuccessfully, in one's and two's over a period between 15.40 and 18.00. The other three got away later; one was shot down, two attacked, also unsuccessfully.

At Leuchars there were fourteen Beauforts but torpedoes for only nine which came south to Manston in Kent and then set out for the target with five Hudsons. The torpedoes were launched but were avoided. The Hudsons succeeded in damaging some of the German escort vessels as will be seen later. Torpedoes for the other five were at an air base in Norfolk but snow on the airfield prevented the Beauforts landing there to pick them up. Meanwhile, from St Eval, twelve Beauforts managed to get away at 14.30–more than three hours after the alarm. Flying first to Coltishall, Norfolk, to collect a fighter escort which did not materialize, it was dusk before they reached the estimated position of the German squadron. They failed to deliver any attack but two of their number were shot down. As for Bomber Command from stations spread over the south of England, no less than 242 bombers were despatched during the afternoon of which only 39 succeeded in attacking –unsuccessfully. Fifteen were lost.

While the main force upon which Operation Fuller depended was thus being fruitlessly expended, the Royal Navy had been doing what it could with the meagre forces available. The MTB's—essentially night-fighting craft—could not hope to penetrate the immense screen in daylight. They were forced to launch their torpedoes ineffectively at long range or were driven off.

There now occurred an episode, futile and forlorn it must be conceded, but involving peerless gallantry, as the six lumbering Swordfish, led by Lieutenant-Commander E. Esmonde, with an escort of ten Spitfires, flew at their stately eighty knots towards the enemy to be set upon by Messerschmitt 109s and—those that survived—an impenetrable wall of gunfire. Two, at least, even succeeded in launching their torpedoes; but all were shot down; five crew members were later picked up.

Finally, five of the six old destroyers from Harwich, led by Captain C. T. M. Pizey in the *Campbell*, had steered to intercept and, at 15.45, raced boldly in amongst the enemy screen. The *Worcester* was heavily hit, set on fire and brought to a halt with forty-six casualties. The other four got through to launch their torpedoes (all of which were avoided by the German ships) and miraculously escaped unscathed.

Such were the various attempts made to disrupt the passage of the German squadron. This is the story of the *Scharnhorst*, however, and it must now be given from her viewpoint. Her first sight of enemy action came as she led the German line at twenty-seven knots through the Dover Straits when at 12.18 out of the water on the port side, tall white columns of water spouted—splashes of shells fired by the big coastal guns near Dover. All fell short. Then there came a flurry of gunfire amongst the escorts as the British MTB's made their vain effort. It had hardly died away when it broke out again. Fighter planes were seen diving with their guns blazing. Suddenly out of the smoke staggered a solitary Swordfish. The *Scharnhorst*'s huge battery of close-range guns concentrated on it; yet it penetrated to a range of barely 2,000 yards before it burst into flame and crashed. This was the only Swordfish to attack the flagship—almost certainly Esmonde's plane. Others were seen making similar gallant attempts against the rear of the line where the *Prinz Eugen* was seen to destroy three and Messerschmitts two more.

Unscathed, the German formation swept on. Ciliax's bold plan was working out perfectly. Then, suddenly at 14.31 the *Scharnhorst* was shaken by an explosion under her starboard bow. She had struck a mine. Hoffman pulled her out of the line and stopped engines. The *Gneisenau* and *Prinz Eugen* swept by and soon disappeared into the haze. The Admiral called the destroyer *Z-29* alongside. After some difficulty in the steep seas which had risen he transferred with his staff to her and sped away to catch up with the remainder.

Anti-aircraft gun crew of the cruiser *Prinz Eugen* during gunnery practice at Brest. The battleship *Scharnhorst* is to be seen in the background, left.

The damage to the *Scharnhorst* proved less serious than appearances had indicated. Although the explosion had torn a long gash in the hull, flooding was confined to two double-bottomed compartments. By 16.00 she was under way and again working up to twenty-seven knots. Four torpedo-boats and a section of the fighter force had been detached to escort her. She was fortunate not to have been caught immobilized by the bombers which at this time found her and, dodging in and out of the low cloud base, attacked. The battleship's AA batteries drove off many; but others braved the intensive fire to aim their bombs, though none fell nearer than a few hundred yards.

Hardly had these aircraft made off when, at 16.00, two Beaufort torpedo planes came in low, one from either side. As one of them swept by, strafing the battleship's decks with her machine guns, a torpedo was seen approaching and Hoffman had to turn hard-a-starboard to avoid it. At about the same time bombers dropped out of the clouds to attack the torpedo-boat escorts, one of which, the *T-13*, was damaged and brought to a halt by bomb-splinters and cannon-fire. Out of the mist and rain ahead loomed the destroyer *Friedrich Ihn* and the torpedo-boat *Jaguar*, both evidently crippled by air attack. Several further attacks developed later and, by the time darkness fell, all aboard the battleship were glad of a respite. Gun barrels were red-hot; a 20-mm gun barrel had burst; gun mountings had jammed.

By 21.15 the *Scharnhorst* was threading her way through the reputedly swept channel off Terschelling when there came once again the shock of an underwater explosion—far worse than the previous one. The ship came to a stop with her starboard main engine out of action and the other two jammed. Electrical

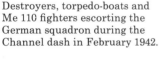
Vice-Admiral Ciliax addressing the crews of *Scharnhorst* and *Gneisenau* at Brest before their escape home up Channel with the *Prinz Eugen* in February 1942, during which the Admiral flew his flag in the *Scharnhorst*.

Destroyers, torpedo-boats and Me 110 fighters escorting the German squadron during the Channel dash in February 1942.

equipment throughout the ship, including the gyro compass and other navigational equipment, had failed. A gale had risen which was driving her towards the nearby shoals. By 22.00 the situation was becoming desperate, with the sandbanks barely two miles to leeward. The destroyer *Hermann Schoemann*, to which Admiral Ciliax had transferred when the *Z-29* had been crippled, attempted vainly to pass a tow-line. In the nick of time the *Scharnhorst*'s engineer announced that one engine had been got back into operation. With heartfelt relief Hoffman steered back into the swept channel at ten knots.

Groping through the stormy night Hoffman succeeded in reaching the River Jade at dawn. There he found the *Prinz Eugen* which had also had narrow escapes from stranding owing to a failure in her navigational equipment. As for the *Gneisenau*, she, too, had exploded a mine but, though seriously damaged, she had reached the anchorage under her own steam.

So Hitler had got his precious ships home; the propaganda value of this was great. The British navy, it seemed, had been worsted in its own waters—a view unjustly held by the British public also. But the two battleships

had, in fact, been so seriously damaged that it would require six months to repair them. In the event the *Gneisenau*, again badly damaged by an air raid while in dry-dock, was never to go to sea again. The *Scharnhorst*, where Captain Hoffman was replaced in April by Captain Friedrich Hüffmeier, did not become fully battleworthy until the end of 1942. When she sailed for Norway on 7 January 1943 accompanied by the *Prinz Eugen* she was at once discovered by British air reconnaissance. The squadron was ordered back into the Baltic where, exercising off Gdynia, the *Scharnhorst* was run aground requiring more repairs which took until 8 March.

Three days later, under cover of darkness, she slipped unobserved through the Great Belt and in wild wintry weather and snow storms arrived to join the battleship *Tirpitz*, flying the flag of Vice-Admiral Kummetz, and the *Lützow* in Altenfiord, near the North Cape, on 22 March 1943. The task of this squadron was to lie in wait for Allied convoys for Murmansk whose route passed within 200 miles of the North Cape. These convoys had, however, been suspended for the summer when the almost continuous daylight made them too vulnerable to the combined air and surface threat. For the next six months, therefore, the German ships lay idle in Altenfiord except for occasional sorties for training.

At the beginning of September the *Tirpitz* and *Scharnhorst* put to sea accompanied by ten destroyers and headed for Spitzbergen. Their purpose—a petty one indeed for so powerful a force—was to destroy the weather station maintained there for the benefit of the Allies by a small band of Norwegians. During the 8th, troops from the destroyer landed under cover of the big ships' gunfire and demolished the installations. The next day the ships were back again behind the net defences of their anchorage.

The sortie had somewhat frivolously used much of the dwindling oil fuel available to the German navy. Nevertheless Captain Hüffmeier was permitted to take his ship out for two days of gunnery practice on 21 September. Thus she was absent from her usual berth

when, on the 22nd, the *Tirpitz* was heavily damaged by the heroic exploit of British midget submarines, putting her out of action for eight months. The *Lützow* having returned to Germany for urgent refit, the *Scharnhorst* and six destroyers became the total naval force in the north.

This reduction of the surface threat and the shortening hours of daylight now led to a resumption of the Allied convoys to Murmansk. The German High Command was very doubtful of the wisdom of risking their last capital ship against them, however, particularly as any action that resulted might be in the long Arctic night when the British, whose ship-borne radar equipment had by this time become far more effective than that of the Germans, would have a great advantage. The weeks passed with the convoys steaming to and fro unmolested and the *Scharnhorst* lying idle at her moorings. In October Captain

Hüffmeier was relieved in command by Captain Fritz Hintze, recently promoted after serving for most of the war as navigating officer of the cruiser *Hipper*. When a directive from the Naval Staff dated 20 November gave the Commander-in-Chief North, Admiral Schniewind, the impression that she was unlikely to be used except under exceptionally favourable circumstances and if no British battleship covering force was in a position to intervene, Vice-Admiral Kummetz was permitted to go on an extended leave, his place being taken by Rear-Admiral Bey.

Nevertheless Grand Admiral Dönitz, who had become Commander-in-Chief of the navy in January 1943 and had seen his U-boat campaign collapse four months later, could hardly sit idle while convoys carried past his doorstep war supplies of immense importance to Russia where the military situation was becoming increasingly disastrous for Germany.

Lieutenant Commander Eugène Esmonde VC, DSO, who led the 'forlorn hope' attack by Swordfish torpedo planes against the German squadron escaping up Channel. He was shot down and killed and was posthumously awarded the Victoria Cross.

The *Scharnhorst*'s fire power. Her six forward 11-inch guns can be seen, and some of her secondary armament of twelve 5·9-inch guns. Her anti-aircraft battery was of fourteen 4·1-inch guns.

111

A torpedo-boat comes to the aid of the *Scharnhorst* after she had been crippled by two mines off the Dutch coast during the Channel dash in February 1942. Anti-aircraft gunners scan the sky anxiously for British bombers. The battleship eventually limped into Wilhelmshaven under her own steam.

opposite, top
Grand-Admiral Karl Dönitz who commanded the U-boat arm until January 1943, when he became Commander-in-Chief of the German Navy in succession to Admiral Raeder. It was at Dönitz's orders that the *Scharnhorst* made the sortie on Christmas Day 1943 which ended in her destruction.

opposite, bottom
A convoy for Russia moves through the Arctic twilight.

So when Convoy JW55B for Russia was located on 22 December, soon after sailing, the decision was taken to launch the *Scharnhorst* and the five available destroyers against it as it passed into the Barents Sea on the 26th.

On Christmas Day 1943, therefore, for the first time for three months steam was raised in the great ship, converting her from the dead hulk she had been into the living, throbbing entity that was a battle-ready capital ship of war. That evening Bey led his force out of the calm waters of the fiords into the open where heavy seas were running. He and his men were spurred on by a signal from Dönitz exhorting them to help 'our eastern army in its heroic struggle'; to 'exploit tactical situations with skill and daring and not end the battle with half a victory'. His plan of action called for the co-operation of his destroyers, firstly to aid in interception, then to shadow and finally to fight a delaying, rearguard action if the *Scharnhorst* were forced by enemy heavy ships to break off the attack. It soon became clear, however, that, in the weather conditions prevailing, the destroyers' fighting efficiency would be reduced almost to vanishing point.

Bey signalled for advice from the Commander-in-Chief North; Admiral Schniewind passed the problem on to the Chief of the Naval Staff; he referred it to Dönitz himself. The reply, transmitted after some hours' delay, left the decision to Bey. He decided to carry on and through the night the squadron steered north, rolling in the huge seas thrown up by the south-westerly gale.

Bey's radio signal had been picked up by British monitoring stations, betraying the fact that he was at sea to the Commander-in-Chief of the British Home Fleet, Admiral Sir Bruce Fraser, in the battleship *Duke of York* which, in company with the cruiser *Jamaica* and four destroyers, was hovering—all unknown to the Germans—to the westward to cover the convoy against just such an eventuality. Similarly unknown to Bey was Vice-Admiral Burnett's cruiser squadron—*Belfast*, *Norfolk* and *Sheffield*—to the eastward and steering to close the convoy. Such information as Bey did have came at 08.00 from a U-boat shadowing the convoy and it misled him into thinking he had already crossed ahead of it. He at once swung round to a south-westerly course, spreading his destroyers five miles apart across his front to search.

It was still dark at 09.30 as the *Scharnhorst* punched her way through the foam-topped rollers when the darkness was suddenly split by the bright yellow glare of a starshell bursting overhead; and then tall columns of white leapt upwards from the water as the first salvo of 8-inch shells from Burnett's cruisers fell around her. Almost at once two of these hit—one against the *Scharnhorst*'s fore-top, causing many casualties and wrecking her forward radar, another bursting on her forecastle. The surprise brought about by the superiority of British radar was complete.

Captain Hintze steered round at once at full speed on to a southerly course to bring all his guns to bear upon his assailants, distinguishable only by the intermittent flashes of their gunfire. His one ostensibly serviceable radar was giving him no information whatever.

Radio touch with the destroyers had been lost also; so that when, by means of the *Scharnhorst*'s speed, he was able to draw out of range of the British cruisers and he swung round first to south-east, then east, to circle round them to get at the convoy, he could not tell the destroyers to conform. They steamed on to the south-west, oblivious of what was going on astern of them. Not until 10.00 were communications restored and though they then turned north-east to try to rejoin, they were in fact to play no further part, being finally ordered back to base at 14.20.

Meanwhile, Bey's manœuvre had been anticipated by Burnett; unable to keep up with the speeding *Scharnhorst*, he turned back north-westerly to place himself between her and the convoy, being joined by four destroyers from the escort. It was an astute move. Night had given way to dim Arctic winter daylight, but it was again the *Belfast*'s radar which made the first contact at 12.05 and fifteen minutes later came mutual sighting. Able to see his target this time, Commander Bredenbreuker, the *Scharnhorst*'s gunnery officer, directed the fire of his 11-inch guns effectively, scoring

twice on the *Norfolk*, putting her after turret out of action, killing an officer and six men and seriously wounding five others.

However, this second confrontation with Burnett's squadron evidently took the heart out of Bey. He had as yet no knowledge of Fraser's force which, kept informed by Burnett, was hurrying eastwards to get between the *Scharnhorst* and her base. Nevertheless, he ordered a withdrawal; at 12.40 the ship swung away to a south-easterly course and increased speed to twenty-eight knots.

The range opened out and the gunfire died away. Though Bey must have known from his earlier experience of British radar capability that the enemy cruisers would not lose contact, he had no fear as yet of being brought to action again.

A much delayed report reached Bey from German air reconnaissance at 15.29 of a second enemy force far to the westward; but even now he was not unduly disturbed, for the signal failed to say that the force included a battleship. Thus it was all the more shattering when, at 16.50, the yellow flare of a starshell blossomed overhead and, almost at once, a salvo of

Rear-Admiral 'Bob' Burnett who commanded the cruiser force which intercepted the *Scharnhorst* as she steered to attack the convoy for Murmansk off the North Cape on 26 December 1943 and fought her off until the arrival on the scene of the *Duke of York*.

The swing to starboard on to a south-westerly heading, however, put the *Savage* and *Saumarez* in a good firing position. They raced in through a storm of fire which killed eleven and wounded another eleven in the *Saumarez*. When they turned to fire, the *Saumarez*, heavily damaged, got four torpedoes away, the *Savage* eight. Three times the *Scharnhorst* leaped and shuddered as explosions ripped holes in her hull. Thousands of tons of water poured in to flood compartments, including a boiler room. The great ship's speed slowed to a crawl.

And now the guns of the *Duke of York*,

shells fell close around which from the size of the splashes must be from a battleship. One of the first to arrive scored a hit abreast the foremost turret where ammunition was set ablaze. The forward magazine had to be flooded, putting the turret out of action. Desperately, Hintze turned north, only to find the British cruisers barring the way and adding the fire of their 8-inch guns to the 14-inch of the *Duke of York*. Only to the eastward was the way clear and in that direction the *Scharnhorst* sped, hitting back as best she could at her pursuer, twice sending shells through the battleship's mast though they failed to explode. That any hope of escape from the trap into which Bey had fallen was melting away is to be seen from the despairing signal–his last, made at 17.02–'We shall fight to the last shell.' Nevertheless, the *Duke of York* could not match the *Scharnhorst*'s speed and the range steadily opened. Even Fraser's four destroyers and those attached to Burnett which had been ordered forward to attack with torpedoes, were gaining only with agonizing slowness. It seemed as though the *Scharnhorst*, racing on under the glare of starshells which lit her up in all her silver-grey beauty might even now escape.

But then, with awful suddenness, the fate of the great ship was sealed as, at 18.20, a 14-inch shell plunged through her armour to explode in her No. 1 boiler room. Smothered in clouds of steam, her speed fell away; the exultant destroyer captains found they were over-hauling fast. Fraser's four had divided into pairs which steered to attack from opposite sides. *Savage* and *Saumarez* to port were the first to be seen and engaged by the battleship's 5·9-inch guns. They replied with their 4·7-inch and were soon causing confusion in the *Scharnhorst*'s gunnery control. Certainly Captain Hintze and the staff on the bridge must have been distracted; for the first they knew of the approach of the *Scorpion* and the Norwegian *Stord* was the sight of sixteen torpedo tracks on the starboard bow. Full starboard wheel and stopping the starboard engine enabled the tracks to be combed though it is possible one torpedo found its target.

Jamaica and *Belfast*, which had ceased while the destroyers were attacking, re-opened in full fury. The *Scharnhorst* was being torn to pieces, fires blazing up and ammunition round the guns exploding. Her own gunfire had become quite ineffective. To hasten the agonizing end of the dying giant, Admiral Fraser again ordered the *Duke of York* to cease fire and the *Jamaica* and *Belfast* to go in and finish her off with torpedoes. At about the same time the *Belfast*'s destroyers had also reached the scene and three of them were able to launch torpedoes.

All that could be seen of the *Scharnhorst* by this time was a huge cloud of smoke shot through with lurid flames. Just which torpedoes hit can never be certainly known; British estimates give two from the cruisers and six from the second group of destroyers to attack *Musketeer*, *Opportune* and *Virago*, making a total of eleven; German survivors were to say twelve or thirteen.

At 19.45 a heavy underwater explosion felt in the British ships marked the *Scharnhorst*'s end. They closed in to search for survivors, but out of 1,903 officers and men and 40 cadets, only 36 ratings survived to be picked up by the *Scorpion* and *Matchless*.

The 14-inch guns of the *Duke of York* during battle practice. The British battleship delivered the blow that crippled the *Scharnhorst* on the evening of Christmas Day, 1943.

HMS ARK ROYAL

It is curious that the name of Britain's most famous warship of the Second World War, *Ark Royal*, should have remained out of the list of ships of the Royal Navy for more than 300 years. Although it had been a household word in the history of the Royal Navy since the heroic episode of the defeat of the Spanish Armada in 1588, when the *Ark Royal* was the flagship of the Lord High Admiral, Howard of Effingham, it was not until 1914 that a king's ship was again given the name; and then it was to a humble ship, indeed, a tramp steamer, bought by the Admiralty while still on the stocks, for conversion to a tender for the primitive seaplanes of that era. As such and, after 1918, as much for the Royal Air Force as for the Navy, she operated until 1934 when she was renamed *Pegasus*.

The laying-down of the ship to which the name *Ark Royal* was now to be given marked the first stirrings of the Royal Navy's efforts to modernize its air arm. Operating its own RN Air Service, the Royal Navy had, by the end of the First World War, established a long lead in ship-borne air power by having one aircraft carrier, *Argus*, in service, and three more, *Hermes*, *Eagle* and *Furious*, under construction or conversion before any other navy had any.

This lead was lost, however, following the conclusion of the Washington Naval Treaty in 1922 which limited both the total tonnage and individual size of carriers the major naval powers might acquire. The United States and Japan built up a modern carrier force from scratch, while Britain contented herself with conversion of the *Furious'* sister ships *Courageous* and *Glorious*. This left her some 20,000 tons available for further construction, but it was not until 1934, with war clouds again looming on the horizon, that it was decided to design a new carrier, the *Ark Royal*. When completed in November 1938 she displaced 22,000 tons at normal load, 685 feet long at the waterline, her flight deck was 800 feet long and 98 feet broad at its widest point. Below this deck were two hangar decks capable of housing 70 of the contemporary aircraft, for which three lifts were provided to range them up or strike down. Two aircraft-launching catapults were fitted at the fore end. Steam turbines developing 100,000 shaft horse-power drove her at nearly thirty-two knots on trials. An unusual feature at that time was her all-welded construction which saved no less than 500 tons of dead weight.

While the *Ark Royal* was still under construction, the Admiralty's efforts to regain control and administration of its own air arm from the Air Ministry had, in 1937, at last borne fruit. This left little time for reorganization and modernization before the outbreak of war in September 1939. Thus of the five squadrons embarked by that time, three (Nos. 818, 810 and 821) were equipped with Swordfish biplane torpedo-bomber-reconnaissance (TBR) planes; only the two fighter Squadrons (800 and 803) flew the new, monoplane Blackburn 'Skua' which doubled in the role of dive-bomber and fighter. It is hardly surprising that as the latter they were to prove less than adequate. Apart from an inevitable lack of manœuvrability they were more than 100 mph slower than the contemporary RAF Hurricane. The Swordfish were to chalk up an impressive record of successes in spite of their stately 80 knots cruising speed (154 mph maximum); but this was to be due rather to the gallantry with which they were operated than to their effective performance.

Commanded by Captain Arthur John Power (later Admiral Sir Arthur J. Power), the *Ark Royal* was at sea with the Home Fleet, wearing the flag of the Vice-Admiral, Aircraft Carriers, Vice-Admiral L. V. Wells, when, at noon on 3 September, the signal was received that war had been declared against Germany. That same day, Kapitän-Leutnant Lemp, commanding the German submarine *U.30*, torpedoed without warning and sank the passenger liner *Athenia*. Once again, as in the First World War, the unrestricted *guerre-de-course* against Allied merchant shipping had seemingly been declared. In 1917 and 1918 it had been defeated by the re-institution of the system of convoys. They had been escorted both by surface ships and aircraft.

The age-old lesson that that was the only effective way to counter raiders, whether surface or submarine, had long since been forgotten, however. And when it now became clear that a number of U-boats were operating in the approaches to the British Isles, the mistaken notion that it was better to employ more offensive methods, led to the deployment of the carriers *Courageous* and *Hermes* in the Western Approaches and the *Ark Royal* to the north-west of Ireland.

Each carrier had her screen of destroyers but as they patrolled to and fro in a fairly limited area they were very vulnerable. And, sure enough, on the morning of 14 September, as a flight of three Skuas was being ranged up on the *Ark*'s deck to fly off to investigate a U-boat reported some 100 miles away attacking the merchant ship *Fanad Head*, Korvetten Kapitän Glattes of *U.39* held her in the cross-wires of his periscope sight as he gave the order to fire torpedoes from a perfect position off the carrier's port bow. The subsequent progress of the war at sea must have been very different but for the fact that, unknown as yet to the Germans, their torpedoes suffered from fatal defects. Not only were the magnetically-operated pistols of the warheads unreliable, often causing them to explode at a distance from their targets, but the torpedoes themselves either ran too deep or on the surface. In this case it was the latter which raised the alarm. The spray and wake of a 'porpoising' torpedo was sighted in time for the ship to be swung parallel to its track; the torpedoes passed harmlessly down the side, though two exploded in the *Ark Royal*'s wake.

The track of the faulty torpedo also betrayed the U-boat's position to the destroyers, making it easy for them to establish Asdic (sonar) contact. Depth-charges forced it to surface where the crew abandoned ship and were made prisoners when *U.39* plunged to the bottom, the first U-boat to be sunk during the Second World War.

Meanwhile, the three Skuas, led by Lieutenant-Commander D. R. F. Cambell (now Rear-Admiral, Retd), had located the *Fanad Head*, stopped and abandoned, with Lemp's *U.30* surfaced nearby. The submarine crash-dived, leaving on the surface its dinghy taking a demolition party to scuttle the merchant ship; the Skuas swooped and released their bombs, too late to score a kill, and, in two of them, so low that the explosions shattered their rear part, killing the air gunners, Petty Officers McKay and Simpson, and forcing the pilots Lieutenant Griffiths, RM and Lieutenant Thurstan, RN, to 'ditch' their aircraft and take to their rubber dinghies. As soon as the other Skua had left to return to the carrier, Lemp surfaced and picked them up as well as his demolition party, three of whom had been wounded by bomb splinters. Six Swordfish sent from the *Ark* again attacked *U.30*. An airborne depth-charge had yet to be devised and their bombs were ineffective to destroy; but enough damage had been sustained to force the U-boat to return to base.

The destruction of *U.39* and the near-success against *U.30* seemed at first encouraging. But three days later the *Courageous* was torpedoed and sunk by *U.29* in the Western Approaches.

This painful loss so soon after the *Ark Royal*'s narrow escape as well as the proven ineffectiveness of ocean sweeps for the elusive U-boats–particularly in those days before airborne radar–brought such misuse of the carriers to an end. The *Ark* returned to the Home Fleet where, on 26 September, one of her Skuas, flown by Lieutenant B. S. McEwen had the distinction of shooting down the first enemy aircraft to be brought down by any of the forces–a Dornier flying-boat which had been shadowing the fleet. On the same day the carrier was shaken by a near miss by a bomb from a Heinkel plane. The German pilot believed he had scored a hit. Nazi propaganda seized upon the story and broadcast to the world that she had been sunk, a claim that was to be repeated again and again throughout her action-filled life.

During the winter months that followed, the war at sea was largely confined to hunting down the commerce-raiding pocket battleship, *Admiral Graf Spee*, in the South Atlantic and eliminating her supply ships and a number of merchant ships trying to get back to Germany through the blockade. The *Ark Royal*, with the battle-cruiser *Renown* and four destroyers formed one of several hunting groups, known as Force K.

Luck did not permit them to be in at the death of the *Graf Spee*; but the *Ark Royal*'s Swordfish located the blockade runner *Uhenfels* which was duly taken in prize by Force K's destroyers; and in February while returning to England, her aircraft located five of the six other merchant ships attempting to get home to Germany at that time.

The royal galleon *Ark Royal*, first of her name. Flagship of Lord Howard of Effingham, Lord High Admiral of England and Commander-in-Chief in the fight against the Armada, 1588.

HMS *Ark Royal*, first British carrier since the *Hermes* (1917) to be designed as such, after being launched at Cammell Laird's yard, Birkenhead in 1937. Displacing 22,000 tons, she had a speed of nearly 30 knots and could operate some 60 contemporary aircraft.

The Phoney War or, as Churchill more felicitously called it, the Twilight War, was about to erupt into the Norwegian campaign; but so unprepared for it was the Admiralty that when first news of the German invasion of Denmark and Norway was received, the *Ark Royal* and the *Glorious* were both with the Mediterranean Fleet at Alexandria. The old *Furious* was the only large carrier with the Home Fleet; she was caught completing a refit and repairs and in the haste to get her to sea she was forced to leave her fighter squadrons on shore. The lack of fighter protection during the first sixteen days of the Norwegian operations forced the fleet to operate farther and farther out at sea—which sadly restricted its effectiveness either to intercept the German warships taking part or to give effective air support to the Allied amphibious expeditions.

What the *Ark Royal* might have achieved had she been present was demonstrated by two of her Skua squadrons, Nos. 800 and 803, left behind at Hatston in the Orkneys. Led by Captain R. T. Partridge, RM and Lieutenant W. P. Lucy, RN, with Lieutenant-Commander John Hare navigating, they flew blindly through low cloud to make a perfect landfall and swoop undetected upon the light cruiser *Königsberg* at Bergen to send her to the bottom—the first major warship ever to be sunk by air attack.

The *Ark Royal* and *Glorious*, hastily recalled from the Mediterranean, replaced the *Furious* on 24 April 1940 and on the following day twenty of their Skuas, and fourteen of the *Ark*'s Swordfish attacked the enemy-held airfield of Vaernes, near Trondheim, causing extensive damage to grounded aircraft and to installations. A second attack by the *Ark*'s planes on the 28th completed the destruction including in it more than a dozen grounded aircraft. In their role as fighters, the Skuas shot down eighteen enemy aircraft and damaged more than a score in combat in spite of their poor performance, which gave them a speed 125 mph slower than a Messerschmitt

110 and 50 mph slower even than a Heinkel 111 bomber, and their puny armament of four ·303 machine guns. They themselves suffered only three shot down in combat but ten others were lost through accidents.

All too late the essential role to be played by a ship-borne air arm was being appreciated; for the Royal Air Force was unable to take any effective part in the Norwegian campaign. Its high bombers found themselves unable to hit ships; its fighters had not the endurance to operate from Scotland nor were any local airfields available to them in central Norway. A squadron of RAF Gladiators brought over in the *Glorious* to operate from a frozen lake survived just forty-eight hours until they and their landing area were broken up by bombs.

Unfortunately the Fleet Air Arm was unable to fill the gap entirely with its inferior aircraft and too few carriers. Both *Ark Royal* and *Glorious* had had to withdraw to replenish when the land campaign in central Norway ended with the evacuation of the Allied expeditions from Namsos and Aandalsnes, harried throughout by unopposed German air attack. While at Scapa, Captain Power (soon to receive his Rear-Admiral's flag) was relieved by Captain C. S. Holland. Allied operations were thereafter confined to the far north where the Germans continued to defy all efforts to dislodge them from Narvik. While the Allied forces fought to hold off the northward advance of the German army to the relief of the beleaguered port, and preparations for its capture were being slowly progressed, until 18 May when she was relieved by the *Glorious* and *Furious*, the *Ark Royal*'s Skuas provided the only Allied fighter cover, claiming 6 kills and 9 enemy damaged for the loss of 2 Skuas in combat, one of them being that of Lucy, who, with is observer, Mike Hanson, was killed.

By this time an airfield at Bardufoss had been prepared and RAF Hurricanes and Gladiators brought across the sea in the *Glorious* and *Furious* were at last able to operate.

Narvik was finally captured on 28 May; but the German advance into France had already begun and it was clear that it would be beyond Allied resources to hold on to northern Norway. Evacuation was ordered and the *Ark Royal* returned to cover the transport convoys while the *Glorious* re-embarked the ten Gladiators and seven Hurricanes which had survived operations from the shore base. Though the aircraft were not fitted with arrester hooks and the pilots had never before landed on a carrier's deck, all got down safely. Tragically, on 8 June, the *Glorious*, steaming home accompanied only by the destroyers of her screen, *Ardent* and *Acasta*, and without an operational aircraft either in the air or ranged on deck, was surprised by the battleships *Scharnhorst* and *Gneisenau*. All three British ships were sunk with very heavy loss of life; but before she was overwhelmed, the *Acasta* succeeded in torpedoing the *Scharnhorst*, forcing the Germans to return to base and perhaps thus saving the troop convoys from disaster.

It fell to the Skuas of 800 and 803 Squadrons, commanded by Captain Partridge – newly decorated with the DSO for his part in the sinking of the *Königsberg* – and Lieutenant-Commander John Casson, the strike leader, to try to exact vengeance on the damaged *Scharnhorst* where she lay in Trondheim harbour. To give the slow Skuas a chance of survival in the face of opposition by the Me 109s and 110s and a thick concentration of flak, four RAF Beaufort bombers were to make a synchronized attack on Vaernes, where the fighters were based, and six long-range Blenheim fighters would provide escort.

When the fifteen Skuas took off in the first minutes of 13 June, no fighter escort had arrived; and as they approached Trondheim, smoke billowing up from Vaernes showed that the Beauforts had attacked prematurely: the alerted enemy had massed their fighters over the harbour. The Skuas pressed home their attacks through the storm of flak, but only one direct hit was achieved and the 500-pound bomb failed to explode. As they turned away they were set upon by the Messerschmitts. Eight were shot down including the whole of the contingent from 800 Squadron. Half their air crews survived to be made prisoner, including Partridge and Casson; but the loss of so many experienced airmen from the ranks of the rapidly expanding Fleet Air Arm was a bitter blow. This was the final episode in the disastrous Norwegian campaign. One third of the air-crew strength of the Fleet Air Arm at the beginning of the war had become casualties.

The primary need for ship-borne aviation now shifted to the Mediterranean where the collapse of France left the western half unprotected until the British Force H under Admiral Sir James Somerville was assembled at Gibraltar on 28 June, centred on the *Ark Royal*, flying the flag of Vice-Admiral L. V. Wells, and the battleships *Hood, Valiant* and *Resolution*. Tragically, its first task was that of trying to persuade the French naval squadron at Oran to neutralize their ships to ensure their not falling into enemy hands, and, when all persuasions failed, to attack and immobilize them as ordered by the British government.

In the cruelly distasteful action which followed, the *Ark Royal*'s offensive role was confined to an attempt by her torpedo planes and dive-bombers to prevent the battle-cruiser *Strasbourg* escaping, in which they were unsuccessful.

Admiral Somerville expressed the feelings of all in his squadron when he wrote to his wife the next day: 'It was an absolutely bloody business to shoot up these Frenchmen who showed the greatest gallantry . . . We all feel thoroughly dirty and ashamed that the first time we should have been in action was an affair like this.' His distress was made almost unbearable when he received orders to return to the attack three days later to complete the disablement of the *Dunkerque* which the French had wrongly reported to be only slightly damaged. To avoid further casualties – inevitable if the ship, ashore quite close to the town of St André, were again brought under gunfire, Swordfish torpedo planes of 820 and 810 Squadrons of the *Ark Royal* were sent in. At the cost of two aircraft shot down, they put the *Dunkerque* out of action for the rest of the war. Somerville was able to write: 'And so that filthy job is over at last.'

For the *Ark Royal*'s airmen there was unfortunately to be yet more fighting with recent allies in time to come. During July and August, however, the carrier operated in the western Mediterranean against the Italians whom Mussolini had brought into the war when the collapse of France seemed to offer easy glory. The Mediterranean Fleet put to sea from Alexandria on 7 July 1940 to cover convoys to Malta: and on the 9th there came the first clash with the Italian battle fleet

Three Swordfish torpedo-reconnaissance aircraft circling the *Ark Royal*. Slow, outmoded biplanes with open cockpits and a cruising speed of some 85 knots, they were the strike aircraft upon which the Royal Navy had principally to rely until 1943.

which fled when its flagship was hit by a 15-inch shell from the *Warspite*. Meanwhile Force H, sent out to create a diversion, was offering itself up to air attacks by Savoia twin-engined bombers from Sardinian bases. Although the high-level bombing favoured at that time by the Italian air force was impressively accurate and their salvoes of bombs fell close around or alongside their targets during raids on 9 July, the *Ark Royal* and others escaped with no more than a shaking–an outcome which was to be repeated on many occasions until the enemy adopted dive bombing and airborne torpedo attack. Nevertheless, the Italians followed the German example by claiming to have hit and heavily damaged both *Ark Royal* and *Hood*.

In spite of their unsuitability as fighters and the lack of air-warning radar to provide fighter direction, Skuas from the carrier scored the first successes against the new enemy by shooting down five of the bombers and damaging as many more. A pattern for future operations in the struggle for control of the Mediterranean had been established, though it was to become more fiercely contested later when the Germans came to the aid of their allies.

The key to the situation was Malta whence the Italian sea supply lines to the Axis armies in Libya could be kept under harassment by naval and air forces. Unfortunately no steps to defend the island had been taken by the British Chiefs of Staff who had been convinced by the exaggerated claims of the air-power prophets that it was indefensible in the face of attack from the nearby Sicilian airfields. Now, however, when the Italians confined their efforts to sporadic air raids, it was decided to build up the island's fighter defence, hitherto restricted to three biplane Gladiators, known as *Faith*, *Hope* and *Charity*, by ferrying Hurricanes on board carriers to within flying range. The first of a great many such trips, which were to play a decisive role in saving Malta from enemy hands, was made at the beginning of August by the old *Argus* carrying 12 Hurricanes.

Force H put to sea to cover the operation and once again to hit at the Cagliari airfield. Though the patrolling Skuas shot down three Italian shadowing planes during the following day, that evening the Italian bombers, flying very high–too high for the *Ark*'s Skuas to intercept them–arrived to repeat their spectacular but ineffective attacks. Then, in the clear, dark, early hours of 2 August nine Swordfish armed with bombs and three with mines to be laid in Cagliari harbour rumbled ponderously off the carrier's deck. Four hours later through the low clouds and poor visibility which had developed at dawn, the aircraft returned at intervals to report four Italian hangars flattened and a number of grounded planes destroyed. One Swordfish piloted by Lieutenant Humphries, had been forced to land on the airfield he had been attacking, but the remainder got back with only minor damage from the heavy but not very accurate AA fire directed at them.

It was only a minor affair when compared with the huge naval air operations mounted later in the war. But it must be remembered that the navigational aids for aircraft which were to become commonplace did not then exist. As Somerville commented: (the Swordfish) 'took off in the pitch dark to fly 140 miles to a place they had never seen and *then*, mark you, to have to fly over the sea to find that tiny floating aerodrome with the knowledge that if they don't find it, they're done'.

When Force H got back to Gibraltar a reorganization took place. The *Valiant* and *Hood* returned home, the former to be equipped with the new radar sets now being produced. Somerville went with the *Hood*, returning in the battle-cruiser *Renown*, when Vice-Admiral Wells hauled down his flag. The *Ark Royal* was thus a 'private' ship again when she sailed with Force H on 30 August to cover the passage of reinforcements for the Mediterranean Fleet in the shape of the now

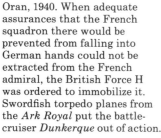

Oran, 1940. When adequate assurances that the French squadron there would be prevented from falling into German hands could not be extracted from the French admiral, the British Force H was ordered to immobilize it. Swordfish torpedo planes from the *Ark Royal* put the battle-cruiser *Dunkerque* out of action.

radar-equipped *Valiant* and the new aircraft carrier *Illustrious*. Once again the opportunity was taken to attack the Italian airfield at Elmas near Cagliari in the early hours of 1 September. The nine Swordfish of the strike, led by Lieutenant-Commander 'Johnnie' Johnstone of 810 Squadron, wreaked considerable damage and were all back safely on board by 08.00. It was no doubt a result of this raid that Force H was left unmolested by enemy bombers as it made its way back to Gibraltar having parted company with the Mediterranean Fleet units at the entrance to the Sicilian Narrows.

By this time constant high-speed running and inadequate harbour periods for self-maintenance were causing mechanical defects to develop in the *Ark Royal*. A refit was needed and expected; but it was not yet to be. The ship was to be involved again in the distasteful business of fighting our previous allies, though on this occasion it was to be in aid of Frenchmen fighting Frenchmen in the muddled and futile operation staged on behalf of General de Gaulle to win French Equatorial and Occidental Africa to the Free French cause. For this she was detached to join Force M under Vice-Admiral John Cunningham. When Operation Menace was finally launched after much delay on 23 September, the *Ark Royal* had embarked two French Luciolle light aircraft and a number of Free French officers and men whom it was intended to land at Dakar where it was wrongly believed the authorities would be amenable to persuasion.

In the event the Frenchmen in the Luciolles were arrested soon after they had landed, while the Swordfish carrying the others were fired at by the battleship *Richelieu*, the Dakar forts and then escorted firmly seaward by French Curtiss fighters. Threats on one side and defiance on the other led to hostilities during which the *Ark Royal*'s aircraft made unsuccessful attacks on the battleship *Richelieu*, when three Swordfish were shot down,

and on the cruisers *Georges Leygues* and *Montcalm*.

Exchanges of gunfire between the battleships and cruisers on either side achieved little. By the 25th it had become clear that the attitude of the French in Dakar had been badly misjudged; and when the *Resolution* was hit by a torpedo from the French submarine *Bévéziers* and seriously damaged, the decision to withdraw was taken and total failure of Operation Menace was conceded. To the heartfelt relief of all on board the *Ark Royal*, Force M retired and on the 30th the carrier shaped course for home for her overdue refit at Birkenhead.

With the *Ark Royal* and *Illustrious* still the only modern carriers in commission the refit could not be a long one; at the end of October 1941 the *Ark* was at sea again to embark her squadrons. One squadron of Skuas (803) was replaced by the latest fleet fighters of 808, the Fairey Fulmars. Though their performance was greatly superior to that of the Skuas and they mounted eight forward-firing ·303-inch machine guns compared to the Skua's four, they were still inferior to the contemporary shore-based fighters, even the obsolescent Hurricane. The Fulmar was in fact a type rejected by the Royal Air Force and, having been accepted by the Royal Navy prior to the development of any radar-directed direction system or adequate electronic navigational aids, was a two-seater. Many of the *Ark*'s experienced flyers, urgently needed to lead squadrons being raised for the new carriers under construction, had been replaced by only partly trained air crews; no ship could be spared during that critical period to act as a training carrier and some of the new pilots made their first deck-landing on embarkation. This lack of experience and training was to be painfully felt.

Nevertheless, by 6 November the *Ark Royal* had rejoined Force H at Gibraltar and, flying Sir James Somerville's flag in the temporary absence of the *Renown*, was at sea the next

The *Ark Royal* straddled by a salvo of bombs from high-level bombers. Though the Italian Air Force showed themselves very accurate in this type of bombing, experience was to show that its chances of obtaining a hit on ships free to manœuvre were much less than expected.

A Fairey Fulmar two-seater fighter, replacement for the Blackburn Skua in the fighter role, going over the side of the Ark Royal's deck after a crash landing.

day taking part in an operation of an already familiar pattern to cover the passage through the western Mediterranean of reinforcements for the Mediterranean Fleet in the shape of the battleship *Barham*, the cruisers *Berwick* and *Glasgow* and four destroyers.

As before, the *Ark Royal*'s aircraft—nine Swordfish—were sent to divert the enemy's attention by attacking Cagliari air base at dawn on the 9th which they succeeded in doing without loss. The Italians responded with a high-level raid by some twenty S.79s during the forenoon. The Fulmars had their first taste of action, breaking up some enemy formations and inflicting damage. The long 'stick' of Italian bombs laid across the British fleet achieved their usual near misses but no hits. By the next day the *Ark* was back at Gibraltar.

Just another 'Club Run' was what the men of Force H called such forays into the Mediterranean. But when Force H—*Renown* (to which Somerville had again shifted his flag on her return), *Ark Royal*, the cruiser *Sheffield* and four destroyers—put out again on 24 November, they were steering for a much more pregnant encounter with the enemy. The operation was a complex one. Its dual object was to cover the passage to Malta of a convoy consisting of the cruisers *Despatch*, *Manchester* and *Southampton*, the last two carrying 1,400 RAF personnel for Egypt, three fast merchant ships with supplies for the island and four little minesweeping corvettes and to meet and return with three ships leaving the Mediterranean Fleet, the old battleship *Ramillies* and the cruisers *Berwick* and *Newcastle*, forming Force D.

Such a movement was likely to be opposed by the Italian air force and fleet. The latter had been greatly weakened by the famous attack on Taranto by Swordfish from the *Illustrious* when three battleships had been sunk at their moorings or beached. They were still, however, able to field three battleships, including the modern 15-inch gun ship *Vittorio Veneto*, six

heavy (8-inch) cruisers and a number of 6-inch. At sunrise on the 27th, therefore, when south of Sardinia, Somerville launched Swordfish to search north and east. It was a clear, blue Mediterranean day with a light south-easterly breeze flecking the surface of the sea. Sure enough it was not long before reports from the scouting aircraft of enemy forces were on the air. Unfortunately there were communications hang-ups and it was not until 10.15 that it became clear that the Italians were out in force—a squadron centred on two battleships some seventy miles to the northward and another composed of half a dozen cruisers ten miles closer, though the various aerial reports left the situation far from clear.

Instructing the convoy, escorted by the *Despatch* and two destroyers, to steer away to the south-east, the Admiral ordered the carrier to act independently and to prepare a striking force of torpedo planes, while, in the *Renown*, he steered eastward at the battle-cruiser's best speed to meet Force D and called the remainder of his warships to concentrate with him. By noon his concentration had been effected, giving him— on paper—a formidable force comprising, besides screening destroyers, *Renown*, *Ramillies*, the 8-inch cruiser *Berwick*, four 6-inch cruisers, *Sheffield*, *Manchester*, *Southampton* and *Newcastle*, and the *Ark Royal*. All were slower than the enemy, however, the ancient unmodernized *Ramillies* being limited to twenty knots. The Italian force was actually composed of a battle squadron—*Vittorio Veneto* and the old, but modernized battleship *Giulio Cesare*—and two squadrons of three heavy cruisers, each with the usual destroyer screen.

The Italian Admiral Campioni had believed at first he had only Force H opposing him. He had pressed forward, therefore, intent on giving battle until, at 11.55, he had learned from his scouting aircraft that Somerville had been joined by Force D. It is fair to say that, but for the uncertain potentiality of the *Ark Royal*'s air striking force, the Italians were still in superior strength. Nevertheless, Campioni decided that: 'A state of affairs was thus created which . . . was unfavourable to us numerically and qualitatively . . . Under these conditions, in conformity with the spirit and letter of the orders received and with what at the moment I deemed to be my duty, I decided not to become involved in a battle.'

When the opposing cruiser forces came in sight of one another and engaged, therefore, as soon as the initially poor British shooting settled down the Italians turned away. A running fight developed during which the *Berwick* was twice hit and soon the Italians were drawing out of range. Any hopes of bringing them to effective action now depended upon the *Ark Royal*'s striking force. Eleven torpedo Swordfish of 810 Squadron led by Johnnie Johnstone had taken off at 11.30; now, flying at their best torpedo-laden speed of some eighty knots into a fresh easterly wind, they overtook with agonizing slowness the speeding Italian fleet.

Perhaps because of the dense smoke-screen under which the enemy were retiring, the aircraft were not discovered until they were already diving towards their chosen target, the two battleships; but then came a fierce barrage of fire from these and their screen of destroyers. As the Italian Admiral was to record: 'The attack was carried out with resolution and was successfully staved off by the manœuvring and gunfire of our ships and through the presence of the close escort of destroyers.'

Miraculously all the aircraft escaped to return safely to their ship; but their torpedoes were avoided. All hope of slowing up the enemy had now gone and any further chase would take the British squadron close inshore where intensive air attack and perhaps a submarine or mine trap might await them. With the safety of his convoy his primary object, Somerville regretfully turned away. Two further efforts to damage the enemy by air attack were made—by a flight of seven Skuas led by Lieutenant R. M. Smeeton (now Vice-Admiral Sir Richard Smeeton, KCB Retd) and another of nine torpedo Swordfish led by Lieutenant-Commander Stewart-Moore—but neither achieved anything. The inexperience of many of the pilots

Force H, based on Gibraltar, which operated in the Eastern Mediterranean and in the Atlantic. Admiral Sir James Somerville's flagship *Renown* with the *Ark Royal* and, in the background, the cruiser *Sheffield*. It was this force which crippled the *Bismarck* and delivered her to the Home Fleet to destroy with their guns and torpedoes.

and the 'penny numbers' in which the single carrier was forced to employ them combined to make such attacks unprofitable. The navy, indeed, was suffering for the past neglect of its air arm. Nevertheless, it had been the threat posed by the *Ark Royal* which had been mainly responsible for Campioni's refusal to accept battle against a much inferior force of British ships.

The enemy's attempt at retaliation by his shore-based bombers which followed was no more successful, though one which concentrated upon the *Ark Royal* where she was operating separated from the remainder was, in Somerville's words 'a stinker'. As he watched, the carrier was completely obscured by the tall plumes of dirty water thrown up by the bomb bursts, some of them within ten yards of the ship; but, as the spray subsided, she emerged undamaged, her guns blazing. This brought the action to an end. Having seen his convoy safely on its way to Malta, Somerville took Force H back to Gibraltar. Once again the inability of the Italians to interfere with British naval moves in the war in the Mediterranean had been demonstrated.

It was a situation that was soon to be drastically modified, however as the exasperated Germans found themselves forced to go to the aid of their ally. During December the Italian armies in Libya were resoundingly defeated by General Wavell's Army of the Nile. In the following month orders would be given for a German Afrika Korps under General Rommel to be sent across the Mediterranean; but an essential preliminary step was to wrest from the British their control of the Central Basin. Already on the move to Sicilian airfields was Fliegerkorps X of the German air force, its main element composed of dive-bombers whose pilots had received special training in attacking ships.

Meanwhile, the *Ark Royal*, after a brief period of training for her air crews, was out with Force H in the Atlantic on two occasions, firstly patrolling fruitlessly off the Azores in search of a non-existent enemy invasion force, then in connection with a convoy attack by the cruiser *Hipper*. Between 19 and 24 December 1940 there was a Club Run to meet battleship *Malaya* coming west from the Mediterranean Fleet and two empty transports from Malta. Then on 7 January 1941 an operation, more complex, but still of a familiar pattern, was set on foot when Force H left Gibraltar to cover a convoy of four fast transports with the light cruiser *Bonaventure* and five destroyers for the eastern Mediterranean, while the Mediterranean Fleet moved into the Central Basin to cover other transport movements to and from Malta.

So far as *Ark Royal* was concerned, this operation proved just another Club Run, marked chiefly by a smart piece of flying by Lieutenant-Commander R. C. Tillard, commanding 808 Fulmar Squadron who cut out and shot down two of the Italian formation of high bombers which unsuccessfully attacked the force.

Spirits were high as Force H returned to Gibraltar; for the *Ark* was now to have a much-needed rest, being relieved by the new carrier *Formidable*. But it was not to be: on the next day Fliegerkorps X swung into action with a massed dive-bombing attack on the *Illustrious*, so heavily damaging her that it was with great difficulty that she was got into Valetta harbour for temporary repairs and finally on to Alexandria to begin a passage via the Suez Canal to the United States for major restoration. So, instead of taking the *Ark Royal's* place the *Formidable* was allocated to the Mediterranean Fleet. And with the advent of German air power to the Mediterranean, control of that sea was to become the object of a fiercely contested

The German battleship *Bismarck* at Bergen, viewed from the heavy cruiser *Prinz Eugen* at the beginning of their sortie into the Atlantic which ended with the destruction of the battleship.

struggle. The naval airmen of the *Ark Royal* were to be forced to fight in aircraft more than ever inferior in performance and numbers to those of the enemy.

For the time being, and until a really serious need to send reinforcements or supplies eastward from Gibraltar arose, the central Mediterranean was closed to the British. Admiral Somerville's thoughts, therefore, returned to a project he had considered earlier–a foray with Force H to bombard the port of Genoa with the 15-inch guns of *Renown* and *Malaya* and the *Sheffield*'s 6-inch, and to bomb oil refineries at Leghorn and Spezia. Plans were made which included a preliminary attack on the previous day on the important Tirso Dam in Sardinia, using torpedo Swordfish; and on 31 January 1941 Force H put to sea to carry it out.

Ill-fortune attended it. A storm was gathering in the area: the eight torpedo-laden planes of 810 Squadron took off in pitch dark from the *Ark Royal*'s deck to wallow away under rain-clouds at 1,500 feet. Ice rapidly formed on their wings as they climbed to overfly the mountains between them and the target, itself at an altitude of 1,200 feet. On breaking out of cloud cover they were greeted by intense fire from anti-aircraft defences, unexpectedly alerted, perhaps by lack of security at Gibraltar. Only four were able to drop their torpedoes in the lake. None exploded, owing, it was thought, to soft silt protecting the dam; one Swordfish was shot down, the crew being taken prisoner. By the time the remainder returned to the ship a gale from the north-west was blowing; the operation against Genoa was abandoned.

But Somerville was determined it should be only a postponement. Training of air crews was resumed under the *Ark*'s senior observer, Vernon Graves, and, for those who would be spotting for the ships' gunfire, with the aid of a model of Genoa dock area made by Commissioned Gunner Scillitoe of the *Renown*. Strict security was enforced and, when Force H sailed again on 6 February, deceptive ploys were made to mislead enemy watchers on shore and listeners on the radio waves. For complete surprise was necessary if the Force was not to be trapped in the Gulf of Genoa by the superior Italian fleet.

In fact, the Italian Commander-in-Chief, Admiral Iachino, in harbour at Spezia, only forty miles from Genoa, with three battleships, knew at once that Force H had sailed, but could not guess its objective. To try to cover all alternatives he sailed on the evening of the 8th for a rendezvous with three of his heavy cruisers at 08.00 the next day, to the west of Bonifacio Strait between Corsica and Sardinia. Unwittingly he had opened the way to Genoa. But he would be well placed to intercept Force H on its retirement should it go there. Meanwhile, Somerville had passed between Ibiza and Majorca and, with fighters from the *Ark Royal* patrolling overhead during the 8th, checking on any aircraft reported in the vicinity (they all proved to be French), skirted the French coast. Each ignorant of the other's presence, the two fleets passed during the night on opposite courses some fifty miles apart.

Dawn on the 9th found Force H in its planned positions–*Ark Royal* off Spezia, the remainder off Genoa–in an otherwise empty sea. As Somerville was to describe it: 'We steamed up to the beginning of the run–about ten miles off Genoa–and then crash went the broadsides . . . The first salvoes fell exactly where we wanted them and then I felt content. The curtain was up and the tragedy was on. For half an hour we blazed away, and I had to think of Valetta, London, Bristol, etc., to harden my heart.'

Three hours earlier, *Ark Royal*'s aircraft–twelve Swordfish loaded with bombs, four with mines for Spezia harbour, had taken off

May 1941. Fulmars taking off from the *Ark Royal*. The battle-cruiser *Renown* can be seen on the right.

The *Bismarck* travelling at high speed in the Atlantic.

in the dark. By 07.00 all but one were safely back on board, their mission completed. The missing aircraft, manned by Midshipmen Attenborough and Foote RNVR and Leading Airman Halifax, had crashed after striking the balloon barrage, killing the crew.

For Somerville's Force the most dangerous phase of the operation still lay ahead. Though the expected shore-based retaliatory air attacks were confined to a half-hearted effort during the forenoon and shadowing planes were shot down, it seemed hardly possible to avoid an encounter on the homeward passage. But in fact the Italian Admiral was badly served both by his shoreward organization, which failed until 09.50 to get a report of the bombardment through to him, and by his own aerial reconnaissance which failed to locate Force H and misdirected him towards a group of ships which turned out to be a French merchant convoy. In misty weather the two fleets again passed on opposite courses during the afternoon a bare thirty miles apart; on the 11th Force H entered Gibraltar harbour in triumph.

But there was to be no rest for the hard-worked *Ark* and Force H. Indeed, for the next eight months—all that remained of her life—the carrier was to establish what must surely constitute a record for constant, high-speed, wartime operation. The composition of Force H would change as ships came and went but there was none to take the place of the *Ark Royal*. 'Without her,' James Somerville said, 'I am like a blind beggar without his dog.' The very next day she exchanged the comparatively calm blue seas of the Mediterranean for the grey-green turmoil of 'Winter North Atlantic'. The Germans had launched a campaign of convoy-raiding with their major naval units; the fast battleships *Scharnhorst* and *Gneisenau*, the heavy cruiser *Hipper* and the pocket battleship *Admiral Scheer* were all loose in the Atlantic. For the next twelve days Force H formed part of the widespread searches mounted for them, the *Ark Royal*'s Swordfish and Fulmars operating whenever the weather permitted. A break of ten days at

Gibraltar gave opportunity for flying exercises when the indefatigable Commander (Flying) H. A. ('Jane') Traill laboured to achieve slick perfection in the flight-deck operations and Admiral Somerville ('Uncle James' to all) never missed a chance of going up with his flyers to gain experience of their problems.

Then the elusive *Scharnhorst* and *Gneisenau* were located on 8 March and Force H was out on convoy duty. The *Ark*'s planes searched far and wide and, on the 20th, Tillard and his observer, the Admiral's nephew Mark Somerville, located them; but it was too late in the day for an attack to be mounted and the battleships escaped into Brest. On 1 April Force H was back at Gibraltar to sail eastward and the next day to fly off twelve Hurricane reinforcements for hard-pressed Malta, which had been brought out from England in the old *Argus*.

A new squadron (807) of Fulmars had also been brought out in the *Furious* to relieve the Skuas of 800 Squadron. Hardly had they been embarked than rumours of *Scharnhorst* and *Gneisenau* being about to sail called for a blockade of Brest to be established. Who else but Force H to implement it? Until 16 April it was the Atlantic again, therefore. Strains and stresses were mounting in personnel as well as material. One who had reached his 'prudent limit of endurance' was Captain 'Hookie' Holland who was relieved by Captain L. E. H. Maund on the 20th. Another Club Run to cover the passage of reinforcements for the Mediterranean Fleet and fly off more Hurricanes for Malta was successfully accomplished between 24 and 28 April.

Already a larger operation was under way with five transports on their way from the United Kingdom, carrying desperately needed tanks for the Army of the Nile, to be given cover by Force H, the battleship *Queen Elizabeth*, and three cruisers which would go through to join the Mediterranean Fleet. It was the first attempt to mount such a large-scale operation since the arrival of the German air force. The Chiefs of Staff had only reluctantly acceded to Churchill's insistence that the risk be taken; but on 6 May the convoy and fleet were inside the Straits and heading eastwards. Operation Tiger was, indeed, to be a first test of how effective a defence the few fighters operated by a single carrier could put up against the greatly increased striking power of the Italian air force with its newly adopted torpedo planes in conjunction with the German use of massed dive-bombers.

Not until the morning of the 8th was the British force located to the south-west of Sardinia; but from 13.45 attacks followed each other at short intervals for the rest of the day. The Fulmars had a poor record of serviceability and, with only twelve fit to fly, four was the most that could be kept on patrol with a second section ready on deck. When eight torpedo planes came skimming in low over the water, the Fulmars, led by Tillard, had to engage the escorting Italian C42 fighters; but, met by the fleet's intensive gun barrage, three of the torpedo planes were shot down and all launched their 'fish' at long range. The torpedoes were well aimed at the *Ark Royal* and *Renown* but smart manœuvring avoided them all. In the dog-fight Tillard and Mark Somerville were shot down and killed–a particularly poignant loss for the Admiral. The crew of another lost Fulmar were rescued.

This attack was followed by a succession of high-level bombing raids by S.79s which, intercepted by Fulmars or engaged by gunfire, achieved nothing. But late in the afternoon there came the real test as from the direction of Sicily came the Stuka JU 87 dive-bombers in two groups–sixteen and twelve–and half a dozen Me 110 twin-engine fighters. By this time only seven serviceable Fulmars remained. Flown off in three sections they tore into the enemy formations with such skill and fury that they broke them up; many of the bombers jettisoned their loads and fled, not one got through to the fleet or convoy. It was a resounding triumph for 807 and 808 Squadrons and to the organization perfected by Traill, remembering the debacle with the *Illustrious* four months earlier.

One last effort by the enemy before night fell came nearer to success as three torpedo planes approaching at wave-top height achieved a surprise attack on the *Ark Royal* and *Renown*. Once again the two big ships were smartly manœuvred to comb the tracks but two torpedoes passed within fifty yards of the carrier.

The convoys and the Mediterranean reinforcements had now reached the narrows of the Skerki Channel between Sicily and Cape Bon and Force H turned back for Gibraltar, yet another delivery made without loss, though one transport was to be sunk by mine

before the rendezvous with the Mediterranean Fleet south of Malta was made the next day. When the remainder reached Alexandria, their Lordships of the Admiralty signalled their 'deep satisfaction' and congratulations.

More flying exercises, especially for the recently acquired radar-fitted Swordfish, and another run to fly off 48 Hurricanes for Malta occupied the next ten days. Then, shortly before midnight on 13 May 1941 came orders from the Admiralty to Force H at Gibraltar to 'Raise Steam with All Despatch'. The great battleship *Bismarck* and the cruiser *Prinz Eugen* had been located by our cruisers

Survivors from the sunken *Bismarck* are picked up by the cruiser HMS *Dorsetshire*.

breaking out into the Atlantic through the Denmark Strait, west of Iceland. By 02.00 *Renown*, *Ark Royal* and *Sheffield* were racing westwards to play their part in a complex deployment of forces ordered by the Admiralty. The events which followed, the interception of the German ships by the *Hood* and *Prince of Wales* in which the former was sunk, the subsequent loss of contact with the *Bismarck*, the frantic hunt to re-locate her and her eventual destruction, have been the subject of more than one book. Here there is space only for a brief account of the *Ark Royal*'s decisive part in them.

Throughout the 25th and the night that followed, during which the *Bismarck* was lost to view, Force H pounded north-westerly into a rising gale to intercept her should she be steering for Brest—as, indeed, she was. All other forces had been casting in the wrong direction and everything now depended upon the torpedo Swordfish of the *Ark Royal* to slow the *Bismarck* down and allow the battleships of the Home Fleet to bring her to action. By daylight on the 26th the north-westerly gale had reduced Force H to seventeen knots, at which speed even the carrier's flight deck, 62 feet above the waterline, was swept by green seas. To range up aircraft in such conditions, speed had to be brought down to dead slow and the ship turned into wind. Even so, with the ends of the flight deck rising and falling as much as 56 feet and a gale of wind screaming along it, the flight-deck party under Lieutenant-Commander Stringer were hard put to it to keep control. The ten Swordfish taking off on a search were climbing steeply uphill at one moment, plunging towards the huge seas at the next. All got away safely though some actually touched the wave tops before clambering away.

The search plan was well conceived to cover the *Bismarck*'s route. But the honour of first locating her was snatched from the Swordfish crews. At 10.30 a Royal Air Force Catalina flying-boat sighted her and got a report away—the first news of the quarry for thirty-one hours. The Catalina was driven off by gunfire and did not regain touch; but fortunately, three quarters of an hour later, first one and then a second Swordfish located the battleship and from that time contact was never lost.

On board the carrier a striking force of fifteen torpedo Swordfish was prepared and at 14.50 took off. The hopes of the whole fleet were in their hands; but mishap and near disaster befell. Unknown to them, the *Sheffield* had been sent ahead to keep radar touch with the *Bismarck*—and when the cruiser became a contact on their own radar they dived through the low clouds to the attack. Eleven of them had launched their torpedoes before realizing their mistake. Captain Larcom of the *Sheffield* called for full speed and avoided those that ran true. The crestfallen airmen returned to make hazardous landings on the carrier. Yet the episode had not been without its compensating feature. Five of the torpedoes had exploded either on striking the water or in the *Sheffield*'s wake. A defect in the Duplex, magnetically fired pistol of the warheads had been exposed. In future contact-operated pistols would be used.

No doubt in Force H there was a feeling that their luck had deserted them. Little did they know that in a short while Lieutenant-Commander Wolfarth of *U.566* would be gazing through his periscope at *Renown* and *Ark Royal*, passing on a steady course, targets he could not fail to hit—if only he had any torpedoes left. He had expended his last against a convoy and was on his way back to base.

A fresh strike was prepared but it was not until 19.15 that fifteen Swordfish, mostly the same aircraft as before, and led by Lieutenant-Commander T. P. Coode, took off for the last possible chance of crippling the *Bismarck* before she could get under cover of the German air force. This time they made contact first with the *Sheffield* whence they were given the range and bearing of the enemy, before climbing away into cover of the clouds. Coode's intention was to approach

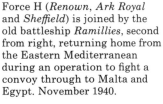

Force H (*Renown*, *Ark Royal* and *Sheffield*) is joined by the old battleship *Ramillies*, second from right, returning home from the Eastern Mediterranean during an operation to fight a convoy through to Malta and Egypt. November 1940.

the target above the clouds which, over the *Sheffield*, rose only to 5,000 feet, and for the five sub-flights into which his force was divided to make a co-ordinated attack from different angles. But over the *Bismarck*, the thick cloud layer of a 'front' towered up from about 700 feet to 10,000 feet and into it the Swordfish plunged. The sub-flights lost touch with each other and had to act independently.

Coode's sub-flight was the first to attack at 20.53; they were met by a storm of fire but escaped with minor damage. They saw no evidence of having scored a hit and seeing no other aircraft attacking and assuming they had failed to find the target, Coode signalled, 'Estimate no hits.' But for the next half an hour the remainder were in fact pressing heroically in to launch their torpedoes. Two of them had achieved hits—one on the armoured side of the battleship which did no fatal damage; but the other hit the *Bismarck*'s Achilles-heel, the starboard quarter abreast the steering-gear compartments, flooding them and jamming the rudder angled 15 degrees to port. The great ship swung round helplessly to a northerly course. All efforts during the night to bring her under control failed: at daybreak the battleships and cruisers of the Home Fleet arrived to batter her to destruction with guns and torpedoes.

When the returning aircraft had landed on (three of them crashing on) the wildly pitching deck, the crews' accounts were heard and pieced together and it became almost certain that two or perhaps even three torpedoes had hit. Later analysis with the aid of information gained from the survivors made it clear that the hit on the port side had been made by the plane flown by Sub-Lieutenant Tony Beale, the other, fatal one by either Lieutenant 'Feather' Godfrey-Faussett or Sub-Lieutenant Kenneth Pattisson who had attacked together. But all shared in the triumph, if for no other reason than that they drew some of the hurricane of gunfire upon themselves. It was to a tumultuous welcome that the *Ark Royal* entered Gibraltar harbour three days later.

While Force H had been (as they considered) teaching the Home Fleet its business, the situation inside the Mediterranean had greatly deteriorated for the British. Back in April, General Wavell had been forced to deplete the strength of his army to send help to Greece which was about to be invaded by the Germans. As a result the Army of the Nile had been driven back to the frontiers of Egypt. Nor had the British reinforcements to Greece been able to prevent the Germans from rapidly overrunning that country. The British troops had had to be evacuated with painful losses to the fleet as well as themselves. In May had come the German assault on Crete, in the vain defence of which the Mediterranean Fleet had lost three cruisers and six destroyers, while two battleships, the only aircraft carrier, two cruisers and two destroyers had been damaged beyond local repair.

On the other hand the Germans had had to withdraw eastwards much of their air strength from Sicily, and Malta had recovered from the first of the air 'blitzes'. Aircraft submarines and destroyers based on the island were wreaking havoc amongst the Axis convoys to and from Libya. But the need to replenish Malta was becoming desperate; so, in July a relief convoy was to be run through under the cover of Force H. Meanwhile, her need was for replacements and reinforcements for her force of Hurricane fighters and during June the *Ark Royal* made three sorties with Force H to fly them off. Two new Swordfish squadrons (820 and 816) joined her also to relieve 825 and 818; between operations these green squadrons had to be trained and exercised. Her arrival back in Gibraltar from the last of the Hurricane operations was on 28 June 1941, the first anniversary of the formation of Force H. Her ceaseless activity during the last twelve months with only the four weeks minor refit in October 1940 was a truly remarkable achievement of her engineers and a tribute to her builders.

While Operation Substance—the convoy to

HMS *Nelson* fires her main armament of 16-inch guns. The battleship was for a time flagship in Force H, to which the *Ark Royal* belonged.

Left: Captain L. E. H. Maund.
Right: Vice-Admiral Sir James
Somerville, on board the *Ark
Royal*.

organized the remainder that their bombs fell
wide. Co-ordinated with this attack, however,
was another by seven torpedo planes, skimming in low. Met by a daunting barrage which
shot three of them down, the remainder,
nevertheless, pressed bravely on to put a
torpedo into the destroyer *Fearless* which had
to be scuttled and the *Manchester* which was
forced to turn back for Gibraltar. Later
attacks were not pressed home with the
same courage; the sight of a Fulmar climbing
up to the attack was enough to cause bombs
or torpedoes to be jettisoned. One Italian
airman taken prisoner thought he had been
shot down by a Hurricane–an unwitting
tribute to the naval pilots rather than the
aircraft.

At dusk that day Force H turned back to
hover south-west of Sardinia to await the
return of Force X and *Hermione* which remained with the still undamaged convoy as it
began the night passage of the Narrows to
Malta. A succession of air raids before dark
were largely neutralized by the escorts' gunfire though one destroyer, the *Firedrake*, was
bomb-damaged and had to be towed back to

Malta–was being mounted, the *Ark Royal*
enjoyed a rare period of rest and recuperation
at Gibraltar. By 20 July all was in train. From
the large troopship *Pasteur*, in the harbour,
troops had been surreptitiously transferred
to the cruisers *Manchester* and *Arethusa*. A
troop transport, *Leinster*, had also arrived,
carrying 1,000 troops. Approaching from
the Atlantic and timed to pass through the
Straits after dark to avoid detection by the
enemy agents on the watch on the Spanish
shore, was the convoy of six storeships
escorted by the battleship *Nelson* (coming to
join Force H), and Force X–the cruiser
Edinburgh, flagship of Rear-Admiral Syfret,
the fast minelayer *Manxman* and five
destroyers. During that night Force H (in
which the cruiser *Hermione* had taken the
place of the *Sheffield*) and the remainder
sailed to join them: caught in a blinding
Levanter followed by a fog, the *Leinster* ran
aground and had to be left behind; but by
daylight the junction had been made inside
the Mediterranean.

Somerville's efforts at deception evidently
succeeded; for it was not until 23 July that
the presence of the convoy off Cape Bon became known to the Italian High Command
and the usual series of air raids mounted.
The first high-level Savoia bombers were
intercepted by sections of Fulmars, led by
Lieutenant-Commander Douglas (later Commander J. S. Douglas, DSO), Lieutenant
Hallett (later Captain N. G. Hallett, DSC)
and Lieutenant Lewin (later Captain R. D. G.
Lewin, CB, CBE, DSO, DSC and bar), who
shot down two and damaged and so dis-

Gibraltar. Italian MTB's then took up the attack and succeeded in torpedoeing the *Sydney Star*, one of the transports but she, too, was able to limp on and reach Malta, protected by the *Hermione*'s guns from attacks by Stuka dive-bombers and Italian Savoias, during 25 July. Their task completed, Force X rejoined Somerville. One last effort by the high bombers of the Italian air force was broken up by the *Ark Royal*'s Fulmars, which tore into them with great *élan*, shooting down four and forcing the remainder to jettison their bombs.

In the course of Operation Substance half of the *Ark Royal*'s Fulmars were lost, though fortunately only two of the air crews. The achievement of these underpowered, out-moded fighters in defence of ships passing through waters which, on paper, were dominated by vastly superior shore-based air power had been magnificent. And when Force H set out again to cover the passage to Malta of the troops from the *Leinster* and *Manchester* in the *Hermione*, *Arethusa* and *Manxman*, by launching the *Ark Royal*'s Swordfish to attack the Sardinian air base at Alghero, the enemy were unable or unwilling to retaliate, being, as Somerville signalled 'completely Botched, Beggared and Bewildered'. Alas, tragedy sullied an otherwise impeccable operation; a bomb which had remained 'hung-up' in the rack of one of the Swordfish exploded when the aircraft landed on the *Ark Royal*'s deck, killing the crew and several of the flight-deck party.

There now came one of the infrequent breaks in operations enjoyed by the carrier during her life, as she waited at Gibraltar for the next relief convoy for Malta–Operation Halberd–to be got together. During that time the flagship *Renown* was replaced in Force H by the battleship *Nelson*. Not that the *Ark Royal* was idle: gunnery, torpedo and flying exercises occupied her; and on the night of 23 August her Swordfish were launched on a raid to set cork woods in Sardinia ablaze as a diversion to distract Italian attention from a minelaying expedition in the Gulf of Genoa by the *Manxman*. But it was another month before Halberd could be mounted. It was correctly calculated that the enemy would make special efforts, even to the extent of

The *Ark Royal* listing, before going down.

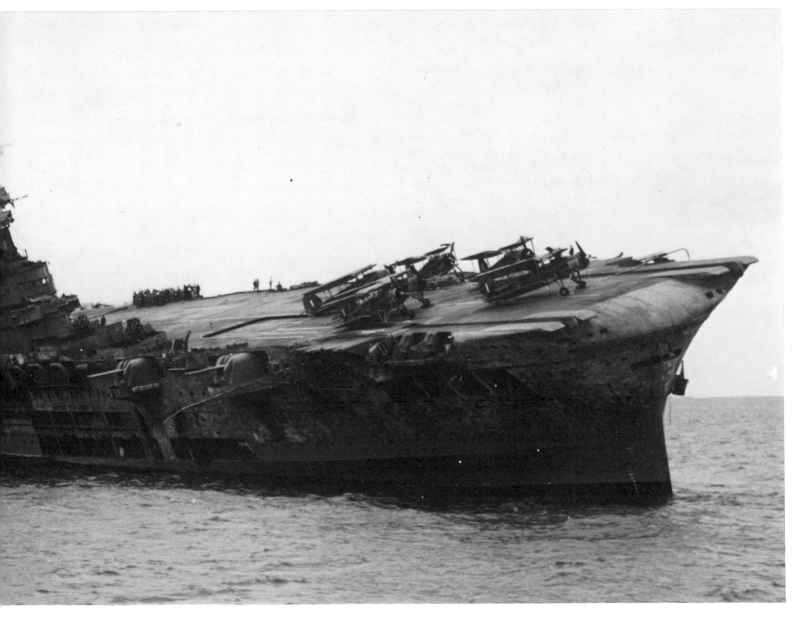

risking the Italian battle fleet, to stop any relief convoy getting through; strong reinforcements for Force H were therefore allocated–the modern battleship *Prince of Wales*, flying the flag of Vice-Admiral A. T. B. Curteiss, the *Nelson*'s sister ship *Rodney* and the cruisers *Sheffield*, *Edinburgh* and *Euryalus*. The convoy was to comprise nine fast transports.

After various deceptive ruses which succeeded in hiding from the Italians his true strength but not the fact of his sortie, Somerville concentrated his force inside the Mediterranean on 25 September. The following evening, therefore, Admiral Iachino led his fleet to sea to confront what he believed to be an inferior force; he had permission from his High Command to engage only so long as he was under cover of Italian shore-based fighters. (A tribute, indeed, to the capabilities of the *Ark Royal*'s stately Swordfish planes.) By midday on the 27th, unknown to Somerville, he was some seventy miles east of Cagliari with his two modern battleships, five cruisers and fourteen destroyers. At the same time Force H, 100 miles south of Cagliari and having been located by Italian air reconnaissance, was preparing to meet the expected air attacks with sixteen Fulmars circling on patrol.

The first raid comprised a dozen torpedo planes coming in low under top cover of six fighters. Half the Fulmars engaged the latter, losing one of their number in the dog-fights that ensued; the other half swooped on the torpedo planes, shooting down one and, in combination with the destroyer barrage, preventing all but six from pressing home their attack; all their torpedoes were avoided. More torpedo planes followed to get the same welcome and only three, coming in from up sun, got through to launch their 'fish' at the flagship before being shot down. The *Nelson* was manœuvred to comb the tracks; but one torpedo, by almost incredible chance, met the battleship head on and exploded under her stem, causing damage that was to force a progressive reduction of speed.

This was the only success achieved, one further attack by twelve torpedo planes being broken up by the gun barrage and all torpedoes avoided. In all, six enemy aircraft had been shot down by gunfire, four more by the Fulmars. But now, at 14.04, came information from an RAF reconnaissance aircraft from Malta of the Italian fleet, seventy-four miles to the north-eastward and steering to intercept the British force, which they would do in less than two hours. Leaving three cruisers and ten destroyers to escort the convoy, near which the *Ark Royal* would operate, Somerville led his battleships and the cruisers *Sheffield* and *Edinburgh* with their destroyer screen to meet the enemy. When it was

reported that Iachino, who had not been given the promised fighter cover, had turned away, it became a chase from which the *Nelson*, her speed reduced to fourteen knots, had to drop out.

The only hope of bringing the Italians to action seemed now to lie with the *Ark Royal*'s torpedo planes, a force of which was being got ready. It was unfortunately delayed by the need to refuel the Swordfish, whose tanks had been drained in expectation of bombing raids, and it did not get off until 15.40. And by that time things had gone awry. After wrongly giving Iachino's course as north-east at 15.03, the RAF reconnaissance reports had abruptly ceased. The torpedo strike was thus misled and finally returned at the end of their endurance without sighting the enemy. At 17.00, convinced that his battle squadron could not come up with Iachino, Somerville recalled it–just when, unknown to him the Italian Admiral, having at last received fighter cover and encouraged by exaggerated claims of the Italian air force, turned once again southwards.

At sunset, however, Iachino was ordered to retire to the eastward of Sardinia for the night; in the meantime the convoy had reached the Narrows. Force H turned westwards to await the return of the escort from Malta. Enemy torpedo planes took advantage of the bright moonlight to make four attacks on the transports and at last managed to hit one of them which had eventually to be scuttled. The remainder arrived unscathed.

Force H was attacked several times by Italian submarines, the only concrete result of which was the destruction of the submarine *Adua* by the destroyers *Gurkha* and *Legion*. Rendezvous with the returning escorts was safely made and Gibraltar was reached on 1 October.

Once again the Italian navy had shown itself incapable of seriously obstructing Force H's use of the western Mediterranean or its ability to keep Malta reinforced and supplied. The German High Command, concerned for Rommel's supply line to Africa, had already in September, ordered Admiral Dönitz, to his disgust, to send six of his U-boats through the Straits of Gibraltar; they now increased this number to ten. So, for the *Ark Royal*'s officers and crew, by this time looking forward to an early return for a refit after having covered more than 200,000 miles since her last trip, a sinister peril was, all unknown to them, building up in the sea area they had always considered their own.

Nevertheless, in mid-October, another Club Run to fly off a squadron of Fleet Air Arm torpedo Albacores and Swordfish to Malta and to cover the passage there of two cruisers and two destroyers, passed off without incident. On 10 November the *Ark Royal* set out with

pages 134–5
The gallant 'forlorn hope' attack by six Swordfish torpedo planes led by Lieutenant Commander Eugène Esmonde against the *Scharnhorst*, *Gneisenau* and *Prinz Eugen* as they broke through the Channel to Germany from Brest in February 1942. The attack was in vain; all the Swordfish were shot down.

left
Defence against aircraft in modern sea warfare. In the foreground a multi-barrelled 2-pounder Pom-Pom, a type of close-range AA gun with which larger British warships were armed at the outbreak of the Second World War. On the left, Oerlikon automatic guns which, together with the larger Bofors automatics, came to replace the Pom-Poms.

below
British submarines played an important part in the Norwegian campaign of 1940, when they sank the *Karlsruhe* and a number of transports and put the pocket battleship *Lützow* out of action for a year. In the Mediterranean they joined naval aircraft in harrying Axis supply convoys to such an extent that Rommel was nearly out of petrol when the Battle of El Alamein began.

left
Admiral of the Fleet Sir James Somerville, commander of the famous Force H which, based on Gibraltar, dominated the western Mediterranean, but operated also in the Atlantic where aircraft from the *Ark Royal* brought about the destruction of the German battleship *Bismarck*. Royal Naval College, Greenwich.

above
A Grumman Wildcat fighter on the deck of HMS *Formidable* during the Allied landings in North Africa in November 1942. The Royal Navy had to re-equip its Air Arm with American aircraft such as this, the Hellcat, Corsair and Avenger in the absence of British types suitable for carrier operation.

Force H for what was expected to be her last before going home. Hurricanes for Malta were flown off from her decks and from the old *Argus* on the 12th and by the next afternoon the Force was within a few hours' steaming of Gibraltar. The presence of submarines in the area had been reported and Somerville had enjoined the greatest vigilance. There had been a number of alarms from the destroyer screen during the day; but poor sonar conditions and the sight of whales disporting themselves had made contacts doubtful.

Since dawn, air operations had been carried on from the *Ark Royal* with Swordfish maintaining an AS patrol while others made training flights. With a fresh breeze from the west, the carrier was able to fly the aircraft on and off with only minor alterations from the course of the fleet; and though this enabled her to remain inside the destroyer screen, it also made her an unusually easy target for Lieutenant-Commander Guggenberger of *U.81* who, at 15.41, undetected by the screening destroyers, hit her with one of a salvo of three torpedoes.

After more than two years of almost uninterrupted active service, during which innumerable bombs and torpedoes had been aimed at her, many only narrowly missing, and repeated claims of her destruction broadcast to the world, the splendid ship had been grievously wounded. The torpedo had exploded alongside her starboard boiler room, flooding that large compartment and causing her to list steeply to that side.

Yet such a wound should not be mortal to so well-designed and modern a ship. And, indeed, after a period when all power was lost leaving her without lighting or capacity to pump, a considerable recovery was made with the aid of destroyers brought alongside and by 17.06 counter-flooding had steadied the list at seventeen degrees. By 20.00 tugs from Gibraltar had taken her in tow, steam had been raised in her port boiler room and it was hoped she might be able to use her main engines soon.

But, alas, the influx of water had not been stemmed. A Board of Enquiry was subsequently to find that the damage-control organization was less efficient than it might have been. Flood water in the starboard and centre boiler rooms rose until it filled the uptakes to the funnel which were common to all three boiler rooms. Fires broke out in the surviving port boiler room and once again steam was lost. Though electrical power was again supplied by a destroyer and the pumps re-started, from this time the ship was doomed. By 04.00 the list was increasing rapidly until it was thirty-five degrees. Captain Maund ordered everyone up from below. All surplus personnel had been taken off in the destroyer *Legion* some hours earlier. Now the last 250

were evacuated. At 06.13 the *Ark Royal* rolled slowly over, lay for a while bottom up and then sank.

It was the end of a ship's life-story which can seldom, if ever, have been equalled for continuity of confrontation with the enemy in time of war. In the years to follow, all who had served in her were proud to call themselves old Ark-Royals.

Today another *Ark Royal* is the last of the Royal Navy's aircraft carriers, soon to be de-commissioned and sent to the breaker's yard. Britain grown soft under socialism and the provisions of the Welfare State is no longer prepared to pay the price of self-defence. The dire consequences have not yet been fully exposed: but they are only too painfully predictable.

USS ENTERPRISE

The United States Navy was some years behind the British in deciding to acquire aircraft carriers; chiefly, no doubt, because they did not have the same stimulus of war between 1914 and 1917 during which the Royal Navy developed this class of ship to provide a shipborne air element for the fleet. Thus it was not until 1922 that the first American experimental carrier, the *Langley*, converted from a collier, was commissioned, at a time when the Royal Navy had been operating the *Argus* for four years and was about to bring into service the *Eagle* and *Hermes* and was completing the *Furious'* third and what was to be her final conversion.

Once started, however, and aided by the restrictions on naval construction agreed in the Washington Treaty, the Americans quickly overtook the British. The latter used up all but about 20,000 tons of the carrier tonnage permitted them under the Treaty when the converted cruisers *Courageous* and *Glorious* joined the fleet in 1928 and 1930, respectively. The Americans, in comparison, had all of the 135,000 tons, less the 11,000 tons of the *Langley* available with which to build an up-to-date carrier force. They converted the partly built battle-cruisers *Saratoga* and *Lexington*, each 36,000 tons, in 1927, followed by the 14,500-ton *Ranger*. Before the latter was commissioned on 4 June 1934, however, it had been decided that 20,000 tons was the ideal size for future ships; and it was for approximately this displacement (19,700 tons) that the *Yorktown* and *Enterprise* (the subject of our story) were designed and laid down in 1934.

The *Enterprise* was built at Newport News, Virginia and was first commissioned under Captain N. H. White on 12 May 1938. She was thus a contemporary of the British *Ark Royal* (whose story is told elsewhere in this book) and, though some 2,000 tons lighter, was of similar dimensions otherwise–length 809½ feet. But she was two knots faster (nearly thirty-four) and could operate 80 aircraft as compared to some 60 in the British ship. For the first year of her life the *Enterprise*, known familiarly as the 'Big E', operated in the Atlantic. She was then transferred to the Pacific; and it was with the surprise Japanese attack on her base, Pearl Harbor, in the Hawaiian island of Oahu that the Second World War began for the United States. The *Enterprise*, however, now commanded by Captain G. D. Murray and flying the flag of Vice-Admiral William F. Halsey, Jr (Commander, Task Force 8) was fortunately absent on that fateful 7 December 1941, having delivered a Marine Corps Fighter Squadron to Wake Island. Nevertheless some of her aircraft became involved.

Eighteen of her 'Dauntless' Scout Dive Bombers (SBD) had been flown off to proceed some 200 miles to the naval airfield on Ford Island in Pearl Harbor and when they saw smoke-puffs blossoming in the air over Oahu they presumed that target practice must be taking place. They were thus 'jumped' by Japanese Zero fighters and though those that survived the first onset fought back, shooting one of their attackers down, only eleven finally got down on the airfield.

The Japanese attack had, for the time being at least, wiped out the battleship force of the US Pacific Fleet. Catastrophic as this seemed at the time and horrifying as was the American list of 2,335 officers and men killed, it had the effect of forcing the United States Navy out of any lingering battleship-governed strategy and to rely upon the types of ship which had become the most effective units–the aircraft carrier and the submarine.

On receiving news of the attack, the *Enterprise* was at once deployed to search for the Japanese carriers; but, perhaps fortunately in view of the much greater strength of the enemy force, she was sent searching in the wrong direction. After a brief visit to Pearl Harbor the *Enterprise* was at sea again on 10 December hunting Japanese submarines–an employment which the British had learned to be unsuitable for such ships two years earlier when they lost the *Courageous* to a U-boat's torpedoes. The 'Big E' came near to suffering the same fate when attacked on the 10th and again on the 11th; and, though her SBD's succeeded in destroying the Japanese submarine *I-170*, the Americans now reached the same conclusion and withdrew her. Together with the carriers *Lexington* and *Saratoga* she was next employed as part of an expedition sent to relieve Wake Island, under attack by the Japanese. The operation was not well handled; Wake fell on 24 December and was to remain in Japanese hands almost until the end of the war.

Shaken by these catastrophes, it was not until 1 February 1942 that Americans could set about hitting back, the *Enterprise* squadron–Task Force 8–being the first to be so employed against Japanese forward bases in the Marshall Islands–Wotje, Maloelap and Kwajalein.

It could not be expected that this first offensive operation of the war should be an unqualified success. Results were considered disappointing although, for the loss of five SBD's, twenty-five enemy planes had been destroyed, two ships had been sunk and a number damaged. A raid on Wake on 24 February, followed by another on Marcus Island on 4 March achieved similar results and like the earlier operation, these were looked upon as primarily of training value. When the *Enterprise* next put to sea from Pearl Harbor on 8 April 1942 with an escort of two

The United States carriers *Enterprise* and *Yorktown* during manœuvres in the Caribbean, 1938.

The USS *Lexington* on fire after being bombed and torpedoed during the Battle of the Coral Sea, 4–8 May 1942. She sank after a violent internal explosion of leaking petrol vapour. Steps to avoid similar catastrophes were taken in later battles by filling the petrol system with inert gas.

Japanese carrier *Shokaku*. She and her sister *Zuikaku* were the first to be designed free of treaty restrictions and were the most successful units of the Japanese Fast Carrier Striking Force which delivered the attacks on Pearl Harbor, Darwin, Colombo and Trincomalee. The *Shokaku* was sunk during the Battle of the Philippine Sea by the US Submarine *Cavalla*; the *Zuikaku* by carrier aircraft of the US 3rd Fleet during the Battle for Leyte Gulf.

cruisers and two destroyers and accompanied by two tankers, she was setting out to take part in an exploit which, materially ineffective, was to have a profound effect on events in the Pacific.

On 13 April rendezvous was made with her new near-sister ship, *Hornet*, on whose decks were ranged sixteen twin-engined B25 bombers. Five days later these Army Air Force planes staggered off with their heavy load of bombs and fuel and set course for Tokyo, more than 700 miles away. Although the American Task Force had been reported that morning by enemy picket vessels, the idea that such long-range planes might be flown off from carriers did not occur to the Japanese. Surprise was thus complete when they arrived over the capital; and, though the damage caused by the bombs of the B25s which flew on to crash-land in China was not serious, the moral effect was tremendous and was to play

a part in leading the Japanese to attempt to widen the ocean area they controlled by capturing Midway Island–a decision which was to prove fatal to them.

Meanwhile, events were moving towards the carrier Battle of the Coral Sea (5–7 May) which, at the cost of the *Lexington* sunk and *Yorktown* damaged, halted similar Japanese expansionist plans in the south-west Pacific and put the two newest Japanese carriers *Shokaku* and *Zuikaku* out of action for the operation against Midway. The *Enterprise* and *Hornet* had been despatched on 30 April to join the other two carriers, but could not arrive in time for the battle.

By the last week in May the American ability to decode Japanese radio messages had supplied the Commander-in-Chief, Pacific, Admiral Nimitz, with the news of the date and many of the details of the planned assault on Midway–an operation in which

virtually the whole Japanese fleet except *Shokaku* and *Zuikaku* was to take part. The *Enterprise* and *Hornet*, Task Force 16, which got back to Pearl Harbor on 26 May with an escort of eight cruisers and fifteen destroyers, were the only ships immediately available to Nimitz to confront the Japanese fleet making for Midway, which comprised a Carrier Striking Force of four large carriers backed by other forces including seven fast battleships and another small carrier, while yet another force centred on two more aircraft carriers were to be deployed against the Aleutian Islands in the north Pacific. The *Yorktown*, however, got back to Pearl Harbor on the 27th. Her damage was estimated to require ninety days' repair; by an amazing display of energy, enterprise and ingenuity, she was patched up and got to sea again on the 30th, joining the others on 2 June 325 miles northeast of Midway.

Rear-Admiral Frank Fletcher in the *Yorktown* (Task Force 17) was overall tactical commander, while *Enterprise* and *Hornet* comprised a separate but subordinate Task Force 16 under Rear-Admiral Raymond A. Spruance, who had hoisted his flag only a few days earlier in place of Vice-Admiral Halsey who had gone sick.

The attack on Midway, as the Americans knew from the deciphered Japanese signals, was scheduled to open with an air strike from the four carriers of Vice-Admiral Chuichi Nagumo's Fast Carrier Force at dawn on the 4th. This force would approach its flying-off position from the north while from the west

would be coming the Occupation Force consisting of a Transport Force of troopships supported by a squadron of two battleships, four cruisers and a flotilla of destroyers, and a bombardment unit of four heavy cruisers to cover the landings. Hovering in the background was the Japanese Main Body centred upon the huge *Yamato*, flagship of the Commander-in-Chief, Admiral Yamamoto, and six other fast battleships.

Much of this plan was known to the Americans through the deciphered Japanese signals. It was no great surprise, therefore, when a scouting Catalina flying-boat from Midway discovered the Transport Force early on 3 June some 650 miles west of the island. Nagumo's Carrier Force, however, remained under a blanket of low cloud and poor visibility all that day and it was not until after their strike of 36 high bombers (known as 'Kates' to the Americans), 36 dive-bombers

A Japanese carrier crew cheer as aircraft take off from the deck for the attack on Pearl Harbor, 7 December 1941.

Vice-Admiral Frank J. Fletcher, Commander of the US Carrier Force in the Battles of the Coral Sea, Midway and Eastern Solomons. Not himself an aviator, he was criticized by the air specialists for his handling of the carriers. Wounded when his flagship *Saratoga* was torpedoed by a submarine, he was superseded by another non-aviator, Thomas Kinkaid.

('Vals') and 36 Zero fighters had set out for Midway that a Catalina reported locating them at 05.52 on the 4th, 200 miles to the westward of Task Forces 16 and 17.

Between 06.30 and 07.00 the Japanese carrier planes, little inconvenienced by the outclassed fighters from the island which were mostly shot down or badly damaged, pounded Midway. In return Army and Navy torpedo planes and Army Flying Fortresses and Marine dive-bombers attacked the carriers without success, while themselves suffering heavy losses at the hands of defending Zeros and ship gunfire. Nevertheless, they made an important contribution in keeping Nagumo pre-occupied, fatally delaying his preparations to launch his second strike force until too late.

On receipt of the Catalina's report, Admiral Fletcher had immediately ordered Spruance's Task Force 16 to 'proceed south-westerly and attack enemy carriers when definitely located'. He himself would follow in the *Yorktown* as soon as he had gathered in his dawn scouting patrol of SBD's. Spruance realized that an opportunity was being presented to catch the enemy carriers off-balance: he decided to throw in his entire striking force at once. They could not all be ranged up and flown off in one body. The first range consisted of 33 dive-bombers from the *Enterprise*, led by Lieutenant-Commander Clarence W. Mc-Clusky, and 35 from the *Hornet*. While waiting overhead for the next launch of torpedo planes (Douglas Devastators) and their fighter-escort of Grumman Wildcats, a Japanese scouting seaplane which had been catapulted from one of Nagumo's cruisers was seen. Nagumo would now know that an enemy carrier strike impended. Not a moment must

Douglas Devastator torpedo-bombers ranged on the flight deck of the *Enterprise* during the Battle of Midway. Of fourteen which set out to attack the Japanese carriers, only four survived.

be lost if he was to be caught unprepared. The SBD force was ordered to set off at once.

Both squadrons steered to intercept Nagumo, assuming he would continue to steer south-easterly towards Midway as he had been first reported. But, in fact, he had turned north-east so that at the expected point of interception the SBD's found an empty ocean. The *Hornet*'s squadron commander decided to turn southwards to look for his target: they, of course, found nothing: running short of fuel, some were able to land on Midway, others seeking their carrier were forced to 'ditch': fourteen were lost and the squadron played no further part in this phase of the battle.

McClusky, instead, made the crucial decision to search northerly, a decision which was to bring about an almost incredible American victory. But that came later, first

disaster befell when the *Enterprise*'s and *Hornet*'s torpedo squadrons, correctly anticipating Nagumo's movements, located the Japanese carriers and, flying under attack from their defensive swarm of Zeros and into an impenetrable wall of gunfire from their two screening battleships and numerous destroyers, skimmed low over the wave tops to launch their torpedoes. Not one of the *Hornet*'s fifteen Devastators and only four of the *Enterprise*'s survived. All their torpedoes were avoided. And when, thirty minutes later, the *Yorktown*'s squadron of twelve Devastators arrived, the same tragedy was played out as every one was shot down.

Those gallant young flyers did not die in vain, nevertheless. The exultant Zero pilots had come down low to deal with them and were now orbiting their carriers waiting to land-on to refuel as soon as a fresh striking force intended for the American carriers had completed arming with torpedoes, bombs and fuel. Thus it was that, high up above in the blue sky, sparsely flecked with clouds, McClusky's squadron and another of seventeen SBD's from the *Yorktown*, led by Lieutenant-Commander Maxwell F. Leslie, arrived unseen. The first that the Japanese knew was the chilling scream of planes diving vertically on to them and the whistle of their bombs.

Making unopposed practice, McClusky's dive-bombers—first to attack—scored four direct hits on the carrier *Kaga*, others on Nagumo's flagship *Akagi*, leaving both flaming, doomed wrecks and forcing Nagumo to transfer his flag to a cruiser. Almost simultaneously Leslie's SBD's swooped on the *Soryu*. There, too, direct hits caused such devastating fires and explosions that within twenty minutes the order to abandon ship was given.

The fourth carrier, *Hiryu*, which became detached from the remainder, escaped detection

The Japanese carrier *Hiryu* blazing after receiving four bomb hits from Dauntless dive-bombers from the *Enterprise* and *Hornet* during the Battle of Midway.

Admiral Raymond A. Spruance, Commander of Task Force 16 (*Enterprise* and *Hornet*), in the Battle of Midway, 4 June 1942. Commander-in-Chief US 5th Fleet in the Battle of the Philippine Sea 19–20 June 1944, and subsequently during the battle for Okinawa in the spring of 1945.

and was left untouched; her strike was at once launched–eighteen Vals and six Zeros–in time to follow the last *Yorktown* planes back to her. Detected by radar at nearly fifty miles, they were intercepted by Wildcats who shot down ten; the remainder pressed on, losing three more to the ships' gunfire; but the survivors scored three direct hits on the *Yorktown*. As in the Japanese carriers, fires blazed up; but lessons learned from the loss of the *Lexington* had been applied to control and extinguish them. Although damage was widespread and the ship brought to a halt, forcing Admiral Fletcher to shift his flag to a cruiser and turn over tactical command of the fleet to Spruance, by the early afternoon the *Yorktown* was again under way and able to fly off fighters. Unfortunately for her, however, she became the target for a second strike from the *Hiryu* of ten Kate torpedo planes with six fighter-escorts. Her Wildcats shot down half the Kates, but the remainder got through to score two torpedo hits, sealing the fate of the *Enterprise*'s sister, though in fact, it was to take more yet to sink her.

But at last the elusive *Hiryu* had been located and from the *Enterprise* fourteen of her own SBD's and ten which had landed on her from the stricken *Yorktown* took off under Lieutenant William E. Gallaher to exact vengeance. And, indeed, they did so as four hits destroyed the *Hiryu*'s flight deck and set off the same fatal train of fire and explosions that had eliminated her squadron mates earlier. Thus, in the space of a few hours were destroyed four of the six ships of Japan's Fast Carrier Force which, by its attacks on Pearl Harbor, followed by a destructive sweep through the East Indies, devastating attacks on Port Darwin, on Colombo and Trincomalee and the sinking of the British cruisers *Cornwall* and *Dorsetshire* and the American *Lexington*, had gained for themselves an awe-inspiring reputation. Japanese naval superiority in the Pacific had been wiped out at a stroke and soon, with new carriers nearing completion in American yards, would be converted into marked inferiority.

Although on the following day the *Enterprise*'s planes were to join with others from the *Hornet* and from Midway in sinking the cruiser *Mikuma* and crippling the *Mogami*, the decisive Battle of Midway–a clear-cut turning point in the history of the war in the Pacific–was over when Admiral Yamamoto learned of the destruction of Nagumo's carriers. He accepted defeat, recalled his scattered units and shaped course for Japan. Only the loss of the *Yorktown* and an attendant destroyer, the *Hamman*, intercepted and sunk by the Japanese submarine *I-168* as the carrier was limping painfully from the battlefield

added to that of so many gallant young airmen, dimmed the triumph of the American fleet when it entered Pearl Harbor.

With Japanese ambitions in the north thus defeated, the centre of activity shifted to the south and south-west Pacific. While Australian troops of General Douglas MacArthur's South-West Pacific Command fought across the towering Owen Stanley Mountains for the possession of Papua, New Guinea, the South Pacific Command under Admiral Ghormley set about the recapture of the Solomon Islands chain; their first objectives were the little island of Tulagi off the south side of Florida Island, where the Japanese had established a seaplane base, and the island of Guadalcanal where they had been discovered to be constructing an airfield.

Continued knowledge of Japanese plans enabled Admiral Nimitz to send three of his carriers, *Enterprise*, *Saratoga*, recently repaired after a torpedoing by submarine, and *Wasp*, newly arrived from the Atlantic theatre, to the south Pacific. Under Vice-Admiral Frank Fletcher in the *Saratoga*, they formed Task Force 61, with each carrier and its escort forming a Task Group. Thus the *Enterprise* where Rear-Admiral T. Kinkaid now flew his flag, with an escort of the new fast battleship *North Carolina*, two cruisers and five destroyers, formed Task Group 61.1.2. When the amphibious assault forces arrived at dawn on 7 August 1942 in the waters between Tulagi to the north and Guadalcanal to the south, it was Task Force 61, operating to the south of Guadalcanal that provided the air cover–the *Wasp* over Tulagi, the other two over Guadalcanal.

At the former there was stiff resistance and it was not until midnight that the US Marines were in full possession, after the *Wasp*'s aircraft had destroyed the base and a number of seaplanes and flying-boats. On Guadalcanal the Marines poured ashore opposed only briefly by the labour battalion constructing the airfield and it was not until the afternoon that the Wildcats of the *Enterprise* and *Saratoga* got into action as a raid by 27 Japanese twin-engined 'Betty' bombers and 18 Zeros developed. This raid and another two hours later, at 15.00, were smashed by the swarm of Wildcats. None of the US transports was hit; the Japanese lost 14 of their bombers and 2 fighters at the cost to the carriers of 11 Wildcats and 1 Dauntless SBD. Nevertheless, the attack was renewed the next day by 26 torpedo-armed Betty planes. All but nine of them were shot down, but a destroyer and a transport were torpedoed and sunk.

That night–8 August–a Japanese cruiser force, arriving undetected, surprised the Allied cruisers defending the anchorage and sank the Australian cruiser *Canberra*, the American cruisers *Vincennes*, *Quincy* and *Astoria* without loss to themselves. And when Admiral Fletcher, taking a decision that was to be much criticized, withdrew Task Force 61 on the 9th on account of the threat from shore-based bombers to his ships, the transports had also to retire without completing unloading. The Marines on Guadalcanal were thus left exposed to Japanese air attack until at last, on the 20th, the runway on Henderson Field was sufficiently completed for Marine Corps Wildcats and SBD's to be based there.

Meanwhile, Admiral Yamamoto had brought the Japanese fleet south to the island base of Truk in the Carolines and planned to use it to cover a Transport Force bringing reinforcements to the Japanese troops on Guadalcanal and to bring on a naval engagement. As before, his intentions were betrayed by the American cryptographers; so that when he sortied from Truk on 21 August, Task Force 61, waiting in the eastern approaches to the Coral Sea, advanced to oppose him in what was to develop into the carrier Battle of the Eastern Solomons.

The Japanese fleet, as at Midway, was organized in several separate groups. Advancing behind a broad scouting line of submarines was an Advance Force of six cruisers and the seaplane carrier *Chitose*. Behind this again came a squadron of two fast battleships and three cruisers. Operating separately within the cover of this wide deployment were Nagumo's two surviving fleet carriers, the *Shokaku* and *Zuikaku*. It had not yet been appreciated by the Japanese that, in an ocean

above
Douglas Dauntless scout dive-bombers over burning ships of the Japanese Carrier Strike Force hit by their bombs during the Battle of Midway, 4 June 1942.

The *Yorktown* sustains a direct hit at the Battle of Midway. She survived three hits by bombs and two by torpedoes, only to be torpedoed again and sunk by Japanese submarine *I-168* as she was limping back to base.

confrontation between major fleets including carrier forces, there was no place for battleships and cruisers on their own. Their function had become one of providing anti-aircraft gunfire support to the carriers which were the main striking force.

Another regular feature of Japanese planning was the decoy force offered up as a sacrifice to draw the sting of the enemy's air striking force. In this case it was the little carrier *Ryujo* which, detached from the remainder, was to mount an air strike against Guadalcanal in support of the transports coming from Rabaul. The Americans, in contrast, were concentrated in the single Task Force 61, with the only fast battleship as yet available to them, the *North Carolina*, on the screen.

By the evening of the 23rd, when Task Force 61 had advanced to the northward of the Solomons, the only Japanese unit located was the Transport Force. Admiral Fletcher, therefore, decided to detach the *Wasp* and her group to refuel at a rendezvous some 240 miles to the south. So it was that when, at last, at about 10.00 on the 24th, news came in from a reconnoitring shore-based seaplane of a carrier group 300 miles north of him, he found himself committed to battle with a third of his strength absent. Nevertheless, he steered to close the enemy and, around noon, launched an armed reconnaissance of twenty-three SBD's from the *Enterprise* to gain further information.

The force which had been located was, in fact, as the Japanese intended, only the *Ryujo* and her escort; but when her air strike heading for Guadalcanal appeared on the *Enterprise*'s radar screen 100 miles to the westward, Fletcher waited no longer. From the *Saratoga*, operating with her own circular screen some dozen miles from the *Enterprise*, a force of thirty SBD's and eight of the new Grumman Avenger torpedo planes (TBF's) which had replaced the outdated Devastators in all the carriers, was flown off. Unfortunately, when some of the *Enterprise*'s scouting planes, searching in pairs, located and reported the main Japanese carrier squadron, a radio failure prevented the information reaching the *Saratoga*'s strike; it flew on to expend its full force upon the *Ryujo* which fulfilled its sacrificial role, going down under a smother of 1,000 lb bombs and torn open by a torpedo. The *Enterprise*'s SBD's attacked through defensive patrols of Zeros and a heavy barrage of gunfire. They survived but their bombs were avoided by the skilfully manœuvred *Shokaku* and *Zuikaku*.

And the big Japanese carriers, where news of Fletcher's position had been belatedly received from a reconnaissance plane which managed to get its message through before being shot down, were now free to launch their own striking force in two waves–the first of which, 12 Zeros, 27 Vals and 9 Kate torpedo planes–set off at about 15.40. The *Enterprise*'s radar detected the swarm 88 miles away at 16.08 and from the two carriers every available Wildcat, to a total of 53, was sent up.

The air battle which followed–ostensibly in charge of the fighter direction officer of the *Enterprise*–was a wildly confused affair. Not yet was the need for strict voice-radio discipline appreciated by the tensed-up fighter pilots; few directions could be got through

The Japanese cruiser *Mikuma* after being crippled by Captain Richard E. Fleming, US Marines, who crashed his damaged Vindicator dive-bomber on to her deck (seen amidships). The cruiser was later sunk by aircraft from the *Enterprise* and *Hornet*.

the babble of their excited voices. Though, the Kates, flying low, were well intercepted and not one got through to their target, many Wildcats got involved in dog-fights with the escorting Zeros while, up at 18,000 feet the main body of Vals were not sighted until their leaders were already plummeting vertically down at the *Enterprise*.

Wildcats, nevertheless, caught some of them – Donald Runyan, an *Enterprise* fighter pilot, accounted for three as well as two Zeros. A storm of AA gunfire, including the twenty 5-inch guns of the *North Carolina*, sent many crashing into the sea. But the 'Big E' – for all her wildly weaving thirty-knot manœuvres could not avoid all the bombs: three hit her in quick succession. The first and most serious, at the corner of her No. 3 elevator, plunged through the flight deck and hangar to burst below, killing 35 men and starting fires. Then one burst in a gun casement, killing 39. The last, though its explosion was less violent, holed the flight deck behind the island superstructure and damaged No. 2 elevator.

The *Saratoga* had been left alone and she was able to accept *Enterprise* planes during the next hour during which damage-control parties strove successfully to make temporary repairs. Yet it might have still gone fatally for the 'Big E'; just as she again began to land aircraft on her patched-up deck, and with the second Japanese strike showing at some fifty miles on the radar screens, her helm jammed. For the next thirty-eight minutes she was forced to circle slowly or lie motionless and would have been an easy target. But the second strike failed to find their objective, and soon afterwards faded from the radar.

Both sides now withdrew their carrier forces; and though the Japanese sent forward their heavy cruisers during the night in the belief that at least one crippled American carrier awaited the *coup-de-grâce* from their guns, the Battle of the Eastern Solomons was over. Though the *Shokaku* and *Zuikaku* had escaped all efforts to destroy them, they had lost 38 of their hard-to-replace carrier-trained air crews. Another 18 had been lost from the sunken *Ryujo*. Only 17 American planes had been lost in the day. Though a short-term view might be that the Japanese had had the best of the encounter, in the long run these figures, added to more in other phases of the Guadalcanal campaign were to prove crucial to the progress of the war.

The *Enterprise* set off on the long haul across the wide Pacific to Pearl Harbor for repairs. These took until 16 October. Then she returned to the vital south Pacific theatre where she was desperately needed to replace the *Saratoga* and *Wasp*, both of which had fallen victims to the torpedoes of Japanese submarines, the latter being sunk, while the *Saratoga* was to be out of action for three months. The 'Big E', indeed, arrived on 24 October just in time to play a vital part in the next big carrier engagement – the Battle of the Santa Cruz Islands. With a screen composed of the fast battleship *South Dakota* (the *North Carolina* had also been damaged by submarine attack), two cruisers and eight destroyers, and again flying the flag of Rear-Admiral Kinkaid, she formed Task Force 16 alongside a similar Task Force 17 centred on the *Hornet*.

The battle on shore for Guadalcanal was

Admiral Thomas C. Kinkaid who commanded Task Force 16, with his flag in the *Enterprise* in the Battle of Santa Cruz Islands, 26 October 1942, and in subsequent operations during the battles for Guadalcanal. Later he commanded the US 7th Fleet, the naval element of General Douglas MacArthur's command in the re-occupation of the Philippines and the Battle for Leyte Gulf.

The US cruiser *Vincennes*, one of three American and one Australian cruisers sunk by Admiral Mikawa's cruiser squadron without loss during the night Battle of Savo Island, 9 August 1942.

The US cruiser *Quincy*, destroyed in the Battle of Savo Island, 9 August 1942.

at its climax. Admiral Yamamoto had sent a powerful carrier fleet, including the *Shokaku* and *Zuikaku*, the new large carrier *Junyo* and the little auxiliary *Zuiho*, operating between them 87 Zero fighters, 68 Val dive-bombers and 57 Kate torpedo planes, to the area north of the Solomons to await the expected capture of Henderson Field. Admiral Halsey, who had taken over the South Pacific Command from Admiral Ghormley, ordered forward the two Task Forces (the whole forming Task Force 61) under the command of Kinkaid. The *Hornet*'s complement of aircraft was 36 Wildcats, 36 Dauntless SBD's and 16 Avenger TBF's. *Enterprise*'s hangars held 34, 36 and 13 respectively of the same types. Halsey's shore-based reconnaissance Catalinas located two of the enemy carriers at about noon on the 25th more than 360 miles to the north-west of Task Force 61. This was beyond the prudent range of Kinkaid's SBD's. Furthermore the Japanese carrier force under Admiral Nagumo, who was as yet unaware of the advance of his American opponent, turned north shortly afterwards. So when Kinkaid launched an armed reconnaissance of twenty-four SBD's and six torpedo-armed Avengers from the *Enterprise*, they found nothing; and, persisting too long with their search, they were benighted before getting back with fuel almost exhausted. Three SBD's and three Avengers came down in the sea or crashed on deck.

The Japanese fleet again turned south during the night; two torpedo-armed Catalinas reported and unsuccessfully attacked the carriers at about 03.00 on the 26th some 200 miles to the north-west. Kinkaid, deciding on this occasion to wait for confirmation from his own aircraft, limited his dawn fly-off at 05.00 to an armed reconnaissance by

eight pairs of Dauntless scout and dive-bombers. Nor did he change his mind when a signal came in from his thrusting Commander-in-Chief Halsey – 'Attack – Repeat – Attack'. Thus it was not until his SBD's, having first located the usual Japanese advanced force of battleships and cruisers at 06.50, reported Nagumo's carriers again 200 miles to the north-west that he gave orders to launch his strike force of aircraft. They left in three waves between 07.30 and 08.15 – a total of 27 SBD's and 23 TBF's with escorts of 23 Wildcats.

Nagumo had at last received a report of Task Force 61 and at about 07.00 a force of 21 Vals, 20 Kates with torpedoes and an escort of 21 Zeros from *Shokaku*, *Zuikaku* and *Zuiho* set out to the attack. Preparations for a second strike were at once begun. It was still in progress when, without any warning, two SBD's, flown by Lieutenant-Commander S. B. Strong and Ensign C. B. Irvine of the *Enterprise*, swooped out of the sky to score two hits on the *Zuiho*'s deck which put her out of action for further flying operations.

First blood to the 'Big E'. But revenge was taken when the two opposing air strikes passed on opposite courses in mid-air. Zeros from the more compact Japanese force 'jumped' the strung-out *Enterprise* group, shooting down three Wildcats and three Avengers and forcing one more of each type to turn back, damaged, at the cost of four of their own number.

Now the opposing carrier squadrons were each awaiting the onslaught from the air which would decide the outcome of the Battle of the Santa Cruz Islands. Task Force 61 was the first to go into action. The approaching swarm of aircraft appeared on the radar screens at 08.40 and the Wildcat defence overhead was increased to a total of 38. Soon

afterwards the *Enterprise*–the luck of the 'Big E' still holding up–steamed into cover of a rain squall, leaving the *Hornet*, some thirteen miles away, in the clear. Thus it was upon the latter that the enemy's fury was concentrated. Interception by the defending Wildcats was belated and, though some Vals and Kates were caught and destroyed, 15 dive-bombers and some 20 torpedo planes were left to make a skilfully co-ordinated attack. The gun barrage shot down 20 or more but the remainder pressed bravely on. In the space of a few minutes the *Hornet* shuddered under the explosion of seven bombs–three of them delivered by suicide planes–and two torpedoes. The bombs set her ablaze: the torpedoes deprived her of all power and communications. As the handful of surviving Japanese aircraft flew away, low over the water, the carrier, a flaming wreck, lay motionless with a heavy list.

At about the same time, 200 miles to the north-west, the first of the American air strike to arrive–15 SBD's and four escorting Wildcats from the *Hornet*–had located their target and attacked Nagumo's flagship *Shokaku*. Six direct hits mangled her flight deck putting her out of action for flying operations. But the remainder of the scattered air strike failed to co-ordinate their attack, or, indeed, to find the Japanese carriers. So, unlike the doomed *Hornet*, the *Shokaku* was able to limp away for repairs which would take nine months to complete.

Some measure of revenge for the *Hornet* had been taken: but the Japanese had by no means expended their strike effort yet. The second wave from *Shokaku* and *Zuikaku*–19 Vals, 16 Kates and nine Zeros–arrived over Task Force 61 just when attention was being concentrated upon avoiding the attack of a

Japanese submarine which had torpedoed a destroyer of the screen. The Vals were undetected, therefore, until they plummeted down. Few survived the hurricane of gunfire that met them, but two bombs tore through the *Enterprise*'s flight deck. Forty men of a repair party on a lower deck were killed. Yet the 'Big E' was, in fact, still enjoying her fabled luck and displaying her fighting skill. For not only was the damage to her deck repairable and her speed and manœuvrability unaffected; but her gunners made the enemy pay a painful price for their success as plane after plane was shot down–26 was the official total for the day, a record. Many others were destroyed by her Wildcats. The Kates had not co-ordinated their attack and when they did arrive the carrier was able to avoid the nine torpedoes aimed at her. Furthermore, when yet another air strike of 29 planes from the *Junyo* (operating separately from the others) suddenly dropped out of cloud to attack her, not one of the 17 dive-bombers succeeded in hitting her.

The 'Big E', her deck patched up, was now able to gather in most of her own and the *Hornet*'s waiting aircraft, in spite of a jammed elevator which could not be repaired by ship's resources. Having finally been forced to give up attempts to salvage the *Hornet*, Task Force 61 withdrew, leaving her a blazing wreck for Japanese torpedoes to sink that night. Superficially the Americans had suffered a tactical and material defeat, being left without a battle-worthy carrier in the South Pacific whereas the Japanese had the *Zuikaku* and *Junyo* undamaged as well as the smaller *Hiyo*. But the true measure of the outcome of the battle was the slaughter inflicted on the Japanese carrier-trained air crews who could not be quickly or easily replaced and, indeed,

USS *Wasp*. She was sunk, and the battleship *North Carolina* damaged, by the Japanese submarine *I-19* on 15 September 1942 in the area between the Solomons and Espiritu Santo, known as Torpedo Junction, in which the *Saratoga* had been torpedoed on 31 August and the *Hornet* and *North Carolina* narrowly missed six days later.

Admiral William F. Halsey Jnr, who, as Vice-Admiral, was flying his flag in the *Enterprise* at the time of the attack on Pearl Harbor. His Task Force 8 was the first to hit back at Japanese-held islands. On 13 April 1942, with the *Enterprise* and *Hornet*, he launched from the latter the Doolittle raid on Tokyo by B25 bombers. Missing the Battle of Midway through ill-health, he later held the South Pacific Command and subsequently the US 3rd Fleet during the Battle for Leyte Gulf and the air assault on Japan in the final months of the war.

right
The Japanese carrier *Hiyo*, launched in June 1941, could operate fifty-three aircraft. She was sunk during the Battle of the Philippine Sea, 20 June 1944, by planes of the US 5th Fleet.

below
The US carrier *Hornet*'s wrecked superstructure after a Japanese dive-bomber had been crashed into it suicidally. Its bombs, with three torpedoes, sealed the fate of the ship during the Battle of the Santa Cruz Islands, 26 October 1942.

opposite, top
The crew of the Japanese carrier *Zuikaku*, torpedoed during the Battle for Leyte Gulf by aircraft from the US 3rd Fleet, salute their Emperor with a last *Banzai!* before abandoning ship.

opposite, bottom
Devastation caused by fire amongst aircraft ranged on the deck of the *Enterprise*, started by a shell accidentally fired from another ship.

whose quality was never again to be matched.

Nevertheless, in the battle still raging for Guadalcanal, the Americans were in desperate need of carrier-borne air power. At their Noumea base, feverish efforts to repair the *Enterprise*'s flight deck and lift were made. But when the crisis in the campaign came in mid-November with a series of surface-ship battles by night and air battles by day, repair parties were still trying to get the damaged lift working when the *Enterprise* was sent racing north to play her part.

She arrived in time to join in the aftermath of the night battle 12/13 November in which American cruisers and destroyers suffered heavily, but left the Japanese battleship *Hiei* crippled. *Enterprise* Avenger torpedo planes played the major part in finally reducing her to a helpless wreck to be scuttled by her own crew. That night, Japanese cruisers took up the night assault on the American position ashore by bombarding Henderson Field. They were made to pay heavily by the subsequent air attack at daylight in which, once again the carrier's SBD's and Avengers helped to sink the heavy cruiser *Kinugasa* and damage three others. Meanwhile, scouting SBD's from the *Enterprise* had located and attacked a convoy of eleven transports bringing Japanese reinforcements to Guadalcanal, an attack which, joined by shore-based aircraft, was to go on intermittently until dark, by which time only four of the troopships were left.

The last of the decisive sea battles which decided the fate of Guadalcanal took place that night when the Japanese battleship *Kirishima* was battered to destruction by the 16-inch guns of the USS *Washington*. Thereafter, Henderson Field, where the *Enterprise*'s strike planes were now based, could assume the task of air defence and the carrier was able to return once again to Noumea to complete repairs. Not until 28 January 1943 did she return to take part in the continuing Solomon Islands campaign until at last in May she was recalled to Pearl Harbor. There, on the 27th at the hands of Admiral Nimitz she was presented with the first Presidential Unit Citation to be won by an aircraft carrier. Then on to the Bremerton Navy Yard in Puget Sound for overhaul and a rest, surely never better earned.

Up to this time the burden of supplying the vital ship-borne air element of Allied sea-power in the Pacific had been more continuously on the shoulders of the *Enterprise* than any other carrier. By the time she sailed again to join the Pacific Fleet in November 1943, there had been a huge access of fresh carrier strength to it with the arrival of the new carrier *Essex* and three others of her class as well as five light carriers of the

A Japanese suicide dive on the USS *Essex*, November 1944.

Independence class converted from light cruisers. So from then on our heroine operated as one of a Task Group of carriers sharing between them the circular screen of battleship, cruisers and destroyers. Those Groups would more and more often be associated with one or more others to form Task Forces until by the end of the war the final operations were carried out by an Allied fleet incorporating no less than ten American and four British fleet carriers with another six US light carriers.

It was as part of Task Group 50.2—with the light carriers *Belleau Wood* and *Monterey*—that the 'Big E' struck her next blow at the enemy when aircraft from the three ships pounded the Japanese-held Makin Island on 19 and 20 November 1943, as part of the operation to recapture the Gilbert Islands. Five days later, during the same operations, it was planes from the *Enterprise* that made the first carrier-based night-fighter interceptions, when her new Hellcat fighters, which had replaced the outmoded Wildcats, co-operated with a radar-equipped Avenger to shoot down several enemy bombers.

It was Task Force 50 again which hammered the Japanese defences in the Marshalls to soften them up for re-capture, the *Enterprise* with the (new) *Yorktown* striking at Kwajalein. How the war had swung in the Allies' favour can be judged by comparing with the early island operations of early 1942. On this occasion planes of Task Force 50 accounted for 65 of the enemy at a cost of 5 carrier planes.

On 6 January 1944, Task Force 50 became Task Force 58 under command of that famous carrier commander Rear-Admiral Marc Mitscher. Of its four Task Groups, *Enterprise*, *Yorktown* and *Belleau Wood* formed Task Group 50.1. Further softening up of the Marshall Islands by this huge carrier force ended with the capture of Kwajalein on 3 February. For the next four months the *Enterprise*'s story was one of incessant similar smothering strikes on Japanese-held islands and atolls. On 17 February it was Truk, where

the 'Big E' again made history by launching the first radar-directed night bombing raid by twelve of her Avengers. Then it was Emirau, Yap, Ulithi, Woleai and the Palaus before taking part in General MacArthur's operations in New Guinea.

It was the month of June, however, which saw the 'Big E' take part in the biggest naval air battle of the war–the Battle of the Philippine Sea which arose out of the Japanese attempt with their whole fleet to prevent the capture of the Marianas. With the remainder of Task Force 58, the *Enterprise* bombers blasted the islands of Saipan, Rota and Guam between 11 and 14 June and gave direct support to the landings on Saipan from the 15th and 17th. Then, on the 19th, the Task Force of seven large and eight light carriers, operating more than 900 aircraft, of which 483 were Hellcat fighters, concentrated to the west of Saipan at news of the approach of the Japanese under Admiral Ozawa with five large and four light carriers.

The American fleet was vastly superior to the Japanese in ships and aircraft, particularly in fighters of which type the former had more than three times the number of the latter and they were all Hellcats, which had established a clear supremacy over the Zeros. The Japanese trusted to the support by island-based air power promised in their operation plan, and to the greater endurance of their

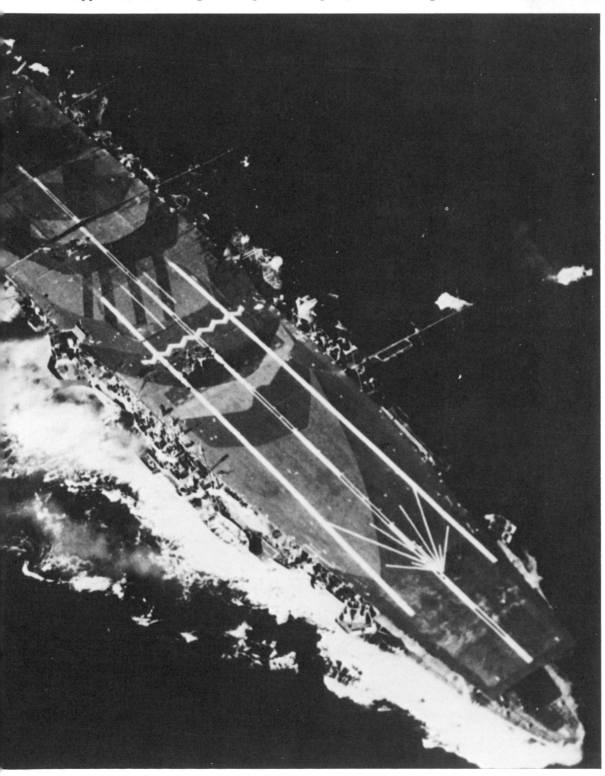

The Japanese carrier *Zuiho* under attack by aircraft from the *Enterprise* during the Battle of the Philippine Sea. She was finally sunk by numerous bomb hits during the Battle for Leyte Gulf.

carrier aircraft, enabling them to operate from beyond the range of the American carrier strike planes. They were to suffer a defeat of devastating magnitude.

The island-based air strength had been almost wiped out during the previous week of continuous air strikes by the planes of Task Force 58. Reinforcements arriving early on the 19th were now intercepted and cut to pieces by waiting Hellcats. And when Ozawa's carrier planes were launched during the day in four waves to a total of some 326, they were met by an overwhelming swarm of Hellcats which shot down 220 of them at a trifling loss to themselves. The handful of bombers that got through failed to do any significant damage to the American fleet. No wonder that the gleeful Americans called that day's action The Great Marianas Turkey Shoot. To add to the débâcle, Ozawa's flagship, the new large carrier *Taiho*, as well as the *Shokaku* were torpedoed – eventually to sink – by American submarines.

By 15.00 the skies over Task Force 58 were clear of enemy aircraft and the American Commander-in-Chief, Admiral Spruance, ordered the carriers forward to seek out and attack the enemy whose ships had not yet been located. Through the night they raced westwards and on through the forenoon and afternoon. But Ozawa had turned away to make rendezvous with his supply tankers and no American reconnaissance could find him. Had he now admitted defeat and pressed on for home, he would have escaped further losses – but he decided to refuel first; and at 15.40 a searching Avenger, flown by Lieutenant R. S. Nelson of the *Enterprise* at last caught up with him at a range of 280 miles.

Already the day was so advanced that strike planes launched by Task Force 58 would get back to their carriers after dark. Nevertheless, Vice-Admiral Mitscher did not hesitate. A strike composed of 85 fighters, 77 dive-bombers and 54 Avengers (most of these armed with bombs, not torpedoes), was on its way by 16.30. Two hours and ten minutes later, with the sun already sinking, they sighted their enemy and went into the attack. Some 75 Zeros were sent up to meet them but were brushed aside – 65 of them being shot down. For twenty minutes all was wild confusion. When the last American plane left the scene, the carrier *Hiyo* had been torpedoed and would later sink, as would two fuel ships hit by bombs. The *Zuikaku*, had been set so furiously ablaze by a bomb that the order to abandon ship was to be given before, as hope of saving her was fading, her fire parties at last gained control. The carriers *Junyo* and *Chiyoda*, also damaged by bombs, managed to limp home.

The Japanese fleet air arm, as a ship-borne air force had, indeed, virtually ceased to

exist and was never again to be a force to be reckoned with. But for the 401 American pilots and other air-crewmen now flying into the gathering darkness, some wounded, some in damaged planes with fuel running low, a desperate ordeal remained. Few had ever made night deck-landings. Radio homing signals guided them back to the vicinity of the sprawling fleet of carriers, but after that all was confusion. Mitscher ordered illuminations of every sort to be used, including floodlighting and starshells. Pilots did not bother to find their own particular ship; any deck would do as the last pints of petrol fed their coughing engines. Thus on to the 'Big E's' deck came 17 'strangers', while 14 of her own got down on others.

Nevertheless, there were many that did not make it. Of the 216 planes of the strike sent out, 100 were lost; of these, six fighters and 14 bombers were shot down; 17 fighters and 63 dive-bombers either 'splashed' in the sea as their fuel ran out, or crashed on deck. Fortunately all but 16 pilots and 33 air-crew men were later located and picked up from their rubber dinghies.

The Battle of the Philippine Sea over, Task Force 58 returned to support the Pacific Fleet's amphibious operations, planes from the *Enterprise* making destructive strikes on Yap and Ulithi Atoll. A month of rest at Pearl Harbor and the 'Big E' was off again with the Carrier Task Force – now Task Force 38 – as Rear-Admiral Ralph E. Davison's flagship of Task Group 38.4. In preparation for the next advance towards the Japanese homeland, carrier planes of Task Group 38.4 hammered the Bonins, Yap, Ulithi and the Palaus, while the remainder swarmed over the Philippines. Then, on 20 October 1944 an Allied Armada landed an American army on the Philippine Island of Leyte – a move which, once again brought the whole Japanese fleet out in an effort to destroy the vast amphibious force.

The three-day Battle for Leyte Gulf followed, the most tremendous widespread naval battle of all time. In this, the aircraft of Task Force 38 were launched, in wave after wave throughout 24 October against the Japanese battle fleet under Admiral Kurita, comprising five battleships (including the two largest ever built, *Yamato* and *Musashi*, each mounting eight 18 inch guns) ten cruisers and a screen of light cruisers and destroyers, as it advanced through the Sibuyan Sea towards the San Bernardino Strait. Torpedo planes from the *Enterprise* took a leading part in sinking the giant *Musashi* which took no less than nineteen torpedo hits and at least ten bombs. A heavy cruiser was hit and forced out of the battle. The *Yamato* and the smaller battleship *Nagato* were each hit by bombs too; but these did not breach their massive armour protection and they were not stopped.

While this was going on, the long-awaited news of the Japanese carrier force came in. The *Zuikaku*, *Chitose*, *Chiyoda* and *Zuiho* had been located far to the north, off the north-east corner of Luzon. That they had only a handful of aircraft on board, flown by only partly trained aviators; that, in fact, they represented only a decoy force sent out under Admiral Ozawa to draw Task Force 38 away from the decisive area round Leyte Gulf, was not appreciated by Admiral Halsey, Commander-in-Chief of the US 3rd Fleet. And that evening he gathered together the three Task Groups which had been hammering Kurita and headed north through the night. At dawn on the 25th their air striking forces swarmed into the sky. By the early afternoon the *Zuikaku*–last survivor of those which had begun the war by striking at Pearl Harbor–the *Chitose* and *Zuiho* had all been sent to the bottom by bombs and torpedoes. The *Chiyoda*, lying immobilized by bomb hits, survived till the evening when she was destroyed by the guns of American cruisers.

It was the end of the Imperial Japanese Navy of the day as a balanced fighting force. Kurita's battle squadron, less shattered than Halsey had been led to believe by the reports of his aviators, had, indeed, steamed through the San Bernardino Strait into the Philippine Sea to threaten the amphibious 7th Fleet as planned. But it had been driven back by ship-borne air strikes mounted in the escort carriers of the 7th Fleet and in Halsey's fourth Carrier Task Group which was diverted to the scene of action as it was returning from a replenishment visit to its forward base at Ulithi. The Japanese ships, in various degrees damaged, got back to base; but lacking ship-borne air support they could never again confront the American fleet. Only the *Yamato* was later to make a suicidal death-ride to go down under the same kind of assault as had her sister, the *Musashi*.

The war in the Pacific, meanwhile, reverted to its 'island-hopping' progress towards Japan, in which the *Enterprise* continued to play a full part in the carrier-borne air support to the amphibious expeditions upon which the whole strategy depended. The opposition, now by shore-based air power, was no less formidable than in the early days of the veteran carrier's career when she faced such odds at Midway and off the Solomons. The fine flower of the Japanese fleet air arm had been eliminated in those battles and the Battle of the Philippine Sea. But in place of the highly trained and skilful dive-bombers and torpedo-plane crews there now swarmed out fleets of *kamikaze* planes flown by pilots committed to crashing their bomb-laden aircraft suicidally on to their targets. They had made their debut during the Leyte battle, sinking the escort carrier St Lo. On 28 October the *Intrepid* became the first fleet carrier to be so hit and damaged.

She was followed on 30 October by the *Enterprise*'s Task Group comrades *Franklin* and *Belleau Wood*. Both were severely damaged and suffered many casualties; the *Enterprise*–not for the last time–seemed to enjoy a charmed life as a flaming *kamikaze* passed a bare fifteen feet over the aircraft thronging her flight deck. During November the *Lexington*, the *Intrepid* (again) and the *Cabot* were all badly damaged.

December saw the *Enterprise* enjoying a respite at Pearl Harbor and working up a new night-flying air group composed of 18 Hellcats and 27 Avengers, all radar-equipped,

Admiral Jisaburo Ozawa replaced Nagumo in command of the Carrier Force in November 1942 and was subsequently the sea-going commander of the Fleet under the Commander-in-Chief Toyoda, who exercised his command from ashore in Japan. Defeated in the Battle of the Philippine Sea, his resignation was refused. In the Battle for Leyte Gulf, he commanded the decoy Carrier Force which was duly massacred, though he himself survived.

The Japanese super-battleship *Yamato*. She and her sister, the *Musashi*, were the biggest (64,170 tons standard displacement) battleships ever built; each mounted nine 18·1-inch guns and had a speed of $27\frac{1}{2}$ knots. The *Musashi* was sunk during the Battle for Leyte Gulf. The *Yamato* was sunk on 7 April 1945 by at least twelve torpedoes when she made a suicidal sortie with fuel for a 'one-way trip' only, against the US 5th Fleet off Okinawa.

the operation of which, together with a similar group in the light carrier *Independence* making up Task Group 38.5, was to be her special contribution to the operations. The Task Group Commander, whose flag she flew, was Rear-Admiral Matthias B. Gardner who had been the 'Big E's' captain when she pioneered such operations in December 1943. The Group joined the fleet on 5 January 1945. From then on with brief intervals of rest, recreation or repair at the fleet base at Ulithi Atoll, the *Enterprise* was in the thick of the fight for the next four months.

Her luck continued to hold. On 18 March a bomb which hit her failed to explode though it killed one man and caused damage which sent her briefly back to Ulithi for repairs. During the operations supporting the assault on Okinawa the explosion of a near-miss *kamikaze* alongside on 11 April set a plane on deck ablaze, but the damage was again repairable at Ulithi and the *Enterprise* was back in action by 6 May.

Such luck could not last for ever. Yet even

when at last on 14 May 1945 a *kamikaze* made a direct hit behind the carrier's forward lift, penetrating deep into the ship before exploding and starting blazing fires which took thirty minutes to put out, she suffered far less than others similarly hit. Her casualties were confined to 14 killed and 34 wounded. Nevertheless, the time had come for the great veteran to make for a home yard for full repairs and, when she arrived at Puget Sound Navy Yard on 7 June 1945 her fighting career was at last over.

During it, besides the Presidential Unit Citation, the *Enterprise* had received the Navy Unit Commendation and the record number of twenty Battle Stars. She had earned a rest, it might be thought. But when she left the Yard she was as good as new and was to be employed transporting troops returning home from the war for four months before at last paying off in January 1946. Today, the famous name is borne by the fast nuclear-powered aircraft carrier USS *Enterprise* (CVAN-65).

Part of the US 5th Fleet at its advanced base – Ulithi Atoll in the Caroline Islands. Fleet carriers of the Essex-class, six of which are seen here, constituted the main striking strength of the fleet.

ACKNOWLEDGEMENTS

The lower illustration on page 23 is reproduced by gracious permission of her Majesty the Queen, the left-hand lower illustration on page 136 by courtesy of the Admiral President Royal Naval College, Greenwich and that on pages 82 and 83 by the authority of the Ministry of Defence.

Photographs

A.C.L., Brussels 15 bottom; Barnabys, London 58; Bildarchiv d. Osterreichische Nationalbibliothek, Vienna 54–55, 59 top, 65 top; Bildarchiv, Preussischer Kulturbesitz, Berlin 47; British Museum, London 117; Central Press Photos, London 16–17 bottom, 99 top; E.C.P.–Armées, Ivry-sur-Seine 33; Fujiphotos, Tokyo 53 bottom, 54 bottom, 97, 98, 99 bottom, 150 top, 151 top; Giraudon, Paris 21 bottom right; Hamlyn Group Picture Library 136 top; Hamlyn Group–Graham Portlock 52 bottom, 81 top, 81 centre, 81 bottom; Hamlyn Group–G. Routhier 62–63; Hamlyn Group–John Webb 61, 136 bottom left; Robert Hunt Library–US Navy 93, 95 bottom, 103; Robert Hunt Library–Associated Press 151 bottom; Imperial War Museum, London 4–5, 16–17 top, 57, 59 bottom, 65 bottom, 66, 67 top, 67 bottom, 68 top, 68–69, 69 top, 70–71 top, 70–71 bottom, 74 top, 77, 78, 79 top, 79 bottom, 80, 85, 86–87, 87, 88, 91, 92 bottom, 94–95 top, 94 bottom, 96, 102, 104, 105, 106, 107, 108, 109, 110 top, 110 bottom, 111 top, 111 bottom, 112, 113 top, 113 bottom, 114 top, 114–115, 119, 121, 122, 123, 124, 125, 126, 128, 129, 130 top, 130–131, 133 top, 133 bottom, 136 bottom right, 137, 140 bottom, 142–143, 143, 145 bottom, 146, 150 bottom, 156–157; Keystone Press Agency, London 139; Kyodophoto Service, Tokyo 155 top; Mansell Collection, London 48 top, 48 bottom, 49 top, 49 bottom, 52 top, 52 centre, 60, 73; Mariners Museum, Newport News, Virginia 35, 41, 42; Mas, Barcelona 8 top, 14; Metropolitan Museum of Art, New York 40 top; Ministry of Defence, London 82–83; Musée de la Marine, Paris endpapers, 19 bottom, 21 top, 23 top, 29, 120; Musées Nationaux, Paris 20; National Archives, Washington D.C. –Chief of Naval Operations 142 top; National Archives, Washington D.C.–Navy Department 145 top, 147 bottom, 148, 149 bottom; National Archives, Washington D.C.–U.S. Bureau of Ships 36 top, 37 top, 37 bottom, 44; National Maritime Museum, London 8 bottom, 9, 10, 11, 13, 15 top, 19 top, 22, 26–27, 31, 32, 36 bottom, 38, 39, 43, 74–75, 84 bottom, 101, 134–135; National Portrait Gallery, London 25, 28; Popperphotos, London title page, 76; Radio Times Hulton Picture Library, London 12, 40 bottom, 51, 89, 118; Roger-Viollet, Paris 24, 50 bottom, 53 top; Science Museum, London 155 bottom; Crown Copyright, Science Museum, London 7; Bradley Smith, New York 64 bottom; Syndication International, London 127; U.S. Naval Academy, Annapolis, Maryland 45 bottom, 64 top; U.S. Navy, 59 top, 92 top, 140–141, 141 bottom, 144, 147 top, 149 top, 152 top, 152–153; Weidenfeld & Nicolson–National Maritime Museum 84 top.

INDEX

Figures in italics refer to illustrations

Acasta 67, 103–4, 119
Achille 24
Addu Atoll 87, 88
Admiral Graf Spee 117
Admiral Hipper 101, 102, 103, *103*, 104, *104*, 106, *106*, 124, 126
Admiral Scheer 92, 104, 106, 126
Adua 132
Adzumo 53
Aeolus 37–8
Africa 37
Akagi 143
Alabama 99
Alexander III 51, 54
Algeciras, Battle of (1801) 20, *21*
Altenfiord 110
American Pacific Fleet 138–57
American Task Forces; '8' 138, 139; '16' 93–4, 96, 141, 142, 147; '38' 155, 156; '50' 152; '58' 152, 153, 154; '61' 144, 145, 146, 148, 149; '64' 92–4, 96, 97, 99; '99' 91
Amiens, Peace of (1802) 19
Anton Schmitt 77
Apraxin 54
Aquidaban 55
Arbuthnot, Rear-Admiral Sir Robert 66
Ardent 103–4, 119
Arethusa 58, 130, 131
Argus 116, 120, 137, 138
Ark Royal (aircraft carrier) 104, 106, 116–17, *118*, *121*, *125*, *128*, 131; Norwegian campaign 118–19; Operation Menace 121; Mediterranean action 119–26, *121*, *123*, 127, 137, *137*; Atlantic action 126–9; and *Bismarck* 127–9; Operation Substance 129–31; Operation Halberd 132
Ark Royal (galleon) 8, 9, 10, 11, 116, *117*
Ark Royal (*Pegasus*) 116
Arnim 78, 102
Asahi 46, 49, 50, 51, 53
Asama 53
Astoria 92, 144
Atago 96
Athenia 116
Atlanta 96
Atlantis 103
Ayanami 97, 98
Aylwin, Lieutenant John C. 40
Azores 14, 15, 16

Bahia 39, 40
Bainbridge, Commodore William 38, 39, 40, *40*
Baker, Matthew 6
Bardia 80
Barham 66, 72, 73, 74, 80, 85, 122
Bart, Jean 21
Battle Cruiser Fleet, Admiral Beatty's 57–9, 60, 65–6, 69, 73
Bazan, Captain-General Alonzo de 15, 72
Beale, Sub-Lieutenant Tony 129
Bear 10
Beatty, Admiral Lord; Battle of the Dogger Bank 57–8; Battle of Jutland 60–6, *68*, 73; see also Battle Cruiser Fleet, Admiral Beatty's
Bedouin 77
Bedout, Rear-Admiral 20
Belfast 112, 113, 114, 115
Belleau Wood 152, 155
Belvedere 38
Benedetto Brin 55
Benham 96, 98
Bernd von Arnim 77, 101
Berwick 122
Bévéziers 121
Bey, Rear-Admiral 111, 112, 113, 114
'Big E' see *Enterprise*
Bismarck 90, 106, 107, *124*, 126, 127–9
Blücher 56, 58, 59, *65*, 77, 102
Boedecker, Rear-Admiral 60
Bomber Command 108
Bonaparte, Napoleon 19, 20, 21, 24
Bonne Citoyenne 39
Borodino 51, 54
Boston Harbour 34, 36, 38, 39, 40, 45

Bouvet, Rear-Admiral 19
Bredenkreuker, Commander 113
Brest 18, 19, 20, *20*, 21, 105, 106–8, 126
Bridport, Lord 18, *18*
British Channel Fleet 18
British Grand Fleet 57, 60–70, 72–4; 5th Battle Squadron 60–70; 72–4, *85*; First Cruiser Squadron 74; see also Battle Cruiser fleet, Admiral Beatty's
British Home Fleet 76, 91, 101, 112, 117, 128
British Mediterranean Fleet 78–80, 85–6, 119–20
British Naval Forces; D 122; H 119, 121–2, *123*, 124, 125, 126–37, *128*; K 117; X 130, 131
British North Sea Fleet 18
Broke, Captain Philip 37, *39*
Brown, Lieutenant-Commander W. L. M. 77
Bruix, Vice-Admiral 19
Bucentaure 18, 24, 29, 30
Bulwark 55
Burnett, Vice-Admiral 'Bob' 112, 113, *114*

Cabot 155
Cadiz 7
Cagliari 120
Calais Roads *24*
Calder, Sir Robert 22
Callaghan, Rear-Admiral David 94
Cambell, Rear-Admiral D. R. F. 117
Campbell 109
Campbell, Flying Officer K. 106, *108*
Camperdown, Battle of 19
Campioni, Admiral Inigo 78–9, 122
Canberra 92, 144
Cape Verde Islands 43
Casson, Lieutenant-Commander John 119
Cavour 80
Central Basin 122, 124
Cerebus, Operation 108
Ceylon 87
Chads, Lieutenant Henry 39–40
Charity 120
'Chatham Chest' 14
Chester 67
Chitose 145, 155
Chiyoda 154, 155
Chokai 96
Ciliax, Vice-Admiral 100, 107, 109–10, *110*
'Club Runs' 122, 124, 126
Cochrane, Lord 33
Collier, Captain Sir George Ralph 44
Colombo 87
Colorado 90
Congress 44
Conqueror 66
Constitution ('Old Ironsides') 34–45, *35*, *38*, *40*, *44*, *45*, *64*
Conte di Cavour 78
Convoys; JW55B 112; PQ17 91–2, *95*
Coode, Lieutenant-Commander T. P. 128–9
Coral Sea, Battle of the 140
Cornwall 87, 144
Corunna 8, 14
Cossack 77
Courageous 103, 116, 117, 138
Crete 86
Cromarty 57
Crutchley, Captain Victor 77
Cumberland, Earl of 14, 15
Cunningham, Admiral Lord 76, 78–80, *79*, 85, 88, 89; Operation Menace 121
Curteiss, Vice-Admiral A. T. B. 132
Cyane 41, 42, 44, *44*

Dacres, Captain 38, 39
Dakar 121
Davis, Captain Glenn B. 97
Davison, Rear-Admiral Ralph E. 154
Decatur, Stephen 36, *37*
Defence 66, 74
Defiance 14, 15
Derfflinger 56; Battle of the Dogger Bank 57–9; Battle of Jutland 60, 65, 66, 67–9
Despatch 122
Deutschland 100; see also *Lützow*
Devonport 72
d'Eyncourt, Sir Eustace Tennyson 72
Diether von Roeder 77, 78

Disdain 9
Dogger Bank, Battle of the 58–9
Dönitz, Grand Admiral 111, 112, *112*, 132
Dorsetshire 87, *127*, 144
Douglas, Commander J. S. 130
Douglas, The Hon. George 41, 42, 43
Dover Command 108
Dover Straits 109
Drake, Sir Francis 7, 8, 9, 10, 12, *12*, 14, *29*
Dreadnought (1906) 46, 56
Duilio 80
Duke of York 88, 91, 112, 114, 115, *115*
Dumanoir, Admiral 23
Duncan, Admiral 18
Dunkerque 100, 119
Dutch War, Third 72

Eagle 78, 116
Eastern Fleet *85*, 86, 87–8
Eastern Solomons, Battle of the 145–7
Edinburgh 130, 132
Egidy, Captain von 56, 65, 70
Elbing 60, 67, 73
Elizabeth I, Queen 6, 7, 14
Elizabeth Bonaventure 7
Enquist, Rear-Admiral 54
Enterprise ('Big E') 94, 96, 138–40, *138*, 150, 151–2, 156–7; Battle of Midway 141–4, *142*; Battle of the Eastern Solomons 145–7; Battle of Guadalcanal 148, 150; Battle of the Solomon Islands 147–9; Battle of the Philippine Sea 153–4; Battle of Leyte Gulf 154–5
'Enterprise of England' 7
Erich Giese 78
Erich Köllner 77
Ermland 106
Eskimo 77, 78
Esmonde, Lieutenant-Commander E. 109, *111*
Essex 151, *152*
Euryalus 132
Evan-Thomas, Rear-Admiral Hugh 73

Fairey Fulmar *122*
Faith 120
Falcon, Captain Gordon Thomas 41, 42
Fanad Head 117
Fearless 130
Ferrol 20
Fighter Command 108
Fiji 86
Firedrake 130
Fisher, Admiral Lord 56, *73*
Fisher, Captain D. B. 78
Fiume 85
Fleet Air Arm 118, 119
Fleming, Captain Thomas 8
Fletcher, Rear-Admiral Frank 141, 142, *142*, 144–6
Fliegerkorps X 80, 85
Formidable 20, *79*, 85, *85*, 86, 124, *133*
Fougueux 30, 32
Frankfurt 60, 67
Franklin 155
Fraser, Admiral Sir Bruce 112, 114, 115
French Atlantic Fleet 18, 21
French Combined Fleet 21–4, 29
Friedrich Ihn 109
Frobisher, Sir Martin 11, 12, 14
Fuji 46, 47, 53
Fuller, Operation 108
Furious 116, 118

Galatea 60, 73
Gallaher, Lieutenant William 144
Ganteaume, Admiral 21
Gardner, Rear-Admiral Mattias B. 156
Garside, Captain 78
Genoa 125
Georges Leygues 121
Georg Thiele 77, 78
German High Seas Fleet 56–70, *71*, 73, 75
Ghormley, Admiral 144
Gibraltar 119, 120, 121, 124, 126, 129
Giessler, Korvettenkapitän Helmuth 102
Giffen, Rear-Admiral R. C. 91
Giulio Cesare 78, 79, 122
Glasgow 122
Glattes, Korvettenkapitän 117
Glorious 103, 116, 117, 118–19, 138
'Glorious First of June' (1794) 18
Gloucester 78, 80, 86
Glowworm 101–2, *103*

Gneisenau 76, 100, 104–10, 126; Norwegian campaign 101–3, 119
Godfrey, Admiral 78
Godfrey-Fausset, Lieutenant 'Feather' 129
Goeben 56
Golden Hind 8, 10
Golden Lion 11
Goodenough, Commander 73
Gourdon, Rear-Admiral 20
Grand Design, The 21–2
Gran Grifon 10
Gravelines, Battle of 13
Graves, Vernon 125
Gravina, Admiral 21
Great Turkey Shoot, The 154
Grenville, Sir Richard 14, 15, 16, *24*
Greyhound 85, 86
Griffiths, RM. Lieutenant 117
Grosser Kurfürst 66, 74
Guadalcanal 92, 94, 144–5
Guadalcanal, Battle of 94–9, *99*, 147–50
Guerrière 38–9, 40, *40*, *64*
Guggenberger, Lieutenant-Commander 137
Gurkha 132
Gwin 96, 98

Halberd, Operation 131
Hallett, Captain N. G. 130
Halsey Jr, Vice-Admiral William F. 138, 148, *149*, 155
Hamman 144
Hannibal 20
Hans Lüdemann 77
Hanson, Mike 118
Hardy 77
Hardy, Captain 32
Hare, Lieutenant-Commander John 118
Hashimoto, Rear-Admiral 97, 98
Hatsuse 46, 47, 48
Havock 77
Hawkins, Sir John 6, 7, *8*, 11, 12, 14
Hawkins, William 7
Helena 96
Heligoland Bight 60
Henderson Field 92, 94, 96, *97*, 148, 150
Hermann Künne 77
Hermann Schoemann 110
Hermes 87, 116, 117
Hermione 130, 131
Hiei 94, 96
Hintze, Captain Fritz 111, 112, 114
Hipper, Rear-Admiral Franz 56, *59*; Battle of the Dogger Bank 57–60; Battle of Jutland 65, 66, 67, 73, 74
Hiryu 143–4, *143*
Hislop, Lieutenant-General 40
Hitler, Adolf 100
Hiyo 149, *150*, 154
Hoffman, Captain Curt Caesar 100, 104–5, 107, 109–10
Holland, Captain C. S. 118, 126
Hood 75, 100, 107, 119, 128
Hood, Admiral Lord 67–8
Hooper, Lieutenant-Commander Edwin B. 97
Hope 120
Hornet 93, 140, 143, 147, 148, 149, *150*
Horn's Reef 69–70
Horton, Captain Max 60
Hostile 77
Howard, Lord Thomas 11, 14, 15
Howard of Effingham, Lord 7, 8, 9, 10, *10*, 12, 13, 116
Howe, Lord 18
Hüffmeier, Captain Friedrich 110, 111
Hull, Captain Isaac 36, 37–8, *37*, 38–9
Humphreys, Joshua 34, 35
Hunter 77

Iachino, Admiral 85, 125, 132
Idzumo 53
Iéna 55
Illustrious 78, 80–5, 121
Indefatigable 56, 60, 65, 68, 73
Independence 156
Indiana 99
Indomitable 56, 58, 67, 74
Inflexible 67, 74
Ingenohl, Admiral von 57, 58
Intrepid 155
Invincible 56, 67, *67*, 74, *83*
Iowa 99
Iron Duke 66

Iron Duke class 72
Irvine, Ensign C. B. 148
Isuzo 96
Iwate 53

Jaguar 109
Jamaica 112, 114, 115
Japanese Fast Carrier Force 141, 143–4
Java 39, 40, *41*, *42*
Java Sea, Battle of the 86
Jean Bart 90
Jellicoe, Admiral Lord; Battle of the Dogger Bank 57; Battle of Jutland 60, *60*, 65, 68–70, 73
Johnstone, Lieutenant-Commander Johnnie 121, 123
Juneau 96
Juniper 103
Juno, Operation 102
Junyo 148, 149, 154
Jutland, Battle of 60–70, 73–4, *83*

Kaga 143
Kamikaze 99
Kamimura, Rear-Admiral 53
Karlsruhe 102
Kasuga 48, 53
Kawachi 55
Kent 80
Kerr, Captain Alexander Robert 44
Kincaid, Rear-Admiral Thomas 96, 144, 147, *147*, 148
Kinugasa 96, 150
Kirishima 94, 97, 98, *99*, 150
Kniaz Suvarov 51
Kolberg 58
Kondo, Admiral 96, 97, 98
König 66
Königsberg 102, 118
Köllner 77
Kummetz, Vice-Admiral 110, 111

Lagos, Battle of (1759) 72
Lambert, Captain 39, 40
La Morandais, Captain Maillard 19
Langley 138
Larcom, Captain 128
Lauriston, General 24
Leander 44
Lee, Rear-Admiral Willis A. 92, 97, 98, 99
Legion 132, 137
Leinster 130, 131
Leiva, Don Alonso de 10, 11
Lemp, Kapitänleutnant 116
Leslie, Lieutenant-Commander Maxwell F. 143
Levant 41, 42, 43, 44, *44*
Lewin, Captain R. D. G. 130
Lexington 138, 140, *140*, 155
Leyte Gulf, Battle of 99, 154–5
Liaotung Peninsula 46, 55
Liberté 55
Lion 58, *58*, 60, 65, 73
Lion class 56
Littorio 80, 90
London Naval treaty (1936) 90
L'Ouverture, Toussaint 20
Lucas, Captain Jean 20–1, *23*, 24, 29–33
Lucy, RN. Lieutenant W. P. 118
Lüdemann 78
Lütjens, Admiral 101, 102, *102*, 104–7
Lützow (ex-*Deutschland*) 60, *83*, 92, 102, 110, 111

MacArthur, General Douglas 144
McClusky, Lieutenant-Commander Clarence W. 142
Macedonian 39, *43*
MacEwen, Lieutenant B. S. 117
McKay, Petty Officer 117
Madden, Commander Sir Charles 86, 87
Maine 55
Makaroff, Admiral 47, 48, *49*
Malaga, Battle of 72
Malaya 66, 73, 78, 79, 105, *107*
Malta 88, 120, 129–30
Manchester 122, 130, 131
Manxman 130, 131
Marathon 105
Maria Juan 13
Markgraf 66, 73
Marschall, Admiral 100–3
Marshall Islands 139, 152
Mary Rose 10
Matapan, Battle of 85

Matchless 115
Matsushima 55
Maund, Captain L. E. H. 126, *130*, 137
Maya 96
Medina Sidonia, Duke of 9, 10, 11, 13
Menace, Operation 121
Midway, Battle of 140–4, *145*
Mikasa 46–55, *49*, *54*, *64*
Mikuma 144, *146*
Mitscher, Rear-Admiral Marc 152, 154
Mogami 144
Moltke 56, 57, 58, 60, 65, 73
Moncousu, Captain 18
Montcalm 121
Monterey 152
Mount's Bay 89
Murray, Captain G. D. 138
Musashi 90
Musketeer 115
Mussolini, Benito 80

Nagara 94, 97, 98
Nagato 154–5
Nagumo, Vice-Admiral Chuichi 87, 141–3, 148
Naiad 104
Nakhimoff 54
Narvik 101, 102, 103, 118
Narvik, Second Battle of 77–8
Natal 55
Navarin 54
Nelson 76, 90, *129*, 130, 131, 132
Nelson, Admiral Lord 21, 22, *23*, 29, 30, *32*, *60*
Nelson, Lieutenant R. S. 154
Nestor 66
Newcastle 101, 122
New Jersey 99
New Zealand 58, 60, 73
Nikolai I 54
Nimitz, Admiral Chester 140
Nisshin 48, 53
Nomad 65
Nonpareil 12
Nore 18
Norfolk 112, 113
Norreys, Sir John 14
North Carolina 90, 92, 99, 144, 146, 147
Nuestra Señora del Rosario 9, *12*

Oil Pioneer 103
Okinawa 156
'Old Ironsides' *see Constitution*
Opportune 115
Orama 103
Oran 119, *120*
Orel 51, 54
Oslofiord 102
Oslyabya 53, 54, *64*
Ozawa, Admiral 153, 154, 155, *155*

Pallada 47
Parma, Duke of 10, *15*
Partridge, RM. Captain R. T. 118, 119
Pasteur 130
Pattison, Sub-Lieutenant Kenneth 129
Pearl Harbor 138–9
Peresviet 48, 51
Petropavlovsk 48, *50*
Philadelphia 35, 36
Philip II, King 7, *9*
Philippine Sea, Battle of the 99, 153–4
Philippon, Vice-Admiral 107, 108
Philpotts, Captain E. M. 73, 74
Pillau 60, 67
Pique 41
Pizey, Captain C. T. M. 109
Plymouth 8
Pobieda 48, 51
Pola 85
Poltava 48, 50
Port Arthur 46, 47, *47*, 48, *49*, 51, 52, 55
Portland 94, 96
Portland Bill 10
Porto Praya 43, 44
Portsmouth, Peace of 55
Power, Admiral Sir Arthur J. 116, 118
Preble, Commander Edward 35, *36*, 37
President 37, 44
Preston 96, 98
Price, Petty Officer F. R. 77
Prince of Wales 128, 132
Princess Royal 58, 60, 65, 73
Principe de Asturias 29
Prinz Eugen 106, 107, 109, *109*, 110, 127–8
Punjabi 78

Queen Elizabeth 72–3, 126
Queen Elizabeth class 75
Queen Mary 60, 65, 68, 73
Quiberon Bay, Battle of (1759) 72
Quincey 92, 144, 148

Raleigh, Sir Walter 72
Ramillies 104, 122, 128
Ranger 138
Rata Coronada 10, 11
Rawalpindi 100–1
Recalde, Juan Martinez de 10, 14
Redoutable 18–19, 24, 29, 31, 60; at Battle
  of Trafalgar 20–33
Redoutable, Le 33
Regensburg 60
Regulus 33
Renown 75, 76, 100, 102, 106, 120, 122,
  123, 127, 128, 128
Républicain 18
Repulse 75, 100
Resolution 85, 119
Retvizan 47, 48, 49, 51
Revenge (battleship) 17
Revenge (galleon) 6–7; Spanish Armada
  8–13, 12; the Azores 14–16
Revenge (nuclear-powered submarine) 16,
  17
Richelieu 90, 93, 121
Richepanse, General 19
Rodgers, Commodore John 37
Rodney 75, 90, 106, 132
Roebuck 9, 10
Roosevelt, President Theodore 55
Rosario 9, 10
Royal Air Force Coastal Command 108
Royal Oak 66
Royal Sovereign 30, 78, 79, 85
Royal Sovereign class 75, 86
Rozhestvenski, Admiral Zinovi 53, 53,
  54, 55
Runyan, Donald 147
Russian Baltic Fleet 51
Russian Far East Fleet 47
Russo-Japanese War 47
Ryujo 146

Saint Domingue 20
St James Day (1666) 72
Salerno 88
San Andreo 72
San Felipe 13, 72
San Francisco 94, 96
San Lorenzo 12
San Juan de Portugal 10, 12
San Luis de Portugal 11
San Marco de Portugal 13
San Mateo 13
San Martín 9, 10, 12, 13
San Mattias 72
San Pablo 16
San Salvador 9, 10, 13
Santa Cruz Islands, Battle of the 93,
  147–9
Santissima Trinadad 30
San Tomas 72
Saratoga 138, 146, 147
Sasebo 55
Saumarez 114
Savage 114
Savo Island, Battle of 92, 97
Scapa Flow 57, 70, 71, 72, 91
Schanze, Commander Edwin S. 97
Scharnhorst 76, 88, 100, 101, 104–15, 105,
  111, 112, 126, 137; in the Norwegian
  campaign 101–3, 119
Scheer, Admiral Reinhard 60, 65–6, 65,
  68, 69–70, 73
Schlettstadt 104
Schniewind, Admiral 111, 112
Scorpion 114, 115
Sealion 108
Semavin 54
Sendai 97, 98
Sevastopol 48
Seydlitz 56–7, 57, 71; Battle of the
  Dogger Bank 58–9; Battle of Jutland
  60–70, 67, 68, 73, 74
Seydlitz, General Friedrich Wilhelm
  Freiherr von 56
Seymour, Lord Henry 11, 12
Shannon 37
Shark 67
Sheffield 112, 122, 123, 128, 128, 129, 132
Shikishima 46, 47, 50, 53
Shimonoseki, Treaty of 46

Shokaku 140, 140, 145, 146, 147, 149, 154
Sicily 88
Simpson, Petty Officer 117
Sissoi Veliki 54
Skagerrak, Battle of 69
Smeeton, Vice-Admiral Sir Richard 123
Somerville, Admiral Sir James 86, 87–8,
  106, 119, 121, 124, 125, 130, 131, 132, 137
Somerville, Mark 126, 127
Soryu 143
Southampton 73, 80, 122
South Dakota 94, 96, 98, 99, 147
Spanish Armada 7–13, 11, 15
Spanish Main 7
Spezia 125
Spithead 18
Spruance, Rear-Admiral Raymond A.
  141, 142, 144, 144, 154
Stewart, Captain Lord George 44
Stewart-Moore, Lieutenant-Commander
  123
Stord 114
Stralsund 57
Strasbourg 100, 119
Stringer, Lieutenant-Commander 128
Strong, Lieutenant-Commander 148
Strother, Commander John A. 97
Stuart, Captain Lord George 44
Submarines, British: E9 60; E1 60; 133
Substance, Operation 129–31
Suffren, Bailli de 18
Superb 66
Surcouf, Robert 21
Suvarov 53, 54, 64
Suzuya 96
Swiftsure 32, 33
Swordfish 119, 137
Sydney Star 131
Syfret, Rear-Admiral 130

Taiho 154
Takao 97
Téméraire 24, 30, 31, 32, 33
Thunderer 66
Thurston, RN. Lieutenant 117
Tiger 58, 59, 60, 65, 73
Tiger, Operation 127
Tillard, Lieutenant-Commander R. C.
  124, 126, 127
Tirpitz 90, 91, 92, 92, 110, 111
Tirpitz, Admiral von 56
Tirso Dam 125
Togo, Admiral Count Heihachiro 46–50,
  49, 53–4
Tokiwa 53
Tokyo 140
Tone, Wolfe 18
Trafalgar, Battle of 24, 29–33, 31, 32
Traill, Commander (Flying) H. A.
  ('Jane') 126, 127
Trincomalee 87–8
Triumph 12
Trondheim 101, 102, 104, 119
Truk 152–3
Tsakuba 55
Tsarevitch 47, 48, 49, 50, 51, 51
Tsushima, Battle of 53, 54, 81
Tsushima, Straits of 53
Tulagi 144
Tyrwhitt, Commodore Reginald 58, 59

U-boats 60; U.30 116, 117; U.39 117;
  U.64 77; U.81 137 U.566 128
Uckermark 106
Uhenfels 117
Ulithi Atoll 156, 157
United States (frigate) 35, 39, 43
Uranami 97, 98
Ushant 108

Vaernes 119
Valdès, Don Pedro de 9, 10
Valiant 66, 72, 73, 74, 80, 85, 86, 119,
  120–1
Valona 80
Vanguard 55
Versailles, Treaty of 100
Victory 11, 24, 30, 31, 32, 60
Villaret-Joyeuse, Vice-Admiral 18
Villeneuve, Admiral Pierre 21, 22–4,
  21, 29, 33
Vincennes 92, 144, 147
Virago 115
Vitgeft, Admiral 48, 50
Vittorio Veneto 80, 85, 90, 120

Vladimir Monomakh 54
Von der Tann 56, 57, 60, 65, 73

Wake Island 139
Walke 96, 98
Walshe, Commander Harvey T. 97
Warburton-Lee, Captain B. A. W. 77
Warrior 66, 74
Warspite (battleship) 7; Battle of
  Jutland 66, 72–5, 74, 75, 83; Second
  World War 76–89, 76, 79, 85, 86, 87, 88,
  89
Warspite (64-gun 3rd Rate) 72
Warspite (74-gun ship-of-the-line) 72
Warspite (Warspight, galleon) 72
Washington 90–2, 91, 92, 94; Battle of
  Santa Cruz 93; Battle of Guadalcanal
  93–9, 150
Washington Treaty 90, 116, 138
Wasp 96, 144, 146, 149
Wells, Vice-Admiral L. V. 116, 119, 120
West Virginia 90
White, Captain N. H. 138
Whitworth, Vice-Admiral 77
Wiesbaden 60, 67
Wilhelm Heidkamp 77
Wilhelmshaven 57, 60, 100, 101
Wolfarth, Lieutenant-Commander 128
Wolfgang Zenker 77
Worcester 109

Yakumo 53
Yamamoto, Admiral 141, 145, 148, 155,
  155
Yamato 90, 99, 141, 154–5
Yashima 46, 48
Yellow Sea, Battle of the (Battle of
  10 August) 51
Yorktown 138, 138, 140, 141, 142, 144,
  145
Yoshino 48

Zara 85
Zélé 19
Zenker 78
Zuiho 148, 153, 155
Zuikaku 140, 145, 146, 147, 148, 149, 150,
  154, 155

160